ONLY ONE SKY

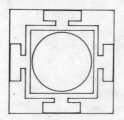

by bhagwan shree rajneesh

- The Book of the Secrets (Vols I and II)
  (discourses on Tantra)
- The Way of the White Cloud
  (talks based on questions)
- Roots and Wings
  (talks based on questions)
- No Water, No Moon
  (discourses on Zen)
- The Mustard Seed
  (discourses on the Sayings of Jesus)
- Neither This Nor That
  (discourses on Sosan)
- . . . and the flowers showered
  (discourses on Zen)
- Just Like That
  (discourses on Sufism)
- I am the Gate
  (talks based on questions)
- The Inward Revolution
  (talks based on questions)
- The Silent Explosion
  (talks based on questions)
- Dimensions Beyond the Known
  (talks based on questions)

translations

- La Rivoluzione Interiore (Italian)
  (published by Armenia Editore)
- Hu-Meditation og Kosmic Orgasme (Danish)
  (published by Borgens Forlag A/S)

Only One Sky

On the Tantric Way of Tilopa's
Song of Mahamudra

Bhagwan Shree Rajneesh

A Dutton  *Paperback*

E. P. DUTTON & CO., INC.
NEW YORK

This paperback edition first published 1976
by E. P. Dutton & Co., Inc.
Copyright © 1975 by Rajneesh Foundation
All rights reserved. Printed in the U.S.A.

FIRST EDITION

10 9 8 7 6 5 4 3 2 1

Library of Congress Catalog Card Number: 76-11869

ISBN: 0-525-47440-4

CONTENTS

INTRODUCTION

After my revolutionary fervour subsided in my early twenties and I realized the futility of my efforts to try and change the outside world, certain teachings which hinted at the more feasible proposition of an inward revolution came to my notice. It was chiefly the Yoga of Tibet that caught my attention and attracted me, but I found that the books on this subject could only sustain a minimal interest in me. Not only was the terminology foreign, obscure and contradictory, but also, once I had ploughed through that, I found the conceptualizations even more alien, confusing and weird. For example, in his *Song of Mahamudra*, Tilopa says:

> . . .*if with the mind one then observes the mind*. . .
> *to conquer distractions is the royal practice;*
> *the path of no-practice is the path of all Buddhas*. . .
> *attain the Non-attainment.*

Well, how to get your teeth into that?

Nevertheless, I found a Guru and a meditation center where Tibetan teachings were practised, but the Guru seemed to be still working out some quite heavy *karma*, which put me off; and sitting quietly doing nothing only seemed to increase the internal chaos and confusion.

I spent the next six years wandering half way round the world and back, in search of . . . only to end up home in England having accumulated a little more knowledge and experience.

Then suddenly a rumour of 'another Indian Guru' reached me, and after some initial hesitation . . . I took a nibble. But once I got the taste, the ravenous hunger which had been gnawing incessantly at my guts for precisely that food, that flavour, drove me to gorge myself on his books, his tapes and his *sannyasins*. The tales told by his disciples were one thing, his written words another, and the spoken voice something else again — a drop of clarity sparkled into my murky depths, an unknown fragrance, or perhaps long-forgotten, was beckoning me to its source. Finally, nothing short of a feast, the living presence, would do.

At first, however, I was disappointed, mainly because I couldn't stomach this exotic new phenomenon. Having lived for so long on all the wrong kinds of foods, this sudden dose of pure, unadulterated nourishment was too much for my system. Along with the physical intestinal discomforts I experienced here in India at the beginning of my stay, I had bouts of emotional and mental diarrhoea as well. I was a mess!

To begin with, the confusion and chaos became even worse as Bhagwan began to tear my ego apart — in the subtlest, kindest possible way, almost unnoticeably in fact. Little knowing what I was letting myself in for at the time, I stayed on way over the four months I had planned to, having been called and caught, hook, line and sinker — and I'm still here two years later.

One of the confusing things about Bhagwan is that he talks on so many different, conflicting subjects: Jesus, Buddha, Lao Tzu, Heraclitus, Zen, Sufism, Chuang Tzu, Tao and of course Yoga and Tantra. Yet on each one of them he speaks so clearly and penetratingly, conveying the very essence of each teaching with such vibrance, that you feel unequivocably: 'This is for me!' — every time. My mind, of course, started cracking up: 'So many contradictions, nowhere to anchor myself, nothing to hang on to.' But slowly, as the mind let go and I began to hear him from somewhere a little deeper, the contradictions began to dissolve.

Bhagwan himself contains all of them. You know even while he's saying that Tantra is the ultimate, tomorrow he will say that Yoga is the greatest — but somehow you know also that both are true. He embraces everything, is a melting-pot of all traditions and teachings, and creates the highest synthesis out of them. Only a being of his stature and bearing, of the grace, serenity and compassion he emanates *can* contain so many paradoxes and yet still be straight with you. He is not only Enlightened but also an incomparable Master.

Sensible teachings, ones with clear-cut directions you can follow easily, small teachings, don't require the all-embracing wisdom and understanding that a Great Teaching does. Says Tilopa:

> *Small teachings lead to acts —*
> *one should follow only teachings that are great.*

Tantra is a Great Teaching and Bhagwan is perhaps the only Master alive today who is a true Tantric Master. He is not concerned with what you do but with what you *are*. 'Do whatsoever you like,' he says, 'but be aware.'

'Loose and natural' is the key phrase in these lectures: Don't deny anything! Be yourself!—sounds simple? It is. But when I tried it I found that because it's more natural for me to be unnatural, and my mind being such as it is, the simplest became the most complex and being natural became perversion. So, of course, I feel it would be much easier to be told what to do rather than stay with all that nonsense. But I also know that unless I ride it, as it were, like the crest of a wave, I will continue to move in circles and never come home to the shore. I felt that Tilopa, through Bhagwan, was telling me again and again in these lectures what this spirituality-trip is *really* all about. Everything else — asceticism, food fads, renunciation, sitting Buddha-like — are all peripheral, and nothing in fact changes unless, through my awareness, my attitude, my relationship with reality changes.

Bhagwan has said that Freud, Jung and Reich have created the situation in the West for a Tantric explosion and now the time is ripe. Not only that, but unless our consciousness explodes, we will soon blow ourselves up as a result of the madness we are indulging in. This Bhagwan, this ultimate alchemist, even helps us to use that very madness, our neurotic drives and energies, to create the inner explosion and transform the inner world. And he says that these are the two possibilities open to humanity today: either global suicide, or the greatest spiritual awakening the world has ever known.

Here in Poona, the first rumblings of the greatest revolution possible can be heard. The inner corruption and decadence is gradually being routed out from where it counts — from the roots of our minds, from our consciousness, not through some outwardly imposed ideology or morality. Political revolutions are nothing by comparison, for this requires that you die to your old self and rise as the phoenix from the ashes to a new birth, to a new order. It is the ultimate suicide, requiring a courage of a totally different sort from ordinary death, for it is not just your body which will die, but your mind-reality, the whole system of your painstakingly created world will be annihilated.

Introduction

Only a Master to whom you can entrust your very being — physical, mental and spiritual — is capable of taking you on such a journey. Listening to Bhagwan, I gradually came to realize that he knows, he has the power, that if I can only say, 'Yes, I leave everything to you,' everything will be taken care of.

Says Tilopa:

Those who disbelieve it (Mahamudra) *are fools*
who ever wallow in misery and sorrow.

And then Bhagwan:

'Why call them fools? He does not call them sinners, he does not call them irreligious, he simply calls them fools — because not believing they are missing the greatest bliss that life can give. They are simply fools! And it cannot happen unless you trust. Unless you trust so much that you can surrender completely, it cannot happen. All bliss, all moments of bliss, happen only when you surrender. Even death becomes beautiful if you can surrender to it, then what to say about life? If you surrender, of course, life is the greatest blessing, it is a benediction. You are missing the ultimate gift because you cannot trust.'

This is Bhagwan's invitation for you to come and celebrate, not through renunciation but acceptance, not through denial but welcoming, not through rules but rejoicing.

Come: eat, drink and be filled. . . .

Ma Yoga Anurag

Poona,
June 1975

In his Song of Mahamudra, Tilopa says:

Mahamudra is beyond all words and symbols,
but for you, Naropa, earnest and loyal,
must this be said:

The Void needs no reliance,
Mahamudra rests on nought.
Without making an effort,
but remaining loose and natural,
one can break the yoke—
thus gaining Liberation.

I   THE ULTIMATE EXPERIENCE
11th February 1975

T HE EXPERIENCE OF THE ULTIMATE is not an experience at all — because the experiencer is lost. And when there is no experiencer, what can be said about it? Who will say it? Who will relate the experience? When there is no subject, the object also disappears — the banks disappear, only the river of experience remains. Knowledge is there, but the knower is not.

That has been the problem for all the mystics. They reach the Ultimate, but they cannot relate it to those who are following. They cannot relate it to others who would like to have an intellectual understanding. They have become one with it. Their whole being relates it, but no intellectual communication is possible. They can give it to you if you are ready to receive; they can allow it to happen in you if you also allow it, if you are receptive and open. But words won't do, symbols won't help; theories and doctrines are of no use at all.

The experience is such that it is more like an experiencing than like an experience. It is a process — and it begins, but it never ends. You enter into it, but you never possess it. It is like a drop dropping in the ocean, or, the ocean itself dropping into the drop. It is a deep merger, it is oneness, you simply melt away into it. Nothing is left behind, not even a trace, so who will communicate? Who will come back to the world of the valley? Who will come back to this dark night to tell you?

All the mystics all over the world have always felt impotent as far as communication is concerned. Communion is possible, but communication, no. This has to be understood from the very beginning. A communion is a totally different dimension: two hearts meet, it is a love affair. Communication is from head to head; communion is from heart to heart, communion is a feeling. Communication is knowledge: only words are given, only words are said, and only words are taken and

3

understood. And words are such, the very nature of words is so dead, that nothing alive can be related through them. Even in ordinary life, leave aside the Ultimate, even in ordinary experiencing when you have a peak moment, an ecstatic moment, when you really feel something and become something, it becomes impossible to relate it in words.

In my childhood I used to go early in the morning to the river. It is a small village. The river is very very lazy, as if not flowing at all. And in the morning when the sun is not yet arising, you cannot see whether it is flowing it is so lazy and silent. And in the morning when nobody is there, the bathers have not come yet, it is tremendously silent. Even the birds are not singing in the morning—early, no sound, just a soundlessness pervades. And the smell of the mango trees hangs all over the river.

I used to go there, to the furthest corner of the river, just to sit, just to be there. There was no need to do anything, just being there was enough, it was such a beautiful experience to be there. I would take a bath, I would swim, and when the sun arose I would go to the other shore, to the vast expanse of sand, and dry myself there under the sun, and lie there, and sometimes even go to sleep.

When I came back my mother used to ask, 'What have you been doing the whole morning?' I would say, 'Nothing,' because, actually, I had not been doing anything. And she would say, 'How is it possible? Four hours you have not been here, how is it possible that you have not been doing anything? You must have been doing something.' And she was right, but I was also not wrong.

I had not been doing anything at all. I had just been being there with the river, not doing anything, allowing things to happen. If it felt like swimming, remember, if it *felt* like swimming, I would swim, but that was not a doing on my part, I was not forcing anything. If I felt like going into sleep, I would go. Things were happening, but there was no doer. And my first experience of *satori* started near that river: not doing anything, simply being there, millions of things happened.

But my mother would insist that I must have been doing something, so I would say, 'Okay, I took a bath and I dried myself in the sun,' and then she was satisfied. But I was not—because what happened there in the river is not expressed by the words: 'I took a bath;' it looks so poor and pale. Playing in the river, floating in the river, swimming in the river, was such a deep experience that to say simply, 'I took a bath,' makes no sense of it; or to just say, 'I went there, had a walk on the bank, sat there,' conveys nothing.

Even in ordinary life you feel the futility of words. And if you don't feel the futility of words, that shows that you have not been alive at all; that shows that you have lived very superficially. If whatsoever you have been living can be conveyed by words, that means you have not lived at all.

When for the first time something starts happening which is beyond words, then life has happened to you, life has knocked at your door. And when the Ultimate knocks at your door, you simply go beyond words—you become dumb, you cannot speak; not even a single word is formed inside. And whatsoever you might say looks so pale, so dead, so meaningless, without any significance, that it seems you are doing an injustice to the experience that has happened to you. Remember this, because Mahamudra is the last, the Ultimate experience.

Mahamudra means a total orgasm with the universe. If you have loved somebody, and sometimes you have felt a melting and merging— the two are no more two; the bodies remain separate, but something between the bodies makes a bridge, a golden bridge, and the twoness inside disappears; one life-energy vibrates on both the poles—if it has happened to you, then only can you understand what Mahamudra is.

> Millions and millions of times deeper,
> millions and millions of times higher, is Mahamudra.
> It is a total orgasm with the Whole, with the universe.
> It is melting into the source of Being.

And this is a song of Mahamudra. It is beautiful that Tilopa has called it a song. You can sing it, but you cannot say it; you can dance it, but you cannot say it. It is such a deep phenomenon that singing may convey a little tiny part of it—not what you sing, but the way you sing it.

Many mystics have simply danced after their Ultimate experience, they could not do anything else. They were saying something through their whole being and body; altogether, body, mind, soul, everything involved in it. They were dancing, and those dances were not ordinary dances. In fact, all dancing was born because of these mystics; it was a way to relate the ecstasy, the happiness, the bliss. Something of the unknown has penetrated into the known, something of the beyond has come to the earth—what else can you do? You can dance it, you can sing it. This is a song of Mahamudra.

And who will sing it? Tilopa is no more. The orgasmic feeling itself is singing. It is not sung by Tilopa; Tilopa is *no* more. The experience itself is vibrating and singing. Hence, the Song of Mahamudra, the song of ecstasy, ecstasy itself singing it. Tilopa has nothing to do with it, Tilopa is not there at all, Tilopa has melted. When the seeker is lost, only then is the goal achieved. Only when the experiencer is no more is the experience there. Seek and you will miss it — because through your seeking the seeker will be strengthened. Don't seek and you will find it. The very seeking, the very effort, becomes a barrier, because the more you seek, the more the ego is strengthened, the seeker. Do not seek.

This is the deepest message of this whole Song of Mahamudra: do not seek, just remain as you are, don't go anywhere else. Nobody ever reaches God, nobody can because you don't know the address. Where will you go? Where will you find the Divine? There is no map, and there is no way, and there is nobody to say where He is. No, nobody ever reaches God. It is always the reverse: God comes to you. Whenever you are ready, He knocks at your door; He seeks you whenever you are ready. And the readiness is nothing but a receptivity: when you are completely receptive there is no ego; you become a hollow temple with nobody in it.

Tilopa says in the song, become like a hollow bamboo, nothing inside. And suddenly, the moment you are a hollow bamboo, the Divine lips are on you, the hollow bamboo becomes a flute, and the song starts — this is the Song of Mahamudra. Tilopa has become a hollow bamboo, and the Divine has come, and the song has started. It is not Tilopa's song, it is the Song of the Ultimate experience itself.

Something about Tilopa before we enter into this beautiful phenomenon. Nothing much is known about Tilopa, because nothing in fact can be known about such persons. They don't leave a trace, they don't become a part of history. They exist by the side, they are not part of the main traffic where the whole of humanity is moving; they don't move there. The whole of humanity moves through desiring, and persons like Tilopa move into desirelessness. They simply move away from the main traffic of humanity where history exists.

And the further away they go from the traffic, the more mythological they become. They exist like myths, they are no longer events in time. And this is as it should be, because they move beyond time, they live beyond time — they live in eternity. From this dimension of our common humanity, they simply disappear, they evaporate. The moment when they are evaporating, only that moment we remember, that much they are part of us. That's why nothing much is known about Tilopa, who he was.

Only this song exists. This is Tilopa's gift, and the gift was given to his disciple Naropa. These gifts cannot be given to anybody — unless a deep love intimacy exists. One has to be capable of receiving such gifts and this song was given to Naropa, his disciple. Before it was given to Naropa he was tested in millions of ways: his faith, his love and trust. When it came to be known that nothing like doubt existed in him, not even a tiny particle of doubt, when his heart was totally filled with trust and love, then this song was given.

I am also here to sing a song, but it can be given to you only when you are ready. And your readiness means that doubt should simply have disappeared from the mind. It should not be suppressed, you should not try to defeat it, because defeated it will remain in you; suppressed, it will remain part of your unconscious and it will go on affecting you. Don't fight your doubting mind, don't suppress it, rather, on the contrary, simply bring more and more energy into trust. Simply be indifferent to your doubting mind, nothing else can be done.

Indifference is the key, simply be indifferent. It is there — accept it. Bring your energies more and more towards trust and love — because the energy which becomes doubt is the same energy which becomes trust. Remain indifferent to doubt. The moment you are indifferent your cooperation is broken, you are not feeding it — because it is through attention that anything is fed. If you pay attention to your doubt, even by being against it, it is dangerous because the very attention is the food, that is cooperation. One just has to be indifferent, neither for nor against : don't be for doubt, don't be against doubt.

So now you will have to understand three words. One word is 'doubt', another word is 'belief', the third word is 'trust' or 'faith', what in the East is known as *shraddha*. Doubt is a negative attitude towards anything. Whatsoever is said, first you look at it negatively. You are against it, and you will find reasons, rationalizations to support your 'againstness'. Then there is the mind of belief. It is just like the mind of doubt only standing upside-down; there is not much difference. This mind looks at things positively and tries to find reasons, rationalizations to support its attitude, how to be for. The mind which doubts suppresses belief; the mind which believes suppresses doubt — but they are both of the same stuff, the quality is not different.

Then there is the third type of mind where doubt has simply disappeared — and when doubt disappears, belief also disappears. Faith is not belief, it is love; faith is not belief because it is not half, it is total. Faith is not belief because there is no doubt in it, so how can you believe?

7

Faith is not a rationalization at all: neither for nor against, neither this nor that. Faith is a trusting, a deep trusting, a love. You don't find any rationalizations for it, it simply is so. So what to do?

Don't create belief against faith. Just be indifferent to both belief and doubt, and bring your energies towards more and more love; love more, love unconditionally. Not only love me, because that is not possible: if you love, you simply love more. If you love, you simply exist in a more loving way — not only towards the Master, but towards everything that exists around you: towards the trees and the stones, and the sky and the earth. You, your being, your very quality of being, becomes a love phenomenon. Then trust arises. And only in such a trust can a gift like the Song of Mahamudra be given. When Naropa was ready, Tilopa gave this gift.

So remember that with a Master you are not on a 'head-trip'. Doubt and belief are both 'head-trips'. With a Master you are on a 'heart-trip'. And the heart doesn't know what doubt is, the heart doesn't know what belief is — the heart simply knows trust. The heart is just like a small child: a small child clings to his father's hand, and wherever the father is going the child is going, neither trusting nor doubting; the child is undivided. Doubt is half, belief is half. A child is still total, whole; he simply goes with his father wherever he is going. When a disciple becomes just like a child, then only can these gifts of the highest peak of consciousness be given.

When you become the deepest valley of reception, then the highest peaks of consciousness can be given to you. Only a valley can receive a peak. A disciple should be absolutely feminine, receptive, like a womb. Only then does such a phenomenon happen as is going to happen in this song.

Tilopa is the Master, Naropa is the disciple, and Tilopa says:

Mahamudra is beyond all words and symbols,
but for you, Naropa, earnest and loyal,
must this be said ...

It is beyond words and symbols, all words and all symbols. Then how can it be said? If it is really beyond all words and symbols, then how can it be said? Is there any way then? Yes, there is a way: if there is a Naropa there is a way; if there is really a disciple there is a way. It depends on the disciple whether the way will be found or not.

If the disciple is so receptive that he has no mind of his own — he does not judge whether it is right or wrong, he has *no* mind of his own,

8

he has surrendered his mind to the Master, he is simply a receptivity, an emptiness, ready to welcome whatsoever is given unconditionally — then words and symbols are not needed, then something can be given. And you can hear it between the words, you can read it between the lines — then words are just an excuse. The real thing happens just by the side of the words.

Words are just a trick, a device. The real thing follows the words like a shadow. And if you are too much of the mind, you will listen to the words, but then it cannot be communicated. But if you are not a mind at all, then the subtle shadows that follow the words, very subtle, only the heart can see them, invisible shadows, invisible ripples of consciousness, 'vibes' . . . then communion is immediately posssible.

Says Tilopa:

> . . . *but for you, Naropa, earnest and loyal,*
> *must this be said* . . .

That which cannot be said, *must* be said for a disciple. That which cannot be said, which is absolutely invisible, must be made visible for the disciple. It depends, not only on the Master, *even more* it depends on the disciple.

Tilopa was fortunate to find a Naropa. There have been a few Masters, unfortunate, who never could find a disciple like Naropa. So whatsoever they had gained disappeared with them, because there was nobody to receive it.

Sometimes Masters have travelled thousands of miles to find a disciple. Tilopa himself went from India to Tibet to find Naropa, to find a disciple. Tilopa wandered all over India and couldn't find a man of that quality, who would receive such a gift, who would appreciate such a gift, who would be able to absorb it, to be reborn through it. And once the gift was received by Naropa, he became totally transformed. Then Tilopa is reported to have said to Naropa, 'Now you go and find your own Naropa.'

Naropa was also fortunate in that way: he was able to find a disciple whose name was Marpa. Marpa was also very fortunate, he was able to find a disciple whose name was Milarepa. But then the tradition disappeared, then no more disciples of that great calibre could be found. Many times religion has come to the earth and disappeared; many times it will come and disappear. A religion cannot become a Church, a religion cannot become a sect; a religion depends on *personal* communication, on personal communion. The religion of

Tilopa existed only for four generations, from Naropa to Milarepa, then it disappeared.

Religion is just like an oasis: the desert is vast, and sometimes in tiny parts of the desert an oasis appears. While it lasts, seek it; while it is there, drink of it — it is very very rare.

Jesus says many times to his disciples, 'A little while more I am here. And while I am here, eat me, drink me. Don't miss this opportunity' — because then for thousands of years a man like Jesus may not be there. The desert is vast. The oasis sometimes appears and disappears, because the oasis comes from the unknown and it needs an anchor on this earth. If the anchor is not there it cannot remain here. A Naropa is an anchor.

The same I would like to say to you: While I am here, a little while more, don't miss the opportunity. And you can miss it in trivial things: you can remain occupied with nonsense, with mental garbage; you can go on thinking for and against — and the oasis will disappear soon. You can think for and against later on. Right now, drink of it, because then there will be many lives for you to think for and against, there is no hurry for it. But while it lasts, drink of it.

Once you are drunk with a Jesus or a Naropa, you are totally transformed. The transformation is very very easy and simple, it is a natural process. All that is needed is to become a soil and receive the seed; to become a womb and receive the seed.

> *Mahamudra is beyond all words and symbols,*
> *but for you, Naropa, earnest and loyal,*
> *must this be said . . .*

It cannot be uttered, it is unutterable — but it has to be said for a Naropa. Wherever a disciple is ready the Master appears, has to appear. Wherever there is a deep need, it has to be fulfilled. The whole existence responds to your deepest need, but the need must be there. Otherwise you can pass a Tilopa, a Buddha, a Jesus, and may not even be able to see that you passed a Jesus.

Tilopa lived in this country. Nobody listened to him — and he was ready to give the Ultimate gift. What happened? And this has happened in this country many times, there must be something behind it. And this has happened more in this country than anywhere else, because more Tilopas have been born here. But why does it happen that a Tilopa has to go to Tibet? Why does it happen that a Bodhidharma has to go to China?

10

This country knows too much, this country has become too much of the head. That's why it is difficult to find a heart — the country of Brahmins and pundits, the country of great knowers, philosophers. They know all the Vedas, all the Upanishads, they can recite from memory all the scriptures: a country of the head. That's why it has been happening so many times.

Even I feel, so many times I feel it, that whenever a Brahmin comes it is difficult to communicate. A man who knows too much becomes almost impossible — because he knows without knowing. He has gathered many concepts, theories, doctrines, scriptures. It is just a burden on his consciousness, it is not a flowering. It has not happened to him, it is all borrowed, and all that is borrowed is rubbish, rot — throw it as soon as you can throw it.

Only that which happens to you is true.

Only that which flowers in you is true.

Only that which grows in you is true and alive.

Remember it always: avoid borrowed knowledge.

Borrowed knowledge becomes a trick of the mind: it hides ignorance — it never destroys it. And the more you are surrounded by knowledge, deep inside at the center, at the very root of your being, the more ignorance and darkness there is. And a man of knowledge, borrowed knowledge, is almost completely closed within his own knowledge; you cannot penetrate him. And it is difficult to find his heart, he himself has lost all contact with his heart. So it is not incidental that a Tilopa has to go to Tibet, a Bodhidharma to China: a seed has to travel so far, not finding a soil here.

Remember this, because it is easy to become very strongly addicted to knowledge — it is an addiction, it is a drug. And LSD is not so dangerous, marijuana is not so dangerous. In a way they are similar, because marijuana gives you a glimpse of something which is not there; it gives you a dream of something which is absolutely subjective — it gives you a hallucination. Knowledge is also the same: it gives you a hallucination of knowing. You start feeling that you know because you can recite the Vedas, you know because you can argue, you know because you have a very very logical, keen mind. Don't be a fool! Logic has never led anybody to Truth. And a rational mind is just a game. All arguments are juvenile.

Life exists without any argument, and Truth needs no proofs — it needs only your heart; not arguments, but your love, your trust, your readiness to receive.

Mahamudra is beyond all words and symbols,
but for you, Naropa, earnest and loyal,
must this be said:

The Void needs no reliance,
Mahamudra rests on nought.
Without making an effort,
but remaining loose and natural,
one can break the yoke —
thus gaining Liberation.

You cannot find more significant words ever uttered. Try to understand every nuance of what Tilopa is trying to say.

The Void needs no reliance . . .

If there is something, it needs a support, it needs a reliance. But if there is nothing, emptiness, there is no need for any support. And this is the deepest realization of all the knowers: that your being is a non-being. To say it is a being is wrong because it is not something, it is not like something. It is like nothing: a vast emptiness, with no boundaries to it. It is an *anatma*, a no-self; it is not a self inside you.

All feelings of self are false. All identifications that 'I am this or that' are false.

When you come to the Ultimate, when you come to your deepest core, you suddenly know that you are neither this nor that — you are no one. You are not an ego, you are just a vast emptiness. And sometimes if you sit, close your eyes and just feel who you are, where are you? Go deeper and you may become afraid, because the deeper you go, the deeper you feel that you are nobody, a nothingness. That's why people become so scared of meditation: it is a death, it is a death of the ego — and the ego is just a false concept.

Now physicists have come to the same truth through their scientific research deepening into the realm of matter. What Buddha, Tilopa and Bodhidharma reached through their insight, science has been discovering in the outside world also. Now they say there is no substance — and substance is a parallel concept to self.

A rock exists, you feel that it is very substantial. You can hit somebody's head with it and blood will come out, the man may even die; it is very substantial. But ask the physicists: they say it is a no-substance, there is nothing in it. They say that it is just an energy phenomenon; many energy currents criss-crossing on this rock give it a feeling of substance. Just as when you draw many lines criss-crossing on a piece of paper: where many lines cross a point, a point arises. The point was not there; two lines crossing and a point arises; many lines crossing and a big point arises. Is that point really there? Or do just lines crossing give an illusion of a point being there?

Physicists say that energy currents criss-crossing create matter. And if you ask what these energy currents are: they are not material, they have no weight, they are non-material. Non-material lines criss-crossing give an illusion of a material thing, very substantial like a rock.

Buddha achieved this illumination twenty-five centuries before Einstein: that inside there is nobody; only energy lines criss-crossing give you a feeling of the self. Buddha used to say that the self is like an onion: you peel it, one layer comes off, another layer is there. You go on peeling, layer by layer, and what remains finally? The whole onion is peeled and you find nothing inside.

Man is just like an onion. You peel layers of thought, feeling, and finally, what do you find? A nothing.

This nothingness needs no support.

This nothingness exists by itself.

That's why Buddha says there is no God; there is no need for a God because God is a support. And Buddha says there is no Creator, because there is no need to create a nothingness. This is one of the most difficult concepts to understand — unless you realize it.

That's why Tilopa says:

Mahamudra is beyond all words and symbols.

Mahamudra is an experience of nothingness —
simply, you are not.

And when you are not, then who is there to suffer?

Who is there to be in pain and anguish?

Who is there to be depressed and sad?

And who is there to be happy and blissful?

Buddha says that if you feel you are blissful you will again become a victim of suffering, because you are still there. When you are not, completely not, utterly not, then there is no suffering and no bliss— and this is the real bliss. Then you cannot fall back. To attain nothingness is to attain all.

My whole effort with you is also to lead you toward nothingness, to lead you to a total vacuum.

The Void needs no reliance,
Mahamudra rests on nought.
Without making an effort,
but remaining loose and natural,
one can break the yoke —
thus gaining Liberation.

The first thing to understand is that the concept of self is created by the mind — there is no self in you.

It happened: A great Buddhist, a man of Enlightenment, was invited by a King to teach him. The name of the Buddhist monk was Nagasen, and the King was a viceroy of Alexander. When Alexander went back from India, he left Minander here as his viceroy; his Indian name is Milinda. Milinda asked Nagasen to come and teach him. He was really interested, and he had heard many stories about Nagasen. Many rumours had come to the court: 'This is a rare phenomenon! Rarely does it happen that a man flowers, and this man has flowered. He has an aroma of something unknown around him, a mysterious energy. He walks on the earth, but he is not of the earth.' The King became interested so he invited him.

The messenger who went to Nagasen came back very much puzzled, because Nagasen had said, 'Yes, if he invites, Nagasen will come — but tell him there is no one like Nagasen. If he invites I will come, but tell him exactly that there is no one like "I am". I am no more.' The messenger was puzzled, because if Nagasen was no more, then who would come? Milinda was also puzzled, he said, 'This man talks in puzzles. But let him come.' He was a Greek, this Milinda, and the Greek mind is basically logical.

There are only two minds in the world, the Indian and the Greek. The Indian is illogical, and the Greek is logical. The Indian moves into the dark depths, wild depths; there are no boundaries, everything is vague, cloudy. The Greek mind walks on the logical line, the straight, where everything is defined and classified. The Greek mind moves into the known. The Indian mind moves into the unknown, and, moreover, into the unknowable. The Greek mind is absolutely rational; the Indian mind is absolutely contradictory. So if you find too many contradictions in me, don't be bothered — it is the way, in the East contradiction is the way to relate.

Milinda said, 'This man seems to be irrational, gone mad. If he is not then how can he come? But let him come, I will see. I will prove it: just by coming he is proving that he is.'

Then Nagasen came. Milinda received him at the gate and the first thing he said was, 'I am puzzled: you have come although you said that you are not.'

Nagasen said, 'Still I say. So let us settle it here.'

A crowd gathered, the whole court came there, and Nagasen said, 'You ask.'

Milinda asked, 'First tell me: if something is not, how can it come? If in the first place it is not, then there is no possibility of its coming — and you have come. It is simple logic that you are.'

Nagasen laughed and he said, 'Look at this *ratha*,' the chariot on which he had come. He said, 'Look at this. You call it a *ratha*, a chariot.'

Milinda said, 'Yes.'

Then he told his followers to remove the horses. The horses were removed and Nagasen asked, 'Are these horses the chariot?'

Milinda said, 'Of course not.'

Then, by and by, everything from the chariot was removed, every part. Wheels were removed and he asked, 'Are these wheels the chariot?'

And Milinda said, 'Of course not!'

When everything was removed and there was nothing left, then asked Nagasen, 'Where is the chariot I came in? . . . and we never removed the chariot, and all that we removed you confirmed was not the chariot. Now where is the chariot?'

Nagasen said, 'Just like this, Nagasen exists. Remove parts and he will disappear.' Just criss-crossing lines of energy: remove the lines and the dot will disappear. The chariot was just a combination of parts.

You are also a combination of parts, the 'I' is a combination of parts. Remove things and the 'I' will disappear. That's why when thoughts are removed from consciousness, you cannot say 'I', because there is no 'I' — just a vacuum is left. When feelings are removed, the self disappears completely. You are and yet not: just an absence, with no boundaries, emptiness.

This is the final attainment, this state is Mahamudra — because only in that state can you have an orgasm with the Whole — now there is no boundary, no self exists; now there is no boundary to you to divide.

The Whole has no boundaries. You *must* become like the Whole — only then can there be a meeting, a merger. When you are empty, you are without boundaries, and suddenly you become the Whole.

When you are not, you become the Whole.

When you are, you become an ugly ego.

When you are not, you have all the expanse of existence for your being to be.

But these are contradictions. So try to understand: become a little like Naropa, otherwise these words and symbols will not carry anything to you. Listen to me in trust. And when I say, listen to me in trust, I mean I have known this, this is so. I am a witness, I bear witness to it, this is so. It may not be possible to say it, but that doesn't mean that it is not. It may be possible to say something, but that doesn't mean that it is. You can say something which is not, and you may be incapable of saying something which is. I bear witness to it, but you will be able to understand me only if you are a Naropa, if you listen in trust.

I am not teaching a doctrine. I would not have been at all concerned with Tilopa if this were not my own experience also. Tilopa has said it well:

The Void needs no reliance,
Mahamudra rests on nought.

On nothing Mahamudra rests.
Mahamudra, the literal word, means the great gesture, or the Ultimate gesture, the last that you can have, beyond which nothing is possible.

Mahamudra rests on nothing.

Be a nothing, and then all is attained.

Die, and you become a god.

Disappear, and you become the Whole.

Here the drop disappears,

and there the ocean comes into existence.

Don't cling to yourself — that's all you have been doing all your past lives: clinging, afraid that if you don't cling to the ego, then you look down and a bottomless abyss is there. . . .

That's why we cling to tiny things, very trivial, we go on clinging to them. The clinging shows that you are also aware of a vast emptiness inside. Something is needed to cling to, but your clinging is your *samsara*, is your misery. Let yourself fall into the abyss. And once you let yourself fall into the abyss, you become the abyss itself.

16

Then there is no death, because how can an abyss die?
Then there is no end to it, because how can a nothingness end?
Something can end, will have to end—
only nothing can be eternal.
Mahamudra rests on nothing.

Let me explain to you through some experience that you have. When you love a person, you have to become a nothing. When you love a person, you have to become a no-self. That's why love is so difficult. And that's why Jesus says God is like love. He knows something about Mahamudra—because before he started teaching in Jerusalem, he had been to India. He had been to Tibet also and he met people like Tilopa and Naropa. He stayed in Buddhist monasteries. He learned about what it is that these people call nothingness. Then he tried to translate his whole understanding into Jewish terminology. There everything got messed up.

You cannot translate Buddhist understanding into Jewish terminology. It is impossible, because the whole of Jewish terminology depends on positive terms, and Buddhist terminology depends on absolutely nihilistic terms: nothingness, emptiness. But here and there in Jesus' words there are glimpses. He says, 'God is love,' he is indicating something. What is the indication?

When you love, you have to become nobody. If you remain a somebody then love never happens. When you love a person, even for a single moment when love happens and flows between two persons, there are two nothingnesses, not two persons. If you have ever had any experience of love, you can understand.

Two lovers sitting by each other's side, or two nothingnesses sitting together—only then is the meeting possible because barriers are broken, boundaries thrown away. The energy can move from here to there, there is no hindrance. And only in such a moment of deep love is orgasm possible.

When two lovers are making love, and if they are both no-selves, nothingnesses, then orgasm happens. Then their body energy, their whole being, loses all identity; they are no more themselves—they have fallen into the abyss. But this can happen only for a moment: again they regain; again they start clinging. That's why people become afraid in love also.

In deep love people are afraid of becoming mad, or that they are going to die, afraid of what will happen. The abyss opens its mouth, the whole existence yawns—and you are suddenly there and you can

17

fall into it. People become scared of love, then people remain satisfied with sex and they call their sex 'love'.

Love is not sex. Sex can happen in love, it can be a part, an integral part of it, but sex itself is not love — it is a substitute. You are trying to avoid love through sex. You are giving yourself a feeling that you are in love, but you are not moving into love. Sex is just like borrowed knowledge: giving a feeling of knowing without knowing; giving a feeling of love and loving without loving.

In love you are not, the other is also not: then only, suddenly, do the two disappear. The same happens in Mahamudra. Mahamudra is a total orgasm with the whole existence.

That's why in Tantra — and Tilopa is a Tantric Master — deep intercourse, orgasmic intercourse, between two lovers is also called Mahamudra, and two lovers in a deep orgasmic state are pictured in Tantric temples, in Tantric books. That has become a symbol of the final orgasm.

Mahamudra rests on nought.
Without making an effort,
but remaining loose and natural . . .

And this is the whole method of Tilopa, and the whole method of Tantra: *Without making an effort . . .* because if you make an effort, the ego is strengthened. If you make an effort, you come in.

So love is not an effort, you cannot make an effort to love. If you make an effort, there is no love. You flow into it, you don't make an effort; you simply allow it to happen, you don't *make* an effort. It is not a doing, it is a happening: *Without making an effort . . .* And the same is the case with the total, the final: you don't make an effort, you simply float with it . . . *but remaining loose and natural.* This is the way, this is the very ground of Tantra.

Yoga says make an effort, and Tantra says don't make any effort. Yoga is ego-oriented, finally it will take the jump, but Tantra is, from the very beginning, non-ego-oriented. Yoga, in the end, attains to such significance, such meaning, such depth, that it says to the seeker, 'Now drop the ego' — only in the end. Tantra says it from the very beginning, from the very first step.

I would like to say it in this way, in such a way: that where Yoga ends, Tantra starts. The highest peak of Yoga is the beginning of Tantra — and Tantra leads you to the Ultimate goal. Yoga can prepare you for Tantra, that's all, because the final thing is to be effortless, 'loose and natural'.

What does Tilopa mean by 'loose and natural'? Don't fight with yourself, be loose. Don't try to make a structure around you of character, of morality. Don't discipline yourself too much, otherwise your very discipline will become the bondage. Don't create an imprisonment around you. Remain loose, floating, move with the situation, respond to the situation. Don't move with a character-jacket around you, don't move with a fixed attitude. Remain loose like water, not fixed like ice. Remain moving and flowing; wherever nature leads you, go. Don't resist, don't try to impose anything on yourself, your being.

But the whole society teaches you to impose something or other: Be good, be moral, be this and that. And Tantra is absolutely beyond society, culture, and civilization. It says that if you are too cultured you will lose all that is natural, and then you will be a mechanical thing, not floating, not flowing. So don't force a structure around you — live moment to moment, live with alertness. And this is a deep thing to be understood.

Why do people try to create a structure around them? So that they don't need alertness — because if you have no character around you, you will need to be very very aware: each moment the decision has to be taken. You don't have a pre-fabricated decision, you don't have an attitude. You have to respond to the situation: something is there, and you are absolutely unprepared for it — you will have to be very very aware.

To avoid awareness people have created a trick, and the trick is character. Force yourself into a certain discipline so that whether you are aware or not, the discipline will take care of you. Make a habit of always saying the truth, make it a habit, then you need not be worried about it. Somebody asks something and you will say the truth, out of habit — but out of habit a truth is dead.

And life is not so simple. Life is a very very complex phenomenon. Sometimes a lie is needed, and sometimes a truth can be dangerous — one has to be aware. For example, if through your lie somebody's life is saved, if through your lie nobody is harmed and somebody's life is saved, what will you do? If you have a fixed mind that you have to be true, then you will kill a life.

Nothing is more valuable than life, no truth, nothing is more

19

valuable than a life. And sometimes your truth can kill somebody's life. What will you do? Just to save your own old pattern and habit, your own ego that 'I am a truthful man', you will sacrifice a life — just being a truthful man, just to be that? This is too much, you are completely mad! If a life can be saved, even if people think that you are a liar, what is wrong in it? Why bother too much about what people say about you?

It is difficult! It is not so easy to create a fixed pattern because life goes on moving and changing, every moment there is a new situation and one has to respond to it. Respond with full awareness, that's all. And let the decision come out of the situation itself, not prefabricated, not imposed. Don't carry a built-in mind, just remain loose and aware and natural.

This is how a real religious man is; otherwise, so-called religious persons are just dead. They act out of their habits, they go on acting out of their habits — this is a conditioning, this is not a freedom. Consciousness needs freedom.

Be loose: remember this word as deeply as possible. Let it penetrate you: Be loose — so that in every situation you can flow, easily, water-like; so that if the water is poured into a glass, it takes the shape of the glass. It doesn't resist, it doesn't say, 'This is not my form.' If the water is poured into a jar, into a jug, it takes the shape of that. It has no resistance, it is loose.

Remain loose like water.

Sometimes you will have to move south and sometimes north, you will have to change directions; according to the situation you will have to flow. But if you know how to flow, it is enough. The ocean is not very far away if you know how to flow.

So don't create a pattern — but the whole society tries to create a pattern, and all the religions try to create a pattern. Only a very few persons, Enlightened Ones, have been courageous enough to say the truth, and the truth is: Be loose and natural! If you are loose you will be natural, of course.

Tilopa doesn't say, 'Be moral,' he says, 'Be natural.' And these are completely, diametrically opposite dimensions. A moral man is never natural, cannot be. If he feels angry he cannot be angry because the morality doesn't allow it. If he feels loving he cannot be loving because the morality is there. It is always according to the morality that he acts; it is never according to his nature.

But I tell you: if you start moving according to moral patterns and not according to your nature, you will never reach the state of Mahamudra, because it is a natural state, the highest peak of being natural. I tell you: if you feel angry, be angry — but perfect awareness has to be retained. Anger should not overpower your consciousness, that's all.

Let anger be there, let it happen, but be fully alert to what is happening. Remain loose, natural, aware, *watching* what is happening. By and by, you will see that many things have simply disappeared, they don't happen any more — and without making any effort on your part. You never tried to kill them and they have simply disappeared.

When one is aware, anger by and by disappears. It becomes simply stupid — *not bad*, remember, because 'bad' has a loaded value. It becomes simply stupid! It is not because it is bad that you don't move into it, it is simply foolish; it is not a sin, but simply stupid. Greed disappears, it is stupid. Jealousy disappears, it is stupid.

Remember this valuation. In morality there exists something good and something bad. In being natural there exists something wise and something stupid. A man who is natural is wise, *not good*. A man who is not natural is stupid, *not bad*. There is nothing bad and nothing good, only wise things and stupid things. And if you are foolish you harm yourself and others; if you are wise you don't harm anybody — neither others, nor yourself.

There is nothing like sin
and there is nothing like virtue —
wisdom is all.
If you want to call it virtue, call it virtue.
And there is ignorance —
if you want to call it sin,
that is the only sin.

So how to transform your ignorance into wisdom? That is the only transformation — and you cannot force it: it happens when you are loose and natural.

. . . remaining loose and natural,
one can break the yoke —
thus gaining Liberation.

And one becomes totally free. It will be difficult in the beginning, because constantly the old habits will be there forcing you to do something: you would like to be angry — but the old habit simply

21

starts a smile on your face. There are people who, whenever they smile, you can be certain that they are angry. In their very smile they show their anger. They are hiding something, a false smile spreads on their faces. These are the hypocrites.

A hypocrite is an unnatural man: if anger is there he will smile; if hate is there he will show love; if he feels murderous, he will pretend compassion. A hypocrite is a perfect moralist — absolutely artificial, a plastic flower, ugly, of no use; not a flower at all, just a pretension.

Tantra is the natural way: Be loose and natural. It will be difficult because the old habits have to be broken. It is difficult because you will have to live in a society of hypocrites. It will be difficult because everywhere you will find a conflict with the hypocrites — but one has to go through it. It will be arduous because there are many investments in false, artificial pretensions. You may feel completely alone, but this will be only a passing phase. Soon others will start feeling your authenticity.

And remember, even an authentic anger is better than a pretended smile, because at least it is authentic. And a man who cannot be authentically angry, cannot be authentic at all. At least he is authentic, true, true to his being. Whatsoever is happening, you can rely on him that it is true.

And this is my observation: that a true anger is beautiful and a false smile is ugly; and a true hate has its own beauty, just like true love — because beauty is concerned with *Truth*. It is neither concerned with hate, nor with love — beauty is of the true. Truth is beautiful in whatsoever form it takes. A truly dead man is more beautiful than a falsely alive man, because at least the basic quality of being true is there.

Mulla Nasrudin's wife died. The neighbours gathered, but Mulla Nasrudin was standing there completely unaffected, as if nothing had happened. Neighbours started crying and weeping and they said, 'What are you doing standing there, Nasrudin? She is dead!'

Nasrudin said, 'Wait! She is such a liar — at least for three days I have to wait and see whether it is true or not.'

But remember this, that beauty is of Truth, authenticity. Become more authentic and you will have a flowering. And the more authentic you become, by and by the more you will feel that many things are falling away — of their own accord. You never made any effort to do it; they are falling of their own accord. And once you know the knack of it, then you become more and more loose, more and more natural, authentic. And, says Tilopa:

> *... one can break the yoke —*
> *thus gaining Liberation.*

The liberation is not very far away, it is just hidden behind you. Once you are authentic the door is open — but you are such a liar, you are such a pretender, you are such a hypocrite, you are so deeply false; that's why you feel that liberation is very very far away. It is not! For an authentic being, liberation is just natural. It is as natural as anything.

As water flows towards the ocean,
as vapour rises towards the sky,
as the sun is hot and the moon is cool,
so for an authentic being is liberation.

It is nothing to be bragged about. It is nothing that you have to tell people that you have gained.

When Lin Chi was asked, 'What has happened to you? People say that you have become Enlightened,' he shrugged his shoulders and said, 'Happened? Nothing — I cut wood in the forest, and carry water to the *ashram*. I carry water from the well and cut wood because the winter is approaching.' He shrugged his shoulders — a very meaningful gesture.

He is saying, 'Nothing has happened. What nonsense you are asking! It is natural: carrying water from the well, cutting wood in the forest. Life is absolutely natural.' Says Lin Chi, 'When I feel sleepy, I go to sleep; and when I feel hungry, I eat. Life has become absolutely natural.'

Liberation is your being perfectly natural. Liberation is not something to be bragged about: that you have attained something very great. It is nothing great, it is nothing extraordinary. It is just being natural, just being yourself.

So what to do?

Drop tensions, drop hypocrisies, drop all that you have cultivated around your natural being — become natural. In the beginning it will be a very very arduous thing, but only in the beginning. Once you get attuned to it, others will also start feeling that something has happened to you, because an authentic being is such a force, such a magnetism. They will start feeling something has happened: 'This

23

man no longer moves as part of us, he has become totally different.'
And you will not be at a loss, because only artificial things will
drop.

And once the emptiness is created by throwing artificial things,
pretensions, masks, then the natural being starts flowing. It needs
space.

Be empty, loose and natural. Let that be the most fundamental
principle in your life.

The Song continues:

If one sees nought when staring into space;
if with the mind one then observes the mind,
one destroys distinctions
and reaches Buddhahood.

The clouds that wander through the sky
have no roots, no home;
nor do the distinctive thoughts
floating through the mind.
Once the Self-mind is seen,
discrimination stops.

In space shapes and colours form,
but neither by black nor white is space tinged.
From the Self-mind all things emerge,
the mind by virtues and by vices is not stained.

II   THE ROOT PROBLEM OF ALL PROBLEMS
12th February 1975

T HE ROOT PROBLEM of all problems is mind itself.
So the first thing to be understood is what this mind is, of what stuff it is made; whether it is an entity or just a process; whether it is substantial, or just dreamlike. And unless you know the nature of the mind, you will not be able to solve any problems of your life.

You may try hard, but if you try to solve single, individual problems, you are bound to be a failure — that is absolutely certain. Because in fact no individual problem exists: mind is the problem. If you solve this problem or that, it won't help because the root remains untouched.

It is just like cutting the branches of a tree, pruning the leaves, and not uprooting it. New leaves will come, new branches will sprout — even more than before; pruning helps a tree to become thicker. Unless you know how to uproot it, your fight is baseless, it is foolish. You will destroy yourself, not the tree.

In fighting you will waste your energy, time, life, and the tree will go on becoming more and more strong, thicker, denser. And you will be surprised at what is happening: you are doing so much hard work, trying to solve this problem and that, and they go on growing, increasing. Even if one problem is solved, suddenly ten problems take its place.

Don't try to solve individual single problems — there are none: *mind itself is the problem.* But mind is hidden underground; that's why I call it the root, it is not apparent. Whenever you come across a problem, the problem is above ground, you can see it — that's why you are deceived by it.

Always remember, the visible is never the root; the root always remains invisible, the root is always hidden. Never fight with the visible, otherwise you will be fighting with shadows. You may waste yourself, but there cannot be any transformation in your life; the same problems will crop up again and again and again. You can observe your own life and you will see what I mean. I am not talking about any theory about the mind, just the 'facticity' of it. This is the fact: mind has to be solved.

People come to me and they ask, 'How to attain a peaceful mind?' I say to them, 'There exists nothing like that: peaceful mind. Never heard of it.'

Mind is never peaceful — 'no-mind' is peace. Mind itself can never be peaceful, silent. The very nature of the mind is to be tense, to be in confusion. Mind can never be clear, it cannot have clarity, because mind is by nature confusion, cloudiness. Clarity is possible without mind, peace is possible without mind, silence is possible without mind — so never try to attain a silent mind. If you do, from the very beginning you will be moving in an impossible dimension.

So the first thing is to understand the nature of the mind, only then can something be done.

If you watch, you will never come across any entity like mind. It is not a thing, it is just a process; it is not a thing, it is like a crowd. Individual thoughts exist, but they move so fast that you cannot see the gaps in between. The intervals cannot be seen because you are not very aware and alert, you need a deeper insight. When your eyes can look deep, you will suddenly see one thought, another thought, another thought — but *no mind.*

Thoughts together, *millions* of thoughts, give you the illusion that mind exists. It is just like a crowd, millions of people standing in a crowd: is there any such thing as a crowd? Can you find the crowd apart from the individuals standing there? But they are standing together and their togetherness gives you the feeling that something like a crowd exists — only individuals exist.

This is the first insight into the mind. Watch, and you will find thoughts, but you will never come across the mind. And if it becomes your own experience — not because I say it, not because Tilopa sings about it, no, that won't be of much help — if it becomes *your* experience, if it becomes a fact of your own knowing, then suddenly many things start changing. Because you have understood such a deep thing about mind, then many things can follow.

Watch the mind and see where it is, what it is. You will feel thoughts floating and there will be intervals. And if you watch long, you will see that the intervals are more than the thoughts, because each thought has to be separate from another thought; in fact, each word has to be separate from another word. The deeper you go, the more and more gaps you will find, bigger and bigger gaps. A thought floats, then comes a gap where no thought exists; then another thought comes, another gap follows.

If you are unconscious you cannot see the gaps; you jump from one thought to another and you never see the gap. If you become aware you will see more and more gaps. If you become perfectly aware, then miles of gaps will be revealed to you.

And in those gaps, *satoris* happen.

In those gaps the Truth knocks at your door.

In those gaps, the guest comes.

In those gaps, God is realized,

or whatsoever way you like to express it.

And when awareness is absolute,

then there is only a vast gap of nothingness.

It is just like clouds: clouds move and they can be so thick that you cannot see the sky hidden behind. The vast blueness of the sky is lost and you are covered with clouds. Then you go on watching: one cloud moves and another has not come into your vision yet — and suddenly a peek into the blueness of the vast sky.

The same happens inside: you are the vast blueness of the sky, and thoughts are just like clouds hovering around you, filling you. But the gaps exist, the sky exists. To have a glimpse of the sky is *satori*, and to become the sky is *samadhi*. From *satori* to *samadhi*, the whole process is a deep insight into the mind, nothing else.

Mind doesn't exist as an entity, the first thing, only thoughts exist.

The second thing: thoughts exist separate from you, they are not one with your nature, they come and go — you remain, you persist. You are like the sky: it never comes, never goes, it is always there. Clouds come and go, they are momentary phenomena, they are not eternal. Even if you try to cling to a thought, you cannot retain it for long, it has to go, it has its own birth and death. Thoughts are not *yours*, they don't belong to you. They come as visitors, guests, but they are not the host.

Watch deeply, then you will become the host and thoughts will be the guests. And as guests they are beautiful, but if you forget completely that you are the host and they become the hosts, then you are

31

in a mess. This is what hell is. You are master of the house, the house belongs to you, and guests have become the masters. Receive them, take care of them, but don't get identified with them; otherwise, they will become the masters.

The mind becomes the problem because you have taken thoughts so deeply inside you, that you have forgotten completely the distance, that they are visitors, they come and go. Always remember that which abides: that is your nature, your *Tao*. Always be attentive to that which never comes and never goes, just like the sky. Change the *gestalt*: don't be focused on the visitors, remain rooted in the host; the visitors will come and go.

Of course, there are bad visitors and good visitors, but you need not be worried about them. A good host treats all the guests in the same way, without making any distinctions. A good host is just a good host: a bad thought comes and he also treats the bad thought in the same way as he treats a good thought. It is not his concern whether the thought is good or bad.

What are you doing once you make the distinction that this thought is good and that thought is bad? You are bringing the good thought nearer to yourself and pushing the bad thought further away. Sooner or later you will get identified with the good thought; the good thought will become the host. And any thought when it becomes the host creates misery — because this is not the truth; the thought is a pretender and you get identified with it. Identification is the disease.

Gurdjieff used to say that only one thing is needed: not to be identified with that which comes and goes. The morning comes, then noon comes, the evening comes, and they go; the night comes and again the morning. You abide: not as you, because that too is a thought — as pure consciousness; not your name, because that too is a thought; not your form, because that too is a thought; not your body, because one day you will realize that too is a thought. Just pure consciousness, with no name, no form; just the purity, just the formlessness and name-lessness, just the very phenomenon of being aware — only that abides.

If you get identified, you become the mind. If you get identified, you become the body. If you get identified you become the name and the form— what Hindus call *nama, rupa,* name and form — then the host is lost. Then you forget the eternal and the *momentary* becomes significant. The momentary is the world; the eternal is Divine.

This is the second insight to be attained, that you are the host and thoughts are guests.

The third thing, if you go on watching, will be realized soon. The third thing is that thoughts are foreign, intruders, outsiders. *No thought is yours.* They always come from without, you are just a passage. A bird comes into the house by one door, and flies out by another: just like that a thought comes into you and goes out of you.

You go on thinking that thoughts are yours. Not only that, you also fight for your thoughts, you say, 'This is my thought, this is true.' You discuss, you debate, you argue about it, you try to prove that, 'This is *my* thought.' No thought is yours, no thought is original — all thoughts are borrowed. And they are not just second-hand, because millions of people have claimed those same thoughts before you. Thought is just as much outside as a thing.

Somewhere, the great physicist Eddington has said that the deeper science goes into matter, the more the realization comes that things are thoughts. That may be so, I am not a physicist, and Eddington may be right that things look more and more like thoughts the deeper you go, but from the other end I would like to tell you that if you go deeper into yourself, thoughts will look more and more like things. In fact, these are two aspects of the same phenomenon: a thing is a thought, a thought is a thing.

When I say a thought is a thing, what do I mean? I mean that you can throw your thought just like a thing. You can hit somebody's head with a thought just like a thing. You can kill a person through a thought just as you can throw a dagger. You can give your thought as a gift, or, as an infection. Thoughts are things, they are forces, but they don't belong to you. They come to you, they abide for a while in you and then they leave you. The whole universe is filled with thoughts and things. Things are just the physical part of thoughts, and thoughts are the mental part of things.

Because of this fact, because thoughts are things, many miracles happen. If a person continuously thinks about you and your welfare, it will happen — because he is throwing a continuous force at you. That's why blessings are useful, helpful. If you can be blessed by someone who has attained no-mind, the blessing is going to be true — because a man who never uses thought, accumulates thought energy, so whatsoever he says is going to be true.

In all the Eastern traditions, before a person starts learning no-mind, techniques are given and much emphasis that he should stop being negative, because if you once attain to no-mind and your trend remains negative, you can become a dangerous force. Before the no-mind is attained, one should become absolutely positive. That is the whole difference between white and black magic.

Black magic is nothing but a man who has accumulated thought energy without throwing his negativity beforehand. And white magic is nothing but a man who has attained to much thought energy, and has based his total being on a positive attitude. The same energy with negativity becomes black; the same energy with positivity becomes white. A thought is a great force, it is a thing.

This will be the third insight. It has to be understood and watched within yourself.

Sometimes it happens that you see your thought functioning as a thing, but just because of too much materialistic conditioning you think this may be just a coincidence. You neglect the fact, you simply don't give any attention to it; you remain indifferent, you forget about it. But many times you know that sometimes you were thinking about the death of a certain person — and he dies. You think it is just a coincidence. At some point you were thinking about a friend and a desire arose in you that it would be good if he came — and he is at the door, knocking. You think it is a coincidence. It is not coincidence. In fact, there is no such thing as coincidence, everything has its causality. Your thoughts go on creating a world around you.

Your thoughts are things, so be careful about them. Handle them carefully! If you are not very conscious, you can create misery for yourself and for others — and you have done that. And remember, when you create misery for somebody, unconsciously, at the same time, you are creating misery for yourself — because a thought is a two-edged sword. It also cuts you simultaneously when it cuts somebody else.

Just two or three years ago, one Israeli, Uri Geller, who has been working on thought energy, displayed an experiment on BBC television in England. He can bend anything just by thinking: somebody else holds a spoon in his hand ten feet away from Uri Geller, and he just thinks about it — and the spoon bends immediately. You cannot bend it with your hand, and he bends it with his thought. But a very rare phenomenon happened on the BBC television; even Uri Geller was not aware that this is possible.

Thousands of people in their homes were watching the experiment. And when he did it, bent things, in many people's houses many things fell and became distorted — thousands of things all over England. It was as if the energy was broadcast. If he was doing the experiment with a distance of ten feet, then from the television screen in people's homes, within the area of ten feet, many things happened: things got bent, fell down, became distorted. It was weird!

Thoughts are things, and very very forceful things. There is one woman in Soviet Russia, Mikhailova. She can do many things to objects from a great distance, she can pull anything towards herself — just by thought. Soviet Russia is not a believer in occult things — a communist country, atheistic — so they have been working on Mikhailova, on what is happening, in a scientific way. But when she does it, she loses almost two pounds in weight; in a half-hour experiment she loses two pounds in weight. What does it mean?

It means that through thoughts you are throwing energy — and you are continuously doing it.

Your mind is a chatterbox.

You are broadcasting things unnecessarily.

You are destroying people around you,

you are destroying yourself.

You are a dangerous thing — continuously broadcasting.

And many things are happening because of you. It is a great network too: the whole world goes on becoming every day more and more miserable because more and more people are on the earth and they are broadcasting more and more thoughts.

The further back you go, the more and more peaceful you find the earth — less and less broadcasters. In the days of Buddha, or in the days of Lao Tzu, the world was very very peaceful, natural; it was a heaven. Why? The population was very very small, one thing. And people were not prone to thinking too much, they were more and more prone towards feeling; also, rather than thinking, people were praying. In the morning, the first thing they would do would be a prayer. In the night the last thing they would do would be the prayer. And throughout the whole day also, whenever they could find a moment, they would be praying inside.

What is prayer?

Prayer is sending blessings to all.

Prayer is sending your compassion to all.

Prayer is creating an antidote to negative thoughts —

It is a positivity.

This will be the third insight about thoughts, that they are things, forces, and you have to handle them very carefully.

Ordinarily, not aware, you go on thinking anything. It is difficult

35

to find a person who has not committed many murders in thought; difficult to find a person who has not been committing all sorts of sins and crimes inside the mind — and then these things happen. And remember, you may not murder, but your continuous thinking of murdering somebody may create the situation in which the person is murdered. Somebody may take your thought, because there are weaker persons all around and thoughts flow like water: downwards. If you think something continuously, someone who is a weakling may take your thought and go and kill a person.

That's why those who have known the inner reality of man, they say that whatsoever happens on the earth, everybody is responsible, everybody. Whatsoever happens in Vietnam, not only are Nixons responsible, everybody who thinks is also responsible. Only one person *cannot* be held responsible, and that is the person who has no mind; otherwise everybody is responsible for everything that goes on. If the earth is a hell, you are a creator, you participate.

Don't go on throwing responsibility on others — you are also responsible, it is a collective phenomenon. The disease may bubble up anywhere, the explosion may happen thousands of miles away from you — that doesn't make any difference, because thought is a non-spatial phenomenon, it needs no space.

That's why thought travels fastest. Even light cannot travel so fast, because even for light space is needed. Thought travels fastest. In fact it takes no time in travelling, space doesn't exist for it. You may be here, thinking of something, and it happens in America. How can you be held responsible? No court can punish you, but in the ultimate court of Existence you will be punished — you are already being punished. That's why you are so miserable.

People come to me and they say, 'We never do anything wrong to anybody, and still we are so miserable.' You may not be doing anything, but you may be thinking something — and thinking is more subtle than doing. A person can protect himself from doing, but he cannot protect himself from thinking. For thinking everybody is vulnerable.

'No-thinking' is a must if you want to be completely freed from sin, freed from crime, freed from all that goes on around you — and that is the meaning of a Buddha.

A Buddha is a person who lives without the mind, so he's not responsible. That's why in the East we say that he never accumulates *karma*, he never accumulates any entanglements for the future. He lives, he walks, he moves, he eats, he talks, he is doing many things, so he must accumulate *karma*, because *karma* means activity. But in the East it is said that even if a Buddha kills, he will not accumulate *karma*. Why? And you, even if you don't kill, you will accumulate *karma*. Why?

It is simple: whatsoever Buddha is doing, he is doing without any mind involved in it.

He is spontaneous, it is not activity.

He is not thinking about it, it happens.

He is not the doer.

He moves like an emptiness.

He has no mind for it,

he was not thinking of doing it.

But if the Existence allows it to happen,

he allows it to happen.

He no longer has the ego to resist,

no longer the ego to do.

That is the meaning of being empty and a no-self: just being a non-being, *anatta*, 'no-selfness'. Then you accumulate nothing; then you are not responsible for anything that goes on around you; then you transcend.

Each single thought is creating something for you and for others. Be alert!

But when I say be alert, I don't mean think good thoughts, no. Because whenever you think good thoughts, by the side you are also thinking of bad thoughts. How can good exist without bad? If you think of love, just by the side, behind it, hate is hidden. How can you think about love without thinking about hate? You may not think consciously, love may be in the conscious layer of the mind, but hate is hidden in the unconscious — they move together.

Whenever you think of compassion, you think of cruelty. Can you think of compassion without thinking of cruelty? Can you think of non-violence without thinking of violence? In the very word 'non-violence', violence enters; in the very concept it is there. Can you think of *brahmacharya*, celibacy, without thinking of sex? It is impossible, because what will celibacy mean if there is no thought of sex? And if *brahmacharya* is based on the thought of no sex, what type of *brahmacharya* is this?

No, there is a totally different quality of being which comes by not thinking: not good, not bad, simply a state of no-thinking. You simply watch, you simply remain conscious, but you don't think. And if some thought enters . . . it *will* enter, because thoughts are not yours; they are just floating in the air. All around there is noe-sphere, a thought-sphere, all around. Just as there is air, there is thought all around you, and it goes on entering of its own accord. It stops only when you become more and more aware. There is something in it: if you become more and more aware, a thought simply disappears, it melts, because awareness is a greater energy than thought.

Awareness is like fire to thought. It is just like when you burn a lamp in your house and the darkness cannot enter; you put the light off — from everywhere darkness has entered; without taking a single moment it is there. When the light burns in the house, the darkness cannot enter. Thoughts are like darkness: they enter only if there is no light within. Awareness is fire: you become more aware, less and less thoughts enter.

If you become *really* integrated in your awareness, thoughts don't enter you at all; you have become an impenetrable citadel, nothing can penetrate you. *Not* that you are closed, remember — you are absolutely open; it is just that the very energy of awareness becomes your citadel. And when no thoughts can enter you, they will come and they will bypass you. You will see them coming, but simply, by the time they reach near you they will turn. Then you can move anywhere, then you can go to hell itself — nothing can affect you. This is what we mean by Enlightenment.

Now try to understand Tilopa's sutra:

If one sees nought when staring into space;
if with the mind one then observes the mind,
one destroys distinctions
and reaches Buddhahood.

If one sees nought when staring into space . . . This is a method, a Tantra method: to look into space, into the sky, *without seeing;* to look with an empty eye. Looking, yet not looking for something: just an empty look.

Sometimes you see an empty look in a madman's eyes — and madmen and sages are alike in certain things. A madman looks at your face, but you can see he is not looking at you. He just looks through you as if you are made of glass, transparent; you are just in the way, he is not looking at you. And you are transparent for him:

he looks beyond you, through you. He looks without looking *at* you; the 'at' is not present, he simply looks.

Look in the sky without looking for something, because if you look for something a cloud is bound to come: 'something' means a cloud, 'nothing' means the vast expanse of the blue sky. Don't look for any object. If you look for an object, the *very look* creates the object: a cloud comes, and then you are looking at a cloud. Don't look at the clouds. Even if there are clouds, don't look *at* them — simply look; let them float, they are there. Suddenly a moment comes when you are attuned to this look of not-looking — clouds disappear for you, only the vast sky remains. It is difficult because your eyes are focused and your eyes are tuned to looking at things.

Look at a small child the first day he is born. He has the same eyes as a sage — or as a madman: his eyes are loose and floating. He can bring both his eyes to meet at the center; he can allow them to float to the far corners — they are not yet fixed. His system is liquid, his nervous system is not yet a structure, everything is floating. So a child looks without looking at things, it is a mad look. Watch a child: the same look is needed from you, because you have to attain a second child-hood again.

Watch a madman, because a madman has fallen out of the society. Society means the fixed world of roles, games. A madman is mad because he has no fixed role now, he has fallen out: he is the perfect drop-out. A sage is also a perfect drop-out in a different dimension. He is not mad; in fact he is the only possibility of pure sanity. But the whole world is mad, fixed — that's why a sage also looks mad. Watch a mad-man: that is the look which is needed.

In old schools in Tibet they always had a madman, just so the seekers could watch his eyes. A madman was very much valued. He was sought after because a monastery could not exist without a mad-man. He became an object to observe. The seekers would observe the madman, his eyes, and then they would try to look at the world like the madman. Those days were beautiful.

In the East, madmen have never suffered like they are suffering in the West. In the East they were valued, a madman was something special. The society took care of him, he was respected, because he has certain elements of the sage, certain elements of the child. He is different from the so-called society, culture, civilization, he has fallen out of it. Of course, he has fallen down; a sage falls up, a madman falls down — that's the difference — but both have fallen out. And they have similarities. Watch a madman, and then try to let your eyes become unfocused.

In Harvard, they were doing one experiment a few months ago, and they were surprised, they couldn't believe it. They were trying to find out whether the world, as *we* see it, is so or not — because many things have surfaced within the last few years. They tried an experiment on a young man: they gave him spectacles with distorted lenses, and he had to wear them for seven days. For the first three days he was in a miserable state, because everything was distorted, the whole world around him was distorted. It gave him such a severe headache that he couldn't sleep. Even with closed eyes those distorted figures would appear: the faces distorted, the trees distorted, the roads distorted. He couldn't even walk because he couldn't trust what was true and what was given by his projection through the distorted lenses. But a miracle happened!

After the third day he became attuned to it, the distortion disappeared. The lenses remained the same, distorted, but he started looking at the world in the same old way. Within a week everything was okay: there was no headache, no problem, and the scientists were simply surprised; they couldn't believe how it was happening. The eyes had completely shifted, it was as if the glasses were no longer there. And the glasses were there, and they were distorting — but the eyes had come to see the world for which they were trained.

We see the world not as it is, we see it as we expect it to be seen, we project something on it.

It happened that in a small island in the Pacific, for the first time a great ship arrived. The people of the island didn't see it, *none of them*! And the ship was so vast — but the people were attuned, their eyes were attuned for small boats. They had never known such a big ship, they had never seen such a thing. Their eyes simply would not catch the glimpse, their eyes simply refused.

Nobody knows what you are seeing, whether it is there or not. It may not be there, it may be there in a totally different way. The colours you see, the forms you see, everything is projected by the eyes. And whenever you look fixed, focused with your old patterns, you see things according to your own conditioning. That's why a madman has a liquid look, an absent look, both looking and not looking. This look is beautiful. It is one of the greatest Tantra techniques:

If one sees nought when staring into space...

40

Don't see, just look. For the first few days, again and again you will see something, just because of the old habit. We hear things because of old habit, we see things because of old habit, we understand things because of old habit.

One of the greatest disciples of Gurdjieff, P. D. Ouspensky, used to insist on a certain thing for his disciples — and everybody resented it. Many people would leave simply because of that insistance. If somebody said, 'Yesterday you told. . .' he would immediately stop him and say, 'Don't say it like that. Say, "I understood that you said yesterday this thing." Add "I understood". Don't say, "What you said." You cannot know that. What you heard, tell about it!' And he would insist so much because we are habitual.

Again someone would say, 'In the Bible it is said . . .' and he would say, 'Don't say that! Simply say that you understand that this is said in the Bible.' With *each* sentence he insisted: 'Always remember that this is *your* understanding.'

We go on forgetting. His disciples went on forgetting again and again, every day, and he was stubborn about it. He would not allow you to go on. He would say, 'Go back. Say first, "I understand you said this, this is my understanding. . ."' because you hear according to yourself, you see according to yourself; because you have a fixed pattern of seeing and hearing.

This has to be dropped.

To know existence, all fixed attitudes have to be dropped.

Your eyes should be just windows, not projectors.

Your ears should be just doors, not projectors.

It happened: One psychoanalyst who was studying with Gurdjieff tried this experiment. At a wedding ceremony he tried a very simple but beautiful experiment. He stood at the side of the reception line; people were passing, and he watched them and he felt that nobody at the receiving end was hearing what they were saying — so many people, some rich man's wedding ceremony. So he also joined in and he said very quietly to the first person in the receiving line, 'My grandmother died today.' The man said, 'So good of you, so beautiful.' Then to another he said it and the man said, 'How nice of you.' And the groom, when he said this, said, 'Old man, it is time you also should follow.'

Nobody is listening to anybody. You hear whatsoever you expect. Expectation is your specs, that is the lenses. Your eyes should be windows — this is the technique.

41

Nothing should go out of your eyes, because if something goes a cloud is created. Then you see things which are not there, then you have a subtle hallucination. Let there be pure clarity in your eyes, in your ears; all your senses should be clear, your perception pure — only then can the Existence be revealed to you. And when you know Existence, then you know that you are a Buddha, a god, because in Existence everything is Divine.

If one sees nought when staring into space;
if with the mind one then observes the mind . . .

First stare into the sky; lie down on the ground and just stare at the sky. Only one thing has to be tried: don't look at anything. In the beginning you will fall again and again, you will forget again and again; you will not be able to remember continuously, but don't be frustrated, it is natural because of so long a habit. Whenever you remember again, defocus your eyes, make them loose and just look at the sky — not doing anything, just looking. Soon a time comes when you can see into the sky without trying to see anything there.

Then try it with your inner sky:

. . . if with the mind one then observes the mind . . .

Then close your eyes and look inside, not looking for anything, 'just the same absent look. Thoughts are floating but you are not looking for them, or at them — you are simply looking. If they come it is good, if they don't come it is also good. Then you will be able to see the gaps: one thought passes, another comes — and the gap. And then, by and by, you will be able to see that the thought becomes transparent, even when the thought is passing you continue to see the gap, you continue to see the hidden sky behind the cloud.

And the more you get attuned to this vision, by and by, the more thoughts will drop, they will come less and less, less and less. The gaps will become wider: for minutes together no thought comes, everything is so quiet and silent inside — you are together for the first time. Everything feels absolutely blissful, no disturbance. And if this look becomes natural to you — it does become so, it is one of the most natural things; one just has to defocus, decondition — then:

. . . one destroys distinctions. . .

then there is nothing good, nothing bad; nothing ugly, nothing beautiful,

. . . and reaches Buddhahood.

Buddhahood means the highest awakening. When there are no

distinctions, all divisions are lost, unity is attained, only one remains. You cannot even say 'one', because that too is part of duality. One remains, but you cannot say 'one', because how can you say 'one' without deep down saying 'two'. No, you don't say that 'one' remains, simply that 'two' has disappeared, the many has disappeared. Now it is a *vast* oneness, there are no boundaries to anything:

. . . one tree merging into another tree, earth merging into the trees, trees merging into the sky, the sky merging into the beyond . . . you merging in me, I merging in you . . . everything merging . . . distinctions lost, melting and merging like waves into other waves . . . a vast oneness vibrating, alive, without boundaries, without definitions, without distinctions . . . the sage merging into the sinner, the sinner merging into the sage . . . good becoming bad, bad becoming good . . . night turning into the day, the day turning into the night . . . life melting into death, death molding again into life . . . then everything has become one . . .

Only at this moment is Buddhahood attained: when there is nothing good, nothing bad, no sin, no virtue, no darkness, no night — nothing, no distinctions.

Distinctions are there because of your trained eyes.

Distinction is a learned thing.

Distinction is not there in existence.

Distinction is projected by you.

Distinction is given by you to the world — it is not there.

It is your eyes' trick, your eyes playing a trick on you.

The clouds that wander through the sky
have no roots, no home;
nor do the distinctive thoughts
floating through the mind.
Once the Self-mind is seen,
discrimination stops.

The clouds that wander through the sky have no roots and no home. . . . And the same is true of your thoughts, and the same is true of your inner sky: your thoughts have no roots, they have no home; just like clouds they wander. So you need not fight them, you need not be against them, you need not even try to stop thought.

This should become a deep understanding in you, because whenever a person becomes interested in meditation he starts trying to stop thinking. And if you try to stop thinking it will never be stopped, because the very effort to stop is a thought, the very effort to meditate is a thought, the very effort to attain Buddhahood is a thought. And how can you stop a thought by another thought? How can you stop mind by creating another mind? Then you will be clinging to the other. And this will go on and on, ad nauseam; then there will be no end to it.

Don't fight — because who will fight? Who are you? Just a thought, so don't make yourself a battle-ground of one thought fighting another. Rather, be a witness, just watch thoughts floating. They stop, but not by your stopping. They stop by your becoming more aware, not by any effort on your part to stop them. No, they never stop that way, they resist. Try and you will find out: try to stop a thought and the thought will persist. Thoughts are very stubborn, adamant; they are *hatha yogis*, they persist. You throw them and they come back a million and one times. You will get tired, but they will not get tired.

It happened that one man came to Tilopa. The man wanted to attain Buddhahood and he had heard that this Tilopa had attained. Tilopa was staying in a temple somewhere in Tibet. The man came, Tilopa was sitting and the man said, 'I would like to stop my thoughts.'

Tilopa said, 'It is very easy. I will give you a device, a technique. You follow this: just sit down and don't think of monkeys. It will do.'

The man said, 'So easy? Just not thinking of monkeys? But I have never been thinking about them.'

Tilopa said, 'Now you do it, and tomorrow morning you report.'

You can understand what happened to that poor man . . . monkeys and monkeys all around him. In the night he couldn't get any sleep, not a wink. He would open his eyes and they were sitting there, or he would close his eyes and they were sitting there, and they were making faces. He was simply surprised: 'Why has this man given this technique, because if monkeys are the problem, then I have never been bothered by them. This is happening for the first time!' But he tried, in the morning he again tried. He took a bath, sat there, but nothing doing: monkeys wouldn't leave him.

He came back by the evening almost mad — because the monkeys were following him and he was talking to them. He came and he said, 'Save me somehow. I don't want this, I was okay, I don't want *any* meditation. And I don't want your Enlightenment — but save me from these monkeys!'

If you think of monkeys, it may be that they won't come to you.

44

But if you want them *not* to come to you, then they will follow you. They have their egos and they cannot leave you so easily. And what do you think of yourself: trying not to think of monkeys? The monkeys get irritated, this cannot be allowed.

This happens to people. Tilopa was joking, he was saying that if you try to stop a thought, you cannot stop it. On the contrary, the very effort to stop it gives it energy, the very effort to avoid it becomes attention. So, whenever you want to avoid something you are paying too much attention to it. If you want not to think a thought, you are already thinking about it.

Remember this, otherwise you will be in the same plight as the poor man who became obsessed with monkeys because he wanted to stop them. There is no need to stop the mind. Thoughts are rootless, homeless vagabonds, you need not be worried about them. Simply watch, watch without looking at them, simply look.

If thoughts come, good, don't feel bad — because even a slight feeling that they are not good and you have started fighting. It's okay, it is natural: as leaves come to the trees, so thoughts come to the mind. It's okay, it is perfectly as it should be. If they don't come, it is beautiful. Simply remain an impartial watcher, neither for nor against, neither appreciating nor condemning — without any evaluation. Simply sit inside yourself and look, looking without looking at.

And it happens that the more you look, the less you find; the deeper your look, the more thoughts disappear, disperse. Once you know this then the key is in your hand. And this key unlocks the most secret phenomenon: the phenomenon of Buddhahood.

The clouds that wander through the sky
have no roots, no home;
nor do the distinctive thoughts
floating through the mind.
Once the Self-mind is seen,
discrimination stops.

And once you can see that thoughts are floating, that you are not the thoughts but the space in which thoughts are floating, then you have attained to your Self-mind, you have understood the phenomenon of your consciousness. Then discrimination stops: then nothing is good, nothing is bad; then all desire simply disappears, because if there is nothing good, nothing bad, there is nothing to be desired, nothing to be avoided.

You accept, you become loose and natural. You simply start floating with existence, not going anywhere, because there is no goal; not moving to any target, because there is no target. Then you start enjoying every moment, whatsoever it brings — whatsoever, remember. And you can enjoy it, because now you have no desires and no expectations. You don't ask for anything, so whatsoever is given you feel grateful. Just sitting and breathing is so beautiful, just being here is so wonderful that every moment of life becomes a magical thing, a miracle in itself.

In space shapes and colours form,
but neither by black nor white is space tinged.
From the Self-mind all things emerge,
the mind by virtues and by vices is not stained.

And then, then you know that in space shapes and colours form. Clouds take many types of shapes: you can see elephants and lions, and whatsoever you like. In space forms, colours, come and go . . . *but neither by black nor white is space tinged* . . . but whatsoever happens, the sky remains untouched, untinged. In the morning it is like a fire, a red fire coming from the sun, the whole sky becomes red; but in the night where has that redness gone? The whole sky is dark, black. In the morning, where has that blackness gone? The sky remains untinged, untouched.

And this is the way of a *sannyasin*: to remain like a sky, untinged by whatsoever comes and happens. A good thought comes — a *sannyasin* doesn't brag about it. He doesn't say, 'I am filled with good thoughts, virtuous thoughts, blessings for the world.' No, he doesn't brag, because if he brags he is tinged. He does not claim that he is good. A bad thought comes — he is not depressed by it, otherwise he is tinged. Good or bad, day or night, everything that comes and goes he simply watches. Seasons change and he watches; youth becomes old age and he watches — he remains untinged. That is the deepest core of being a *sannyasin*, to be like a sky, space.

And this is in fact the case. When you think you are tinged, it is just thinking. When you think that you have become good or bad, sinner or sage, it is just thinking, because your inner sky never becomes anything — it is a *being*, it never becomes anything. All becoming is just getting identified with some form and name, some colour, some form arising in space — all becoming. You are a being, you are already that — no need to become anything.

Look at the sky: spring comes and the whole atmosphere is filled with birds singing; then flowers and the fragrance. Then comes the fall, and then comes summer. Then comes the rain — everything goes on changing, changing, changing. And it all happens in the sky, but nothing tinges it. It remains deeply distant; everywhere present, yet distant; nearest to everything and farthest away.

A *sannyasin* is just like the sky: he lives in the world — hunger comes, and satiety; summer comes, and winter; good days, bad days; good moods, very elated, ecstatic, euphoric; bad moods, depressed, in the valley, dark, burdened — everything comes and goes and he remains a watcher. He simply looks, and he knows everything will go, many things will come and go. He is no longer identified with anything.

Non-identification is *sannyas*, and *sannyas* is the greatest flowering, the greatest blooming that is possible.

In space shapes and colours form,
but neither by black nor white is space tinged.
From the Self-mind all things emerge,
the mind by virtues and by vices is not stained.

When Buddha attained to the Ultimate, the utterly Ultimate Enlightenment, he was asked, 'What have you attained?' And he laughed and said, 'Nothing — because whatsoever I have attained was already there inside me. It is not something new that I have achieved. It has always been there from eternity, it is my very nature. But I was not mindful of it, I was not aware of it. The treasure was always there, but I had forgotten about it.'

You have forgotten, that's all — that's your ignorance. Between a Buddha and you there is *no* distinction as far as your nature is concerned. Only one distinction is there and that distinction is that you don't remember who you are — and he remembers. You are the same, but he remembers and you don't remember. He is awake, you are fast asleep, but your nature is the same.

Try to live it out in this way — Tilopa is talking about techniques — live in the world as if you are the sky, make it your very style of being. Somebody is angry at you, insulting — watch; if anger arises in you, watch; be a watcher on the hills, go on looking and looking and looking. And just by looking, without looking at anything, without getting obsessed by anything, when your perception becomes clear, suddenly, in a moment, in fact in no time it happens, suddenly, without time, you are fully awake: you are a Buddha, you become the Enlightened, the Awakened One.

What does a Buddha gain out of it? He gains nothing. Rather on the contrary, he loses many things: the misery, the pain, the anguish, the anxiety, the ambition, the jealousy, the hatred, the possessiveness, the violence — he loses all. As far as what he attains is concerned, nothing. He attains that which was already there, he remembers.

The Song continues:

The darkness of ages
cannot shroud the glowing sun;
the long kalpas of samsara
ne'er can hide the Mind's brilliant light.

Though words are spoken to explain the Void,
the Void as such can never be expressed.
Though we say 'the Mind is a bright light,'
it is beyond all words and symbols.
Although the Mind is void in essence,
all things it embraces and contains.

III   THE NATURE OF DARKNESS AND OF LIGHT
13th February 1975

LET US FIRST MEDITATE a little on the nature of darkness. It is one of the most mysterious things in existence — and your life is too involved in it, you cannot afford not to think about it. One has to come to terms with the nature of darkness because the same is the nature of sleep, and the same is the nature of death, and the same is the nature of all ignorance.

The first thing that will be revealed to you if you meditate on darkness is that darkness does not exist, it is there without any existence. It is more mysterious than light — it has no existence at all; rather on the contrary, it is just the absence of light. There is no darkness anywhere, you cannot find it, it is simply an absence. It is not in itself, it has no 'in-itself' existence, it is simply that light is not present.

If light is there, there is no darkness; if light is not there, there is darkness. Darkness is the absence of light, it is not a presence of something. That's why light comes and goes — darkness remains; it is not, but it persists. Light you can create, light you can destroy, but you cannot create darkness and you cannot destroy darkness: it is always there *without* being there at all.

The second thing you will come to realize if you contemplate darkness, is that because it is non-existential you cannot do anything to it. And if you try to do anything to it, *you* will be defeated. Darkness cannot be defeated; how can you defeat something which is not? And when you are defeated you will think: 'It is very powerful because it has defeated me.' This is absurd! Darkness has no power; how can a thing which is not have power? You are not defeated by the darkness and its power, you are defeated by your foolishness. In the *first* place you started fighting — that was foolish. How can you fight with some-

53

thing which is not? And remember, you have been fighting with many things which are not, they are just like darkness.

The whole of morality is a fight against darkness, that's why it is stupid. The whole of morality, unconditionally, is a fight with darkness, fighting with something which in itself is not:

Hate is not real, it is just the absence of love.

Anger is not real, it is just the absence of compassion.

Ignorance is not real, it is just the absence of Buddhahood, of Enlightenment.

Sex is not real, it is just the absence of *brahmacharya*.

And the whole of morality goes on fighting with that which is not. A moralist can never succeed, it is impossible. Finally he has to be defeated, his whole effort is nonsense.

And this is the distinction between religion and morality: morality tries to fight with darkness, and religion tries to awaken the light which is hidden within. It doesn't bother about the darkness, it simply tries to find the light within. Once the light is there, darkness disappears; once the light is there, you need not do anything to darkness — simply, it is not there.

This is the second thing, that nothing can be done to darkness directly. If you want to do something with darkness, you will have to do something with light, not with darkness. Put the light off and the darkness is there; put the light on and the darkness is not there — but you cannot put on and put off darkness; you cannot bring it from somewhere, you cannot push it out. If you want to do something with darkness, you have to go via light, you have to go in an indirect way.

Never fight things which are not. The mind is tempted to fight, but that temptation is dangerous: you will waste your energy and life and dissipate yourself. Don't be tempted by the mind; simply see whether something has a real existence or whether it is just an absence. If it is an absence then don't fight with it, then seek the thing of which it is the absence — then you will be on the right track.

The third thing about darkness is that it is involved deeply with your existence in many millions of ways.

Whenever you are angry, your light within has disappeared. In fact, you are angry because the light has disappeared, the darkness has entered. You can be angry only when you are unconscious, you cannot be angry consciously. Try it: either you will lose consciousness and anger will be there, or you will remain conscious and anger

54

will not arise — you cannot be angry consciously. What does it mean? It means that the nature of consciousness is just like light, and the nature of anger is just like darkness — you cannot have both. If the light is there, you cannot have darkness; if you are conscious, you cannot be angry.

People come to me continuously and ask how not to be angry. They are asking a wrong question — and when you ask a wrong question it is very difficult to get the right answer. First ask the right question. Don't ask how to dispel darkness, don't ask how to dispel worries, anguish, anxiety; just analyse your mind and see why they are there in the first place. They are there because you are not conscious enough, so ask the right question: how to be more and more conscious. If you ask how not to be angry, you will become the victim of some moralist. And if you ask the question how to be more conscious, so anger cannot exist, so lust cannot exist, so greed cannot exist, then you are on the right track, then you will become a religious seeker.

Morality is a false coin, it deceives people, it is not religion at all. Religion has nothing to do with morality — because religion has nothing to do with darkness. It is a positive effort to awaken you. It does not bother about your character; what you do is meaningless and you cannot change it. You may decorate it, but you cannot change it. You may colour it in beautiful ways, you may paint it, but you cannot change it.

There is only one transformation, only one revolution, and that revolution comes not by being concerned with your character, with your acts, with your doings, but by being concerned with your *being*. Being is a positive phenomenon; once the being is alert, awake, conscious, suddenly darkness disappears — your being is of the nature of light.

And the fourth thing — then we can enter the *sutra* — is that sleep is just like darkness. It is not accidental that you find it difficult to sleep when there is light, it is simply natural. Darkness has an affinity with sleep; that's why it is easy to sleep at night. Darkness all around creates the milieu in which you can fall into sleep very easily.

What happens in sleep? You lose consciousness by and by. There comes an interim period in which you dream: dreaming means half-conscious, half-unconscious; just on the midway, moving towards total unconsciousness; from your waking state you are moving to total unconsciousness. On the path dreams exist; dreams mean only that you are half-awake and half-asleep. That's why if you dream continuously the whole night, you feel tired in the morning. And if you are not allowed to dream, then too you will feel tired — because dreams exist for a certain reason.

In your waking hours you accumulate many things: thoughts, feelings, incomplete matters hang in the mind. You looked at a beautiful woman on the road and suddenly a desire arose in you. But you are a man of character, manners, civilized, so you simply pushed it down, you would not look at it, you went on with your work — an incomplete desire hangs around you. It has to be completed, otherwise you will not be able to fall into deep sleep. It will pull you back again and again. It will say, 'Come up! That woman was really beautiful, her body had a charm. And you are a fool, what are you doing here? Seek her, you have missed an opportunity!'

The desire hanging will not allow you to fall into sleep. The mind creates a dream: again you are on the road, the beautiful woman passes, but this time you are alone without any civilization around you. No manners are needed, no etiquette is needed; you are like an animal, you are natural, no morality. This is your own private world, no police constable can enter into it, no judge can judge it. You are simply alone, there will not even be a witness. Now you can play with your lust: you will have a sexual dream. That dream completes the hanging desire, then you fall into sleep. But if you continuously dream, then too you will feel tired.

In the United States they have many sleep labs, and they have come to discover this phenomenon: that if a person is not allowed to dream, within three weeks he will go mad. You can awaken someone again and again whenever he starts dreaming, because there are visible signs when a person starts dreaming: his eyelids particularly start fluttering, fast; that means he is seeing a dream. When he is not seeing a dream his eyelids rest, because when he starts seeing a dream his eyes are functioning. Awaken him, and do this the whole night: whenever he starts dreaming, awaken him — within three weeks he will go mad.

Sleep doesn't seem to be so necessary. If you awaken a person whenever he is not dreaming, he will feel tired, but he will not go mad. What does it mean? It means dreams are a necessity for you. You are so illusory, your whole existence is such an illusion — what Hindus have called *maya* — that dreams are needed. Without dreams you cannot exist: dreams are your food, dreams are your strength, without dreams you will go mad. Dreams are a release of madness, and once the release happens you fall into sleep.

From waking you fall into dreaming and from dreaming you fall into sleep. Every night a normal person has eight cycles of dreaming, and just between two dreaming cycles he has a few moments of deep sleep. In that deep sleep all consciousness disappears, it is absolutely dark. But still you are near the boundary, any emergency will awaken you: if the house is on fire, you will have to run back to your waking consciousness; or, if you are a mother and your child starts crying, you will run, rush, towards waking — so you remain on the boundary. You fall into deep darkness, but you remain on the boundary.

In death you fall right to the center. Death and sleep are similar, the quality is the same. In sleep, every day, you fall into darkness, complete darkness; that means you become completely unconscious, the very opposite pole of Buddhahood. A Buddha is totally awakened, and every night you fall to a totally unawakened state, absolute darkness.

In the Gita, Krishna says to Arjuna that when everybody is fast asleep, the yogi is still awake. That doesn't mean that he never sleeps: he sleeps, but only his body sleeps, his body rests. He has no dreams because he has no desires, so he cannot have incomplete desires. And he has no sleep like yours — even in deepest rest his consciousness is clear, his consciousness burns like a flame.

Every night when you fall into sleep, you fall into deep unconsciousness, a coma. In death you fall into a deeper coma. These are all like darkness, and that's why you are afraid of darkness; because it is deathlike. And there are people who are afraid of sleep too, because sleep is also deathlike.

I have come across many people who cannot sleep, and they want to sleep. When I tried to understand their mind, I came to realize that they are basically afraid. They say they would like to sleep because they feel tired, but deep down they are afraid of sleep — and that is creating the whole trouble. Ninety percent of insomnia is fear of sleep, you are afraid. If you are afraid of darkness, you will be afraid of sleep also, and the fear comes from the fear of death.

Once you understand that these are all darknesses and that your inner nature is that of light, things start changing: then there is no sleep for you, only rest; then there is no death for you, only a change of clothes, of bodies, only a change of garments. But that can happen only if you realize the inner flame, your nature, your innermost being.

Now we should enter the sutra:

The darkness of ages
cannot shroud the glowing sun;
the long kalpas of samsara
ne'er can hide the Mind's brilliant light.

Those who have awakened, they have come to realize that . . . *the darkness of ages cannot shroud the glowing sun.*

You may have been wandering in darkness for millions of lives, but it cannot destroy your inner light because darkness cannot be aggressive. It is not: something which is not, how can it be aggressive? Darkness cannot destroy light — how can darkness destroy light? Even a small flame, darkness cannot destroy it, darkness cannot jump on it, cannot be in conflict with it — how can darkness destroy a flame? How can darkness shroud a flame? It is impossible, it has never happened because it cannot happen.

But people go on thinking in terms of conflict: they think darkness is against light. This is absurd! — darkness cannot be against light. How can an absence be against that of which it is the absence? Darkness cannot be against light: there is no fight in it; it is simply the absence, sheer absence, sheer impotency — how can it attack?

You go on saying, 'What could I do? — I had an attack of anger' — it is impossible; 'I had an attack of greed' — it is impossible. Greed cannot attack, anger cannot attack: they are of the nature of darkness — and your being is *light*, so the very possibility doesn't exist. Anger comes, but that shows only that your inner flame has been completely forgotten, you have become completely oblivious of it, you don't know it is there. *This forgetfulness* can shroud it, but not darkness.

So the *real* darkness is your forgetfulness, and your forgetfulness can invite anger, greed, lust, hate, jealousy — they don't attack you. Remember, you send the invitations first and they accept them. Your invitation is there — they cannot attack, they come as invited guests. You may have forgotten that you ever invited them, you can forget because you have forgotten yourself, you can forget anything.

Forgetfulness is the real darkness.

And in forgetfulness everything happens; you are just like a drunkard, you have completely forgotten yourself, who you are, where you are going, for what you are going. All direction is lost, the very

58

sense of direction is not there: you are like a drunkard. That's why all basic religious teachings insist on self-remembering. Forgetfulness is the disease, so self-remembering is going to be the antidote.

Try to remember yourself — but you will say, 'I know myself and I remember myself! What are you talking about?' Then try it: just keep your wristwatch before you, look at the hand that shows seconds and remember only one thing: 'I am looking at this hand which is showing seconds.' You will not be able to remember for even three seconds together; you will forget many times — just a simple thing: 'I am looking and I will remember this, that I am looking.'

You will forget, many things will come in your mind: you have made an appointment and just looking at the watch the association will come in your mind: 'I have to go at five o'clock to meet a friend.' Suddenly the thought comes in and you have forgotten that you are looking at it. Just by looking at the watch you may start thinking of Switzerland because it is Swiss-made. Just by looking at the watch you may start thinking, 'How foolish I am. What am I doing here wasting time?' But you will not be able to remember, even for three consecutive seconds, that you are looking at the hand showing seconds moving.

If you can attain to one minute's self-remembering, I promise to make you a Buddha. Even for one minute, sixty seconds, that will do. You will think, 'So cheap, so easy?' — it is not. You don't know how deep your forgetfulness is. You will not be able to do it for one minute continuously, without a single thought coming in and disturbing your self-remembering.

This is the real darkness.

If you remember, you become light.

If you forget, you become dark.

And in darkness, of course, all sorts of thieves come, all sorts of robbers attack you, all sorts of mishaps happen.

Self-remembrance is the key. Try to remember more and more, because whenever you try to remember more and more, you become centered, you are in yourself; your journeying mind falls back to your own self. Otherwise you are going somewhere: the mind is continuously creating new desires, and you are following and chasing the mind in many directions simultaneously. That's why you are split, you are not one, and your flame, inside flame, goes on wavering — a leaf in a strong wind.

When the inner flame becomes unwavering, suddenly you go through a mutation, a transformation, a new being is born — that being will be of the nature of light. Right now you are of the nature of darkness, you are simply an absence of something which is possible. In fact, you are *not* yet, you are not yet born. You have taken many births and many deaths, but you have not yet been born. Your real birth is still to take place, and this will be the birth: when you transform your inner nature from forgetfulness to self-remembering.

I don't give you any discipline, and I don't say to you, 'Do this and don't do that.' My discipline is very easy. My discipline is: do whatsoever you like — but do it with self-remembering; remember yourself that you are doing it. Walking, remember that you are walking. You need not verbalize this because verbalization will not help; that in itself will become a distraction. You need not walk and say inside, 'I am walking,' because if you say, 'I am walking, I am walking,' this 'I am walking' will be the forgetfulness, then you will not be able to remember. Simply remember; there is no need to verbalize it.

I have to verbalize because I am talking to you, but when you are walking simply remember the phenomenon, the walking; each step should be taken with full awareness. Eating, eat. I don't say what to eat, and what not to eat. Eat whatsoever you like, but with self-remembrance that you are eating. And soon you will see that it has become impossible to do many things.

With self-remembering you cannot eat meat, impossible. It is impossible to be so violent if you remember. It is impossible to harm somebody when you remember, because when you remember yourself, suddenly you see that the same light, the same flame is burning everywhere, within each body, each unit. The more you know your inner nature, the more you penetrate the other. How can you kill for eating? It becomes simply impossible. Not that you practise it — if you practise it, it is false. If you practise not to be a thief it is false; you will be a thief, you will find subtle ways. If you practise non-violence, behind your non-violence there will be violence hidden.

No, religion cannot be practised. Morality can be practised, that's why morality creates hypocrisy, morality creates false faces. Religion creates the authentic being, it cannot be practised. How can you practise the being? You simply become more aware and things start changing. You simply become more of the nature of light, and darkness disappears.

The darkness of ages cannot shroud the glowing sun. . .

For millions of lives, for ages together, you have been in darkness — but don't feel depressed and don't feel hopeless, because even if you have lived in darkness for millions of lives, this very moment you can attain to the light.

Just look: a house has remained closed for one hundred years, dark, and you go into it and you light a light. Will the darkness say, 'I am one hundred years old and this light is just a baby'? Will the darkness say, 'I am not going to disappear. You will have to burn light for at least one hundred years, only then will I disappear'? No, even a baby flame is enough to disperse very very ancient darkness. Why? Because in one hundred years the darkness must have become engrained. But no, darkness cannot become engrained because it is *not*. It was simply waiting for the light — the moment the light comes in the darkness disappears; *it cannot resist* because it has no positive existence.

People come to me and they say, 'You teach that sudden Enlightenment is possible. Then what will happen about our past lives and our past *karmas?*' Nothing — they are of the nature of darkness. You may have murdered, you may have been a thief, a robber, you may have been a Hitler, a Ghenghis Khan, or somebody, the worst possible, but that doesn't make any difference. Once you remember yourself, the light is there and the whole past disappears immediately; not for a single moment can it stay there. You murdered, but you cannot become a murderer; you murdered because you were not aware of yourself, you were not aware of what you were doing.

Jesus is reported to have said on the cross, 'Father, forgive these people because they know not what they are doing.' He was saying simply. 'These people are not of the nature of light, they don't remember themselves. They are acting in complete forgetfulness, in darkness they are moving and stumbling. Forgive them, *they are not responsible* for whatsoever they are doing.' How can a person who does not remember himself be responsible?

If a drunkard kills somebody, even the court forgives him if it can be proved that he acted when he was completely unconscious. Why? Because how can you make a person responsible? You can make him responsible for drinking, but you cannot make him responsible for murder. If a madman kills somebody, he has to be forgiven because he is not himself.

Responsibility means remembering.

Whatsoever you have done, I tell you, don't be worried by it. It has happened to you because you were not aware. Light your inner flame — find it, seek it, it is there — and suddenly the whole past

61

disappears, as if it all happened in a dream. In fact, it did happen in a dream, because you were not conscious. All *karmas* have happened in a dream, they are made of the same stuff as dreams are made of.

You need not wait for your *karmas* to be fulfilled — if you do then you will have to wait for eternity. Even then you will not be out of the wheel because you cannot simply wait for eternity: you will be doing many things meanwhile and then the vicious circle cannot be completed ever. You will move on and on and on, and you will go on doing things, and new things will make you entangled in more future things — then where will the end be? No, there is no need. Simply become aware and suddenly all *karmas* drop. In a single moment of intense awareness, the whole past disappears, becomes rubbish.

This is one of the *most* fundamental things the East has discovered. Christianity cannot understand it; it goes on thinking of judgment, and the Last Day of Judgment, that everybody has to be judged by his acts — then Christ must be wrong when he says, 'Forgive these people because they know not what they are doing.' Jews cannot understand it, Mohammedans cannot understand it.

Hindus are really one of the most daring races, they have penetrated to the very core of the problem: the problem is *not* action, the problem is *being*. Once you realize your inner being and the light, you are no more of this world; whatsoever happened in the past happened in a dream. That's why Hindus say this whole world is a dream — only you are not a dream, only the dreamer is not the dream; otherwise, everything is a dream.

Look at the beauty of this truth: only the dreamer is not a dream, because the dreamer cannot be a dream — otherwise the dream cannot exist. At least somebody, the dreamer, has to be a real phenomenon.

In the day you are awake and you do many things: you go to the shop, you go to the market, you work in a farm, or in a factory, and you do millions of things. By the night when you are asleep, you forget everything about it, it disappears — a new world starts, the world of the dream. And now scientists say that the same time has to be given to dreaming as you give to waking. The same number of waking hours have to be given to dreaming. In sixty years, if twenty years have been devoted to work in the waking state, twenty years have been devoted to dreaming; the *same* time, exactly the same time, has to be devoted to dreaming. So dreaming is not less real, it has the same quality.

In the night you dream, you forget about your waking world. In deep sleep you forget about both your waking world and your dreaming world. In the morning again the waking world comes into existence, you forget about your dreaming and your sleep. But one thing continuously remains — YOU. Who remembers the dreams? In the morning who says, 'I dreamt last night'? In the morning who says, 'Last night I had a very very deep sleep without any dreams'? Who?

There must be a witness to it who stands aside, who always stands aside and goes on looking. Waking comes, dreaming comes, sleep comes, and somebody stands by the side and goes on looking. Only this is real, because it exists in *every* state. Other states disappear but it has to remain in every state, it is the only permanent thing in you.

Attain to this witness more and more. Become more and more alert, and become more and more a witness. Rather than being an actor in the world, be a witness, a spectator. Everything else is a dream, only the dreamer is the truth. He has to be true, otherwise where will dreams happen? He's the base; illusions can happen only if he is there.

And once you remember, you start laughing. What type of life existed without remembering? You were a drunkard, moving from one state to another, not knowing why, drifting with no direction. But:

> *The darkness of ages*
> *cannot shroud the glowing sun;*
> *the long kalpas of samsara·· ·*

many many ages, aeons of this world, *kalpas*,

> *. . . ne'er can hide the Mind's brilliant light.*

It is always there, it is your very being.

> *Though words are spoken to explain the Void,*
> *the Void as such can never be expressed,*
> *though we say 'the Mind is a bright light,'*
> *it is beyond all words and symbols.*

One thing will be helpful to understand. There are three approaches towards reality: one is the empirical approach, the approach of the scientific mind — experiment, experiment with the objective world, and unless something is proved by experiment, don't accept it. Then there is another approach, that of the logical mind. He does not experiment; he simply thinks, argues, finds pros and cons, and just by mind-effort, reason, he concludes. And then there is a third approach, the metaphorical, the approach of poetry — and of religion. These three approaches exist; three dimensions whereby one reaches towards reality.

Science cannot go beyond the object, because the very approach creates a limitation. Science cannot go beyond the outer, because experiments are possible only with the outer. Philosophy, logic, cannot go beyond the subjective, because it is a mind-effort, you work it in your mind. You cannot dissolve the mind, you cannot go beyond it. Science is objective; logic, philosophy, is subjective. Religion goes beyond, poetry goes beyond: it is a golden bridge, it bridges the object with the subject. But then everything becomes a chaos — of course, very creative; in fact, there is no creativity if there is no chaos. But everything becomes indiscriminate, divisions disappear.

I would like to say it in this way: science is a day approach, at full noon; everything is clear, distinct, with boundaries, and you can see the other well. Logic is a night approach, groping in the dark with only the mind, without any experimental support, just thinking. Poetry and religion are twilight approaches, just in the middle:

The day is there no more,
the brightness of noon has gone,
things are not so distinct, clear.
The night has not yet come,
the darkness has not enveloped all.
Darkness and day meet,
there is a *soft* greyness,
neither white nor black —
boundaries meeting and merging,
everything indiscriminate,
everything is everything else.

This is the metaphorical approach.

That's why poetry talks in metaphors — and religion is the ultimate poetry, religion talks in metaphors. Remember, those metaphors are not to be taken literally, otherwise you will miss the point. When I say 'the inner light', don't think of it in literal terms, no. When I say 'the inner is light', it is a metaphor. Something is indicated, but not demarked, not defined; something of the nature of light, not exactly light — it is a metaphor.

And this becomes a problem because religion talks in metaphors, it *cannot* talk otherwise, there is no other way. If I have been to another world and I have seen flowers which don't exist on this earth, and

64

then I come to you and talk about those flowers, what will I do? I will have to use metaphors and similes. I will say 'like roses' — but they are not roses; otherwise why say 'like roses', simply say 'roses'. But they are not roses, they have a different quality about them.

'Like' means I am trying to bridge my understanding of the other world with your understanding of this world — hence similes, metaphors. You know roses; you don't know those flowers of the other world. I know those flowers of the other world, and I am trying to communicate something to you of that world, so I say they are like roses. Don't be angry at me when you reach the other world and you don't find any roses; don't drag me to a court — because I never meant it literally. Just the quality of a rose is indicated; it is just a gesture, a finger pointing to the moon. But don't catch hold of the finger, the finger is irrelevant — look at the moon and forget the finger. That is the meaning of a metaphor; don't cling to the metaphor.

Many people are in deep murky waters because of this: they cling to the metaphor. I talk about the inner light — immediately, after a few days, people start coming to me and they say, 'I have seen the inner light'; they have found the roses in the other world — they don't exist there. Because of this metaphorical language, many people simply become imaginative.

P. D. Ouspensky coined a word; he used to say *imaginazione*. Whenever somebody came and started talking about inner experiences: 'The *kundalini* has arisen; I have seen a light in my head; *chakras* are opening,' he would stop him immediately and say, *'Imaginazione.'* So people would ask, 'What is this *imaginazione?*' He would say, 'The disease of imagination,' and he would simply drop the matter. Immediately he would say, 'Stop! You have fallen a victim.'

Religion talks in metaphors — there is no other way to talk, because religion talks of the other world, of the beyond. It tries to find similes in this world, it uses words which are irrelevant, but somehow those irrelevant words are the only available words, so you have to use them.

Poetry you can understand easily, religion is difficult, because with poetry you already know it is imagination so there is no trouble. Science you can understand easily because you know it is not imagination, it is an empirical fact. Poetry you can understand easily, you know it is poetry, *mere* poetry, finished — it is imagination. Good! Beautiful! You can enjoy it — it is not a truth.

What will you do with religion? — and religion is the ultimate

65

poetry. And it is not imagination. And I tell you, it is empirical, as empirical as science — but it cannot use scientific terms, they are too objective. It cannot use philosophical terms, they are too subjective. It has to use something which is neither, it has to use something which bridges both — it uses poetry.

All religion is ultimate poetry, essential poetry. You cannot find a greater poet than Buddha. Of course, he never tried to write a single poem. I am here with you; I am a poet; I have not composed a single poem, not even a *haiku*, but I am continuously talking in metaphors, I am continuously trying to bridge the gap that is created by science and philosophy. I am trying to give you the feeling of the whole, undivided.

Science is half, philosophy is half — what to do? How to give you the feeling of the whole? If you move deep into philosophy, you will come to what Shankara came to. He said, 'The world is illusory, it doesn't exist — only consciousness exists.' This is too one-sided. If you move with scientists you will come to what Marx came to — Marx and Shankara are the polar opposites — Marx says, 'There is no consciousness — only the world exists.' And I know both are true and both are wrong. Both are true because they are saying half the truth; and both are wrong because they are denying the other half. And if I have to talk about the whole, how to do it? Poetry is the only way, metaphor is the only way out. Remember this:

Though words are spoken to explain the Void,
the Void as such can never be expressed.

That's why sages go on insisting: 'Whatsoever we are saying, we cannot say. It is inexpressible, and still we are trying to express it.' They always emphasize the fact, because the possibility exists that you may take them literally.

The Void is void in the sense that nothing of you will be left there; but the Void is not void in another sense, because the Whole will descend in it — the Void is going to be the *most* perfect, fulfilled phenomenon. So what to do? If you say 'Void', suddenly the mind thinks there is nothing; then why bother? And if you say it is not void, it is the most perfect being, the mind goes on an 'ambition-trip': how to become the most perfect being — then the ego enters in it.

To drop the ego the word 'void' is emphasized. But to make you alert to the fact that the Void is not really a void, it is also said that it is filled with the Whole.

66

When you are not, the whole existence comes into you.
When the drop disappears, it becomes the ocean.

*Though we say 'the Mind is a bright light,' says Tilopa,
it is beyond all words and symbols.*

Don't be deceived by the metaphor, don't start imagining a light
inside. It is very easy—*imaginazione*. You can close your eyes and
imagine a light; you are such a dreamer, you can dream so many
things, why not light?

Mind has a faculty to create anything that you want, just a little
persistence is needed. You can create beautiful women in the mind,
why not light? What is wrong with light? You can create such beautiful women in the mind, that any woman in real life will be unsatisfac-
tory because she will never come up to standard. You can create a
whole world of experiences inside. Every sense has its own imaginative center behind it.

In hypnosis it happens that imagination starts working with
absolute capacity, and reason drops completely because reason goes
to sleep in hypnosis. Hypnosis is nothing but a sleep of reason, the
doubter, then imagination functions perfectly. Then there is no brake
on it, only acceleration — you go on and on, no brake is there.

In hypnosis anything can be imagined: if you give an onion to
a person who is lying hypnotized and say, 'It is a beautiful apple, very
delicious,' he will eat the onion and say, 'It is really beautiful. I have
never tasted such a delicious apple before.' If you give him an apple
and say, 'This is an onion,' his eyes will start shedding tears and he
will say, 'Very very strong' — and he is eating an apple. What is
happening? The doubter is not there, it is a hypnosis, the doubter
has gone to sleep. Now imagination functions and there is no check
on it — and this is the problem with religion also.

Religion needs trust. Trust means the doubting faculty of the
mind goes to sleep, it is like hypnosis. So when people say to you,
'This man Rajneesh has hypnotized you,' they are right in a way: if
you trust me it is like hypnosis; fully awake, you have dropped your
reason — now imagination functions with total capacity, now you are
in a dangerous situation.

If you allow imagination, you can imagine all sorts of things:
kundalini is arising, *chakras* opening; all sorts of things you can imagine,
and they will all happen to you. And they are beautiful — but not true.
So when you trust a person, in the very trusting you have to be aware

of imagination. Trust, but don't become a victim of imagination. Whatsoever is being said here is metaphorical. And remember always, that *all* experiences are imagination; all experiences, I say, unconditionally — only the experiencer is the truth.

So whatsoever you experience, don't pay much attention to it, and don't start bragging about it. Just remember that all that is experienced is illusory — only the one who experiences is true. Pay attention to the witness; focus on the witness and not on the experiences. Howsoever beautiful, all experiences are dreamlike and one has to go beyond all of them.

So, religion is poetic, one has to talk metaphorically. The disciple is in deep trust, he can easily fall a victim of imagination — one has to be very very alert. Trust, listen to the metaphors, but remember that they are metaphors. Trust — many things will start happening, but remember: all is imagination except you. And you have to come to a point where there is no experience; only the experiencer sits in his abode silently, no experience anywhere, no object, no light, no flowers flowering, no—nothing.

Lin Chi was sitting in his monastery, a small monastery on a hilltop. He was sitting under a tree, near a rock, and somebody asked, 'What happens when one has attained?' And Lin Chi said, 'I sit alone here — clouds pass, and I watch; and seasons come and I watch; and visitors come sometimes and I watch. And I sit alone here.'

Finally, just the witness, the consciousness, remains watching everything. All experiences disappear, only the *very* background of all experiencing remains. You remain, everything is lost. Remember this, because with me you trust and I speak in metaphors — and then imagination is possible. *Imaginazione*: be aware of that disease.

> *Though we say 'the Mind is a bright light,'*
> *it is beyond all words and symbols.*
> *Although the Mind is void in essence,*
> *all things it embraces and contains.*

These assertions look contradictory: you say the mind is void, and the next moment you say it contains all and everything. Why these contradictions? It is just the nature of the whole religious experience. Metaphors have to be used — and immediately you have to be alerted not to become a victim of the metaphors.

It is void in essence,
but it contains all things.

When you become totally empty,
then only will you be fulfilled.
When you are no more,
then only for the first time will you be.
Says Jesus,
'If you lose yourself, you will attain.
If you cling to yourself, you will lose.
If you die, you will be reborn.
If you can efface yourself completely,
you will become eternal, you will become eternity itself.'

These are all metaphors — but if you trust, if you love, if you allow your heart to be open towards me, then you will be able to understand. That understanding passeth all understanding. It is not intellectual, it is heart-to-heart. It is an energy jump from one heart to another.

I am here and I am trying to talk to you, but that is secondary. The basic thing is that if you are open I can pour myself into you. If my talking to you can help only this much, that you become more and more open, it has done its work. I'm not trying to say something to you, I am just trying to make you more open — that is enough. Then I can pour myself into you . . . and unless you taste me, you will not be able to understand what I am saying.

The Song continues:

Do nought with the body but relax;
shut firm the mouth and silent remain;
empty your mind and think of nought.
Like a hollow bamboo rest at ease your body.
Giving not nor taking, put your mind at rest.
Mahamudra is like a mind that clings to nought.
Thus practising, in time you will reach Buddhahood.

IV   BE LIKE A HOLLOW BAMBOO
14th February 1975

F IRST, THE NATURE OF ACTIVITY and the hidden currents in it have to be understood, otherwise no relaxation is possible. Even if you want to relax, it will be impossible if you have not observed, watched, realized, the nature of your activity, because activity is not a simple phenomenon.

Many people would like to relax, but they cannot relax. Relaxation is like a flowering: you cannot force it. You have to understand the whole phenomenon — why you are active so much, why so much occupation with activity, why you are obsessed with it.

Remember two words: one is 'action', the other is 'activity'. Action is not activity; activity is not action. Their natures are diametrically opposite. Action is when the situation demands it, you act, you respond. Activity is when the situation doesn't matter, it is not a response; you are so restless within that the situation is just an excuse to be active.

Action comes out of a silent mind — it is the most beautiful thing in the world. Activity comes out of a restless mind — it is the ugliest. Action is when it has a relevance. Activity is irrelevant. Action is moment to moment, spontaneous. Activity is loaded with the past. It is not a response to the present moment, rather, it is pouring your restlessness, which you have been carrying from the past, into the present. Action is creative. Activity is very very destructive — it destroys you, it destroys others.

Try to see the delicate distinction. For example, you are hungry then you eat — this is action. But you are not hungry, you don't feel any hunger at all, and still you go on eating — this is activity. This eating is like a violence: you destroy food, you crush your teeth together and destroy food; it gives you a little release of your inner

73

restlessness. You are eating not because of hunger, you are simply eating because of an inner need, urge to be violent.

In the animal world violence is associated with mouth and hands, the finger-nails and the teeth. These two are the violent things in the animal kingdom. With food, while you are eating, both are joined together; with your hand you take the food, and with your mouth you eat it — violence is released. But when there is no hunger it is not an action, it is a disease. This activity is an obsession. Of course, you cannot go on eating like this because then you will burst. So people have invented tricks: they will chew *pan* or gum, they will smoke cigarettes — these are false foods, without any nutritious value in them, but they work well as far as violence is concerned.

A man sitting chewing *pan*, what is he doing? He is killing somebody. In the mind, if he becomes aware, he may have a fantasy of murdering, killing — and he is chewing *pan*: a very innocent activity in itself; you are not harming anybody — but very dangerous for you, because you seem to be completely unconscious of what you are doing. A man smoking, what is he doing? Very innocent in a way : just taking the smoke in and bringing it out, inhaling and exhaling; a sort of ill *pranayama*, and, a sort of secular transcendental meditation. He is creating a *mandala*: he takes the smoke in, brings it out, takes it in, brings it out — a *mandala* is created, a circle. Through smoking he is doing a sort of chanting, a rhythmic chanting. It soothes, his inner restlessness is relieved a little.

If you are talking to a person, always remember — it is almost one hundred percent accurate — that if the person starts finding his cigarettes, it means he is bored, you should leave him now. He would have liked to throw you out; that cannot be done, that would be too impolite. Instead, he is finding his cigarettes; he is saying, 'Now, finished! I am fed up.' In the animal kingdom he would have jumped on you, but he cannot jump — he is a human being, civilized. He jumps on the cigarette, he starts smoking. Now he is not worried about you, now he is enclosed in his own chanting of the smoke. It soothes.

But this activity shows that you are obsessed. You cannot remain yourself, you cannot remain silent, you cannot remain inactive. Through activity you go on throwing your madness, insanity. Action is beautiful, action comes as a spontaneous response; life needs response. Every moment you have to act, but action comes through the present moment. You are hungry and you seek food! You are thirsty and you go to the well. You are feeling sleepy and you go to sleep. It

74

is out of the total situation that you act. Action is spontaneous and total.

Activity is never spontaneous, it comes from the past. You may have been accumulating it for many years, and then it explodes into the present — it is not relevant. But mind is cunning; the mind will always find rationalizations for activity. The mind will always try to prove that this is not activity, this is action; it was needed. Suddenly you flare up in anger. Everybody else becomes aware that it was not needed, the situation never demanded it, it was simply irrelevant — only you cannot see. Everybody feels: 'What are you doing? There was no need for it. Why are you so angry?' But you will find rationalizations; you will rationalize that it was needed.

These rationalizations help you to remain unconscious about your madness. These are the things that Gurdjieff used to call 'buffers'. You create buffers of rationalization around you so you don't come to realize what the situation is. Buffers are used in trains; between two bogies, two compartments, buffers are used so that if there is a sudden stopping, there will not be too much shock to the passengers — the buffers will absorb the shock. Your activity is continuously irrelevant, but the buffers of rationalizations don't allow you to see the situation. Buffers blind you — and this type of activity continues.

If this activity is there, you cannot relax. How can you relax? Because it is an obsessive need; you want to do something, whatsoever it is.

There are fools all over the world who go on saying, 'Do something rather than nothing.' And there are perfect fools who have created a proverb all over the world that, 'An empty mind is the Devil's workshop.' It is not. An empty mind is God's workshop. An empty mind is the most beautiful thing in the world, the purest. Because how can an empty mind be a workshop for the Devil? The Devil cannot enter into an empty mind, impossible! The Devil can enter only into a mind which is obsessed with activity — then the Devil can take charge of you, and he can show you ways and means and methods to be more active. The Devil never says, 'Relax!' He says, 'Why are you wasting your time? Do something, man! Move! Life is going — do something!' And all the great teachers, teachers who have awakened to the truth of life, have come to realize that an empty mind gives space for the Divine to enter in you.

Activity can be used by the Devil, not an empty mind. How can the Devil use an empty mind? He will not dare to come near because emptiness will simply kill him. But if you are filled with a deep urge, mad urge to be active, then the Devil will take charge of you, then he will guide you — then he is the only guide.

I would like to tell you that this proverb is absolutely wrong. The Devil himself must have suggested it.

This obsession to be active has to be watched. And you have to watch it in your own life, because whatsoever I say, or Tilopa says, will not be of much meaning unless you see it in yourself: that your activity is irrelevant, it is not needed. Why are you doing it?

Travelling, I have seen people continuously doing the same thing again and again. For twenty-four hours I am with a passenger in a train. He will read the same newspaper again, again, not finding what to do. Enclosed in a railway compartment there is not much possibility of being active, so he will read the same newspaper again and again, and I am watching. What is this man doing?

A newspaper is not a Gita or a Bible. You can read the Gita many times because each time you come to it a new significance is revealed. But a newspaper is not a Gita; it is finished once you have seen it! It was not even worth reading once, and people go on reading newspapers again and again, they will start again. What is the problem? Is it a need? No — they are obsessed; they cannot remain silent, inactive. That is impossible for them — that looks like death. They have to be active.

Travelling for many years gave me many opportunities to watch people without their knowing, because sometimes only one person was with me in the compartment, and he would make all sorts of efforts to bring me to talk to him and I would say only yes or no, so he would drop the idea. Then I would simply watch — a beautiful experiment and without any expense.

I would watch him: he would open the suitcase — and I could see that he was not doing anything — then he would look in it, close it. Then he would open the window, and then would close it; then again he would go to the newspaper, then he would smoke, then again open the suitcase, rearrange it, go and open the window, look out . . . what is he doing? And *why?* An inner urge, something is trembling within him, a feverish state of mind. He has to do something otherwise he will be lost. He must have been an active man in life, now there is a moment to relax — he cannot relax, the old habit persists.

It is said that Aurangzeb, a Moghul emperor, imprisoned his father in his old age. Aurangzeb's father, Shah Jehan, built the Taj

Mahal. Aurangzeb dethroned him and imprisoned him. It is said, and it is written in the autobiography of Aurangzeb, that after a few days, Shah Jehan was not worried about imprisonment because every luxury was provided. It was a palace and Shah Jehan was living as he was living before; it was not like a prison; absolutely everything that he needed was there. Only one thing was missing and that was activity—he couldn't do anything. So he told his son Aurangzeb, 'It is okay, you have provided everything for me, and everything is beautiful. If you can do just one thing, I will be grateful forever and ever, and that is, send thirty boys. I would like to teach them.'

Aurangzeb could not believe it: 'Why would my father like to teach thirty boys?' He had never shown any inclination towards being a teacher, he was never interested in any type of education. What had happened to him? But he fulfilled the desire. Thirty boys were sent to him and everything was okay. He became again the emperor — thirty small boys. You go in a primary school, the teacher is almost the emperor: you can order them to sit and they will have to sit; you can order them to stand and they will have to stand. And in that room with thirty boys he created the whole situation of his court — just old habit and the old drug addiction to order people.

Psychologists suspect that teachers are in fact politicians. Of course, not self-confident enough to go into politics, so they move to the schools and there they become presidents, prime ministers, emperors. Small children — and they order them and they force them.

Psychologists also suspect that teachers have an inclination towards being sadistic, that they would like to torture. And you cannot find a better place than a primary school. You can torture innocent children — and you can torture them for their own sake, for their own good. Go and watch! I have been in primary schools, reading, and I have watched teachers. And what psychologists suspect, I am certain of: they are torturers. You cannot find more innocent victims either: unarmed completely, they cannot even resist; they are so weak and helpless—and the teacher stands like an emperor.

Aurangzeb writes in his autobiography: 'My father, just because of old habits, still wants to pretend that he is the emperor. So let him pretend and let him fool himself, there is nothing wrong in it. Send him thirty boys or three hundred, whatsoever he wants. Let him run a *madersa*, a small school, and be happy.'

Activity is when the action has no relevance. Watch in yourself and see: ninety percent of your energy is wasted in activity. And because of this, when the moment for action comes, you don't have any energy. A relaxed person is simply non-obsessive, and the energy starts accumulating within him. He conserves his energy, it is conserved automatically, and then when the moment for action comes his total being flows into it. That's why action is total. Activity is always *half*-hearted, because how can you befool yourself absolutely? Even you know that it is useless. Even *you* are aware that you are doing it for certain feverish reasons within, which are not even clear to you, very vague.

You can change activities, but unless activities are transformed into actions, that won't help. People come to me and they say, 'I would like to stop smoking.' I say, 'Why? This is such a beautiful TM, continue. And if you stop it you will start something else — because the disease doesn't change by changing the symptoms. Then you will chew *pan*, then you will chew gum; and there are even more dangerous things. These are innocent, because if you are chewing gum you are chewing gum yourself. You may be a fool, but you are not a violent man; you are not destructive to anybody else. If you stop chewing gum, smoking, then what will you do? Your mouth needs activity, it is violent — then you will talk, then you will talk continuously: yakety-yakety-yak — and that is more dangerous!'

Mulla Nasrudin's wife came just the other day. She rarely comes to see me, but when she comes I immediately understand there must be some crisis. So I asked, 'What is the matter?' Thirty minutes she took, and thousands of words, to tell me: 'Mulla Nasrudin talks in his sleep, so you suggest something — what should be done? He talks too much and it is difficult to sleep in the same room. And he shouts and says nasty things.'

So I said, 'Nothing is to be done. You simply give him a chance to talk while you are both awake.'

People go on talking. They don't give any chance to anybody else. Talking is the same as smoking. If you talk twenty-four hours a day . . . and you do: while you are awake, you talk; your body is tired, you fall into sleep, but the talk continues. Twenty-four hours, round the clock, you go on talking and talking and talking. This is like smoking, because the phenomenon is the same: the mouth needs movement. And the mouth is the *basic* activity, because that is the first activity you started in your life.

The child is born and he starts sucking the mother's breast; that is the first activity — and the basic activity. And smoking is just like

78

sucking the breast: warm milk flows in; in smoking, warm smoke flows in; and the cigarette between your lips feels just like the breast of the mother, the nipple. If you are not allowed to smoke, chew gum, and this and that, then you will talk, and that is more dangerous because you are throwing your garbage on other people's minds.

Can you remain silent for a long time? Psychologists say that if you remain silent for three weeks, you will start talking to yourself. Then you will be divided into two: you will talk and you will listen also. And if you remain silent for three months, you will be completely ready for the madhouse, because then you will not bother whether somebody is there or not. You will talk, and not only talk, you will answer also — now you are complete, now you don't depend on anybody. This is what a lunatic is.

A lunatic is a person whose whole world is confined to himself. He is the talker and he is the listener; he is the actor and he is the spectator — he is all, his whole world is confined to himself. He has divided himself in many parts and everything has become fragmentary. That's why people are afraid of silence — they know they may crack up. And if you are afraid of silence that means you have an obsessive, feverish, diseased mind inside, which is continuously asking to be active.

Activity is your escape from yourself. In action you are, in activity you have escaped from yourself — it is a drug. In activity you forget yourself, and when you forget yourself there are no worries, no anguish, no anxiety. That's why you need to be continuously active, doing something or other, but never in a state where non-doing flowers in you and blooms.

Action is good. Activity is ill. Find the distinction within yourself: what is activity and what is action; that is the first step. The second step is to be *more* involved in action so that the energy moves into action, and whenever there is activity to be more watchful about it, more alert. If you are aware, activity ceases, energy is preserved, and that same energy becomes action.

Action is *immediate*. It is not ready-made, it is not prefabricated. It doesn't give you any chance to make a preparation, to go through a rehearsal. Action is always new and fresh like the dew-drops in the morning. And a person who is a person of action is also always fresh and young.

The body may become old, but his freshness continues.

The body may die, but his youth continues.

The body may disappear, but he remains —
because God loves freshness.
God is always for the new and the fresh.

Drop activity more and more. But how can you drop it? *You can make dropping itself an obsession.* This is what has happened to your monks in the monasteries: dropping activity has become their obsession. They are continuously doing something to drop it: prayer, meditation, yoga, this and that — now that is also activity. You cannot drop it in that way; it will come from the back door.

Be aware. Feel the difference between action and activity. And when activity takes hold of you — in fact that should be called a possession: when the activity possesses you, like a ghost; and activity is a ghost, it comes from the past, it is dead — when activity possesses you and you become feverish, then become more aware; that's all that you can do. *Watch* it. Even if you have to do it, do it with full awareness. Smoke, but smoke very slowly, with full awareness so that you can see what you are doing.

If you can watch smoking, suddenly some day, the cigarette will fall from your fingers, because the whole absurdity of it will be revealed to you. It is stupid; it is simply stupid, idiotic! When you realize that, it simply falls. You cannot *throw* it because throwing is an activity. That's why I say it simply falls, just like a dead leaf falling from the tree, just like that it falls. If *you* have thrown it, you will pick it up again in some other way, in some other form.

Let things drop, don't drop them. Let activity disappear, don't force it to disappear — because the very effort to force it to disappear is again activity in another form. Watch, be alert, conscious, and you will come to a very very miraculous phenomenon: when something drops by itself, of its own accord, it leaves no trace on you. If you force it, then a trace is left, then a scar is left. Then you will always brag that you smoked for thirty years, and then *you* dropped it. Now this bragging is the same; talking about it you are doing the same thing — not smoking, but talking too much about the fact that you have dropped smoking. Your lips are again in activity, your mouth is functioning, your violence is there.

If a man really understands, things drop — and then you cannot take the credit that, 'I have dropped.' It dropped itself! You have not dropped it. The ego is not strengthened through it. And then more and more actions will become possible. And whenever you have an opportunity to *act* totally, don't miss it, don't waver — act.

80

Act more, and let activities drop of their own accord. A transformation will come to you by and by. It takes time, it needs seasoning, but there is no hurry either.

Now we will enter into the *sutra.*

Do nought with the body but relax;
shut firm the mouth and silent remain;
empty your mind and think of nought.

Do nought with the body but relax. Now you can understand what relaxation means. It means no urge for activity in you. Relaxation doesn't mean lying down like a dead man; and you cannot lie down like a dead man — you can pretend only. How can *you* lie down like a dead man? You are alive; you can *only* pretend. Relaxation comes to you when there is no urge for activity; the energy is at home, not moving anywhere. If a certain situation arises you will act, that's all, but you are not finding some excuse to act. You are at ease with yourself. Relaxation is to be at home.

I was reading one book a few years ago. The title of the book is *You Must Relax.* This is simply absurd, because the 'must' is against relaxation — but such books can only sell in America. 'Must' means activity, it is an obsession. Whenever there is a 'must' an obsession is hidden behind it. There are actions in life, but there is no 'must', otherwise the 'must' will create madness. 'You must relax' — now relaxation has become the obsession. You have to do this posture and that, and lie down, and suggest relaxation to your body from the toes to the head; tell the toes, 'Relax!' and then go upwards.

Why 'must'? Relaxation comes only when there is no 'must' in your life. Relaxation is not only of the body, it is not only of the mind, it is of your total being.

You are too much in activity, of course tired, dissipated, dried up, frozen. The life-energy doesn't move. There are only blocks and blocks and blocks. And whenever you do something you do it in a madness. Of course the need to relax arises. That's why so many books are written every month about relaxation, but I have never seen a person who has become relaxed through reading a book about relaxation — he becomes more hectic, because now his whole life of activity remains untouched. His obsession to be active is there, the disease is there, and he pretends to be in a relaxed state so he lies down. All turmoil within, a volcano ready to erupt, and he is relaxing, following the instructions from a book: how to relax.

There is no book that can help you to relax — unless you read your own inner being, and then relaxation is not a must. Relaxation is an absence, an absence of activity, *not* of action. So there is no need to move to the Himalayas. A few people have done that: to relax, they move to the Himalayas. What need is there to move to the Himalayas? Action is not to be dropped, because if you drop action you drop life. Then you will be dead, not relaxed. So in the Himalayas you will find sages who are dead, not relaxed. They have escaped from life, from action.

This is the subtle point to be understood: activity has to go, but not action — and both are easy. You can drop both and escape to the Himalayas, that's easy. Or, the other thing is easy: you can continue in the activities, and force yourself every morning, or every evening, for a few minutes to relax. You don't understand the complexity of the human mind, the mechanism of it. Relaxation is a state. You cannot force it. You simply drop the negativities, the hindrances, and it comes, it bubbles up by itself.

What do you do when you go to sleep in the night? Do you do something? If you do, you will be an insomniac, you will move into insomnia. What do you *do*? You simply lie down and go into sleep. There is no 'doing' to it. If you 'do', it will be impossible to sleep. In fact, to go into sleep all that is needed is for the continuity in the mind of the activities of the day to discontinue. That's all! When the activity is not there in the mind, the mind relaxes and goes into sleep. If you *do* something to go into sleep, you will be at a loss, then sleep will be impossible. Doing is not needed at all.

Says Tilopa, 'Do nought with the body but relax.' Don't do anything! No yoga posture is needed, no distortions and contortions of the body are needed. 'Do nought!' —only the absence of activity is needed. And how will it come? It will come by understanding. Understanding is the only discipline. Understand your activities and suddenly, in the middle of the activity, if you become aware, it will stop. If you become aware why you are doing it, it will stop. And that stopping is what Tilopa means by, 'Do nought with the body but relax.'

What is relaxation? It is a state of affairs where your energy is not moving anywhere, not to the future, not to the past — it is simply there with you. In the silent pool of your own energy, in the warmth of it, you are enveloped. *This* moment is all. There is no other moment. Time stops — then there is relaxation. If time is there, there is no relaxation. Simply, the clock stops; there is no time. This moment is all.

You don't ask for anything else, you simply enjoy it. Ordinary things can be enjoyed because they are beautiful. In fact, nothing is ordinary — if God exists, then everything is extraordinary.

People come to me and ask, 'Do you believe in God?' I say, 'Yes, because everything is so extraordinary, how can it be without a *deep* consciousness in it?' Just small things:

Walking on the lawn
when the dew-drops have not yet evaporated,
and just feeling totally there —
the texture, the touch of the lawn,
the coolness of the dew-drops,
the morning wind, the sun rising.
What more do you need to be happy?
What more is possible to be happy?

Just lying down in the night on your cool bed, feeling the texture; feeling that the bed is getting warmer and warmer, and you are shrouded in darkness, the silence of the night. With closed eyes you simply feel yourself. What more do you need? It is too much — a *deep* gratitude arises: this is relaxation.

Relaxation means this moment is more than enough, more than can be asked or expected. Nothing to ask, more than enough, more than you can desire — then the energy never moves anywhere.

It becomes a placid pool.
In your own energy, you dissolve.
This moment is relaxation.
Relaxation is neither of the body nor of the mind,
relaxation is of the total.

That's why Buddhas go on saying, 'Become desireless,' because they know that if there is desire, you cannot relax. They go on saying, 'Bury the dead,' because if you are too much concerned with the past, you cannot relax. They go on saying, 'Enjoy this very moment.'

Jesus says, 'Look at the lilies. Consider the lilies in the field — they toil not and they are more beautiful, their splendour is greater than King Solomon's. They are arrayed in a more beautiful aroma than King Solomon was ever. Look, consider the lilies!'

What is he saying? He is saying, 'Relax! You need not toil for it — in fact everything is provided.' Jesus says, 'If He looks after the birds of the air, animals, wild animals, trees and plants, then why are you worried? Will He not look after you?' This is relaxation. Why are you so worried about the future? Consider the lilies, watch the lilies, and become like lilies—then you relax. Relaxation is not a posture; relaxation is a total transformation of your energy.

Energy can have two dimensions. One is motivated, going somewhere, a goal somewhere; this moment is only a means and the goal is to be achieved somewhere else. This is one dimension of your energy, this is the dimension of activity, goal-oriented — then everything is a means; somehow it has to be done and you have to reach the goal, then you will relax. But for this type of energy the goal never comes, because this type of energy goes on changing every present moment into a means for something else, into the future. The goal always remains on the horizon. You go on running, but the distance remains the same.

No, there is another dimension of energy: that dimension is unmotivated celebration. The goal is here, now; the goal is not somewhere else. In fact, you are the goal. In fact, there is no other fulfillment than that of this moment—consider the lilies. When you are the goal and when the goal is not in the future, when there is nothing to be achieved, rather, you are just celebrating it, then you have already achieved it, it is there. This is relaxation, unmotivated energy.

So, to me, there are two types of people: the goal-seekers and the celebrators. The goal-oriented, they are the mad ones, they are going crazy by and by, and they are creating their own craziness. And then the craziness has its own momentum: by and by, they move deeper into it — then they are completely lost. The other type of person is not a goal-seeker — he is not a seeker at all, he is a celebrator.

And *this* I teach to you, be the celebrators, celebrate! Already there is too much: the flowers have bloomed, the birds are singing, the sun is there in the sky — celebrate it! And you are breathing and you are alive, and you have consciousness — celebrate it! Then suddenly you relax, then there is no tension, then there is no anguish. The whole energy that becomes anguish becomes gratitude; your whole heart goes on beating with a deep thankfulness — that is prayer. That's all prayer is about: a heart beating with a deep thankfulness.

Do nought with the body but relax.

No need to do anything for it. Just understand the movement of the energy, the unmotivated movement of the energy. It flows, but not towards a goal, it flows as a celebration. It moves, not towards a goal, it moves because of its own overflowing energy.

A child is dancing and jumping and running around, and you

ask, 'Where are you going?' He is not going anywhere — you will
look foolish to him. Children always think that adults are foolish.
What a nonsense question, 'Where are you going?' Is there any need
to go anywhere? A child simply cannot answer your question because
it is irrelevant. He is not going anywhere. He will simply shrug his
shoulders. He will say, 'Nowhere.' Then the goal-oriented mind asks,
'Then why are you running?' Because to us an activity is relevant only
when it leads somewhere.

And I tell you,
there is nowhere to go:
here is all;
the whole existence culminates in this moment,
it converges into this moment.
The whole existence is pouring already into this moment;
all that is there is pouring into this moment —
it is here, now.

A child is simply enjoying the energy. He has too much. He is running,
not because he has to reach somewhere, but because he has too much;
he has to run.

Act unmotivated, just as an overflow of your energy. Share, but
don't trade, don't make bargains. Give because you have, don't give
to take back — because then you will be in misery. All traders go to
Hell. If you want to find the greatest traders and bargainers, go to
Hell, there you will find them. Heaven is not for traders, Heaven is
for celebrators.

In Christian theology, again and again, for centuries it has been
asked, 'What do angels do in Heaven?' This is a relevant question
for people who are goal-oriented: 'What do angels do in Heaven?'
Nothing seems to be done, nothing is there to do. Somebody asked
Meister Eckhard, 'What do angels do in Heaven?' He said, 'What type
of a fool are you? Heaven is a place to celebrate. They don't do anything. They simply celebrate — the glory of it, the magnificence of
it, the poetry of it, the blooming of it, they celebrate. They sing and
they dance and they celebrate.' But I don't think that that man was
satisfied by Meister Eckhart's answer, because to us an activity is meaningful only if it leads somewhere, if there is a goal.

Remember, activity is goal-oriented, action is not. Action is an
overflowing of energy; action is in this moment, a response, unprepared, unrehearsed. The whole existence meets you, confronts you, and
a response simply comes. The birds are singing and you start sing-

85

ing — it is not an activity. Suddenly it happens. Suddenly you find it is happening, that you have started humming — this is action.

And if you become more and more involved in action, and less and less occupied in activity, your life will change and it will become a deep relaxation. Then you 'do' but you remain relaxed. A Buddha is never tired. Why? Because he is not a doer. Whatsoever he has he gives, he overflows.

Do nought with the body but relax;
shut firm the mouth and silent remain.

The mouth is really very very significant, because that is where the first activity landed; your lips started the first activity. Surrounding the area of the mouth is the beginning of all activity: you breathed in, you cried, you started groping for your mother's breast. And your mouth always remains in frantic activity. That's why Tilopa suggests: 'Understand activity, understand action, relax, and . . . *shut firm the mouth.*'

Whenever you sit down to meditate, whenever you want to be silent, the first thing to do is to shut the mouth completely. If you shut the mouth completely, your tongue will touch the roof of the mouth; both the lips will be completely closed and the tongue will touch the roof. Shut it completely — but that can be done only if you have followed whatsoever I have been saying to you, not before it.

You can do it! Shutting of the mouth does not require a very big effort. You can sit like a statue, with your mouth completely shut, but that will not stop activity. Deep inside the thinking will continue, and if thinking continues you can feel subtle vibrations in the lips. Others may not be able to observe it because they are very subtle, but if you are thinking then your lips quiver a little, a very subtle quivering.

When you really relax, that quivering stops. You are not talking, you are not making any activity inside yourself. *Shut firm the mouth and silent remain.* And then don't think.

What will you do? Thoughts are coming and going. Let them come and go, that's not the problem. You don't get involved; you remain aloof, detached. You simply watch them coming and going, they are not your concern. Shut the mouth and you remain silent. By and by, thoughts will cease automatically — they need your cooperation to be there. If you cooperate, they will be there; if you fight, then too they will be there — because both are cooperations: one for, the other against; both are sorts of activity. You simply watch.

But shutting of the mouth is very helpful. So first, as I have been observing many people, I will suggest to you that first you yawn: open your mouth as wide as possible, tense your mouth as wide as possible, yawn completely so it even starts hurting, and do this two or three times. This will help the mouth to remain shut for a longer time. And then for two or three minutes, speak gibberish loudly, nonsense. Anything that comes to the mind, say it loudly and enjoy it. Then shut the mouth.

It is always easier to move from the opposite end. If you want to relax your hand, it is better to first make it as tense as possible; clench the fist and let it be as tense as possible, do just the opposite and then relax — then you will attain a deeper relaxation of the nervous system. Make gestures, faces, movements of the faces, distortions, yawn, speak nonsense for two or three minutes — and then shut. And this tension will give you a deeper possibility to relax the lips and the mouth. Shut the mouth and then just be a watcher. Soon a silence will descend on you.

There are two types of silence. One, the silence that you can force upon yourself. That is not a very graceful thing, it is a violence; it is a sort of rape of the mind, it is aggressive. Then there is another sort of silence that descends on you, like night descends. It comes upon you, it envelops you. You simply create the possibility for it, the receptivity, and it comes. Shut the mouth, watch, don't try to be silent. If you try, you can force a few seconds of silence, but they will not be of any value — inside you will go on boiling. So don't try to be silent. Simply create the situation, the soil, plant the seed and wait.

Empty your mind and think of nought.

What will you do to empty the mind? Thoughts are coming, you watch. And watching has to be done with a precaution: the watching *must* be passive, not active. These are subtle mechanisms and you have to understand everything, otherwise you can miss anywhere. And if you miss a slight point, the whole thing changes its quality. Watch; watch passively, not actively.

What is the difference? You are waiting for your girl, or your lover — then you watch actively. Then when somebody passes by the door, you jump to see whether she has come. Then, just leaves fluttering in the wind, and you feel maybe she has come. You go on jumping; your mind is very eager, active. No, this will not help. If you are too eager and too active this will not bring you to Tilopa's silence or my silence. Be passive like when you sit by the side of a river and the river floats by, and you simply watch. There is no eagerness, no urgency, no emergency. Nobody is forcing you. Even if you miss, nothing is missed. You simply watch, you just look. Even the word 'watch' is not good, because the very word 'watch' gives a feeling of being active. You simply look, not having anything to do. You simply sit by the bank of the river, you look, and the river flows by. Or, you look in the sky and the clouds float, and you look passively.

It is very very essential that this passiveness be understood, because your obsession for activity can become eagerness, can become an active waiting, then you miss the whole point; then the activity has entered from the back door again. Be a passive watcher.

Empty your mind and think of nought.

This passivity will automatically empty your mind. Ripples of activity, ripples of mind-energy, by and by, will subside, and the whole surface of your consciousness will be without any waves, without any ripples. It becomes like a silent mirror.

Like a hollow bamboo, rest at ease your body.

This is one of Tilopa's special methods. Every Master has his own special method through which he has attained, and through which he would like to help others. This is Tilopa's speciality: *Like a hollow bamboo rest at ease your body.*

A bamboo is completely hollow inside. When you rest, just feel that you are like a bamboo: inside completely hollow and empty. And in fact this is the case: your body is just like a bamboo, and inside it is hollow. Your skin, your bones, your blood, all are part of the bamboo, and inside there is space, hollowness.

When you are sitting with a completely silent mouth, inactive, tongue touching the roof and silent, not quivering with thoughts, mind watching passively, not waiting for anything in particular, feel like a hollow bamboo — and suddenly infinite energy will start pouring within you, you will be filled with the Unknown, with the mysterious, with the Divine.

A hollow bamboo becomes a flute
and the Divine starts playing it.
Once you are empty then there is no barrier for the Divine to enter in you.

Try this; this is one of the most beautiful meditations, the medi-

88

tation of becoming a hollow bamboo. You need not do anything else. You simply become this — and all else happens. Suddenly you feel something is descending in your hollowness. You are like a womb and a new life is entering in you, a seed is falling. And a moment comes when the bamboo completely disappears.

Like a hollow bamboo rest at ease your body.

Rest at ease — don't desire spiritual things, don't desire Heaven, don't desire even God. God cannot be desired — when you are desireless, He comes to you. Liberation cannot be desired because desire is the bondage. When you are desireless, you are liberated. Buddhahood cannot be desired, because desiring is the hindrance. When the barrier is not, suddenly Buddha explodes in you. You have the seed already. When you are empty, space is there — the seed explodes.

Like a hollow bamboo rest at ease your body.
Giving not nor taking, put your mind at rest.

There is nothing to give, there is nothing to get. Everything is absolutely okay — as it is. There is no need for any give and take. You are absolutely perfect as you are.

This teaching of the East has been very much misunderstood in the West, because they say, 'What type of teaching is this? Then people will not strive, and then they will not try to go higher. Then they will not make any effort to change their character, to transform their evil ways into good ways. Then they may become victims of the Devil.' In the West, 'Improve yourself' is the slogan; either in terms of this world, or in terms of the other, but improve. How to improve? How to become greater and bigger?

In the East we understand it more deeply; we understand that this very effort to become is the barrier — because you are already carrying your being with you. You need not become anything — simply realize who you are, that's all. Simply realize who is hidden within you. Improving, whatsoever you improve, you will always be in anxiety and anguish because the very effort to improve is leading you on a wrong path. It makes the future meaningful, the goal meaningful, ideals meaningful, and then your mind becomes a desiring.

Desiring you miss. Let desiring subside, become a silent pool of non-desiring — and suddenly you are surprised, unexpectedly it is there. And you will have a belly-laugh, as Bodhidharma laughed. And Bodhidharma's followers say that when you become silent again,

89

you can hear his roaring laugh. He is still laughing. He has not stopped laughing since then. He laughed because, 'What type of joke is this? You are already that which you are trying to become! How can you be successful if you are already that, and you are trying to become that? Your failure is absolutely certain. How can you become that which you are already?' So Bodhidharma laughed.

Bodhidharma was just exactly a contemporary of Tilopa. They may have known each other, maybe not physically, but they must have known each other — the same quality of being.

> *Giving not nor taking, put your mind at rest.*
> *Mahamudra is like a mind that clings to nought.*

You have achieved if you don't cling; nothingness in your hand — and you have achieved.

> *Mahamudra is like a mind that clings to nought.*
> *Thus practising, in time you will reach Buddhahood.*

What is to be practised then?
To be more and more at ease.
To be more and more here and now.
To be more and more in action,
and less and less in activity.
To be more and more hollow, empty, passive.
To be more and more a watcher —
indifferent, not expecting anything, not desiring anything.
To be happy with yourself as you are.
To be celebrating.

And then, any moment, *any moment,*
when things ripen and the right season comes,
you bloom into a Buddha.

The Song continues:

The practice of mantra and paramita,
instruction in the sutras and precepts,
and teaching from the schools and scriptures,
will not bring realization of the Innate Truth.
For if the mind when filled with some desire
should seek a goal,
it only hides the Light.

He who keeps Tantric precepts, yet discriminates,
betrays the spirit of samaya.
Cease all activity, abandon all desire,
let thoughts rise and fall
as they will like ocean waves.
He who never harms the non-abiding,
nor the principle of non-distinction,
upholds the Tantric precepts.

He who abandons craving
and clings not to this or that,
perceives the real meaning given in the scriptures.

V   *THE INNATE TRUTH*
15th February 1975

T HE TANTRIC ATTITUDE is the very being of Tilopa. You must
understand first what the Tantric attitude is, only then will
it be possible for you to comprehend what Tilopa is trying
to say.

So something about the Tantric attitude — the first thing: it is
not an attitude, because Tantra looks at life with a total vision. It has
no attitude with which to look at life. It has no concepts, it is not a philosophy. It is not even a religion, it has no theology. It doesn't believe
in words, theories, doctrines. It wants to look at life without any philosophy, without any theory, without any theology. It wants to look at
life as it is, without bringing any mind in between — because that will
be the distortion. The mind will then project, the mind will then
mix — and then you will not be able to know that which is.

Tantra avoids mind and encounters life face to face, neither
thinking, 'This is good,' nor thinking, 'This is bad': simply facing
that which is. So it is difficult to say that this is an attitude — in fact
it is a no-attitude.

The second thing to remember is that Tantra is a great yea-sayer;
it says yes to everything. It has nothing like 'no' in its vocabulary,
there is no negation. It never says no to anything, because with 'no'
the fight starts, with 'no' you become the ego. The moment you say
no to anything, you have become the ego already; a conflict has come
in, now you are at war.

Tantra loves, and loves unconditionally. It never says no to anything whatsoever, because everything is part of the whole, and everything has its own place in the whole, and the whole cannot exist with
anything missing from it.

It is said that even if a drop of water were missing,
the whole existence would thirst.
You pluck a flower in the garden,
and you have plucked something out of the whole existence.
You harm a flower,
and you have harmed millions of stars —
because everything is interrelated.

The Whole exists as a whole, as an organic whole. The Whole exists
not as a mechanical thing — everything is related to everything
else.

So Tantra says yes unconditionally. There has never been any
other vision of life which says, 'Yea', without any conditions — simply
yes, 'no' disappears; from your very being 'no' disappears. When there
is no 'no', how can you fight? How can you be at war? You simply
float. You simply merge and melt. You become one. The boundaries
are there no more. 'No' creates the boundary. 'No' *is* the boundary
around you. Whenever you say no, watch — immediately something
closes in. Whenever you say yes, your being opens.

The real atheist is one who goes on saying no to life; his saying
no to God is just symbolic. You may be believing in God, but if you
say no to anything, your belief is of no worth, your God is hocus-
pocus — because only a total 'yes' creates a real God, reveals the real
God. When you say a total 'yes' to existence, the whole existence is
suddenly transformed; then there are no more rocks, no more trees,
no more persons, rivers, mountains — suddenly everything has become one, and that oneness is God.

A real theist is one who says yes to everything, not only to God,
because mind is very cunning. You can say yes to God and no to the
world. This has happened. Millions have lost their whole life because
of this. They say yes to God and they say no to life. In fact, they think
that unless you say no to life, how can you say yes to God? They create
a division: they deny the world in order to accept God. But an acceptance that stands on a denial is no acceptance at all. It is false. It is a
pretension.

How can you accept the Creator without accepting the Creation?
If you say no to the Creation, how can you say yes to the Creator? They
are both one. The Creator and the Creation are not two things: the
Creator is the Creation. In fact there is no division between the
Creator and the Creation, it is a continuous process of creativity. On
one pole the creativity looks like the Creator; on the other pole the

creativity looks like the Creation — but they are both poles of the same phenomenon.

Tantra says that if you say yes, you simply say yes; you don't posit it against some no. But all the religions have done that: they say no to the world and yes to God; and they say no to the world forcibly, so that their yes can become stronger. Many so-called saints have said that: 'God, we accept You, but we don't accept Your world.' But what type of acceptance is this? Is this acceptance? You are choosing. You are dissecting the existence into two. You are putting yourself above God. You say, 'This we accept and that we deny.' All renunciation comes out of this.

One who renounces is not a religious person. In the view of Tantra, one who renounces is an egoist. First he was accumulating things of the world, but his attention was on the world. Now he renounces, but his attention is again on the world and he remains the egoist. The ego has subtle ways of fulfilling itself and coming again and again, in spirals. Again and again it comes back — with a new face, with new colours.

It happened: I was staying in my village and Mulla Nasrudin came to visit me. In those days he used to live in New Delhi, the capital, and he was so full of the capital that he was almost blind. I took him to the small fort of my village; he said, 'What! You call this a fort? You should come to New Delhi and see the Red Fort. This is nothing!' I took him to the river, and he said, 'What! You call this a river? I have never in my life seen such a sick and thin river.' And this happened everywhere.

Then came the full moon night, and I thought that at least he would be happy with the full moon, and that he would not bring this small village in. But no, I was wrong. I took him to the river. It was a beautiful silent evening, and then the moon came up — very big, simply wonderful. I looked at Nasrudin and said, 'Look! What a big moon.'

He looked at the moon, shrugged his shoulders and said, 'Not bad for a small village like this.'

This is the mind: it persists, it comes in spirals — again and again to the same thing. You can renounce the world, but you will not become other-worldly; you will remain very worldly. And if you want to check, go to the Indian monks, *sadhus*: they remain very very worldly, rooted in the world. They have renounced everything, but their focus is on the world, their focus is on renouncing, their focus is ego-centered, ego-oriented. They may be thinking that by renouncing they are nearing God—no. Nobody has ever reached the Divine by saying no to anything.

This is the vision of Tantra: Tantra says, 'Say yes. Say yes to everything. You need not fight, you need not even swim — simply float with the current. The river is going by itself, of its own accord and everything reaches the ultimate ocean. Simply don't create any disturbance, don't push the river, simply go with it.' That going with it, floating with it, relaxing with it, is Tantra.

If you can say yes, a deep acceptance happens to you. If you say yes, how can you be complaining? How can you be miserable? Then everything is as it should be. You are not fighting, not denying — you accept. And remember, this acceptance is different from ordinary acceptance.

Ordinarily a person accepts a situation when he feels helpless; that is impotent acceptance. That will not lead you anywhere; impotence cannot lead you anywhere. A person accepts a situation when he feels hopeless: 'Nothing can be done, so what to do? At least accept, to save face.' Tantric acceptance is not that type of acceptance. It comes out of an overfulfillment, it comes out of a deep contentment — not out of hopelessness, frustration, helplessness. It comes when you don't say no, it suddenly surfaces in you. Your whole being becomes a deep contentment.

This acceptance has a beauty of its own. It is not forced; you have not practised for it. If you practise, it will be false, it will be a hypocrisy. If you practise, you will be split in two: on the outside it will be acceptance; deep down will be the turmoil, the negation, the denial. Deep down you will be boiling up to explode any moment. Just on the surface you will pretend that everything is okay.

Tantric acceptance is total, it doesn't split you. All the religions of the world, except Tantra, have created split personalities. All the religions of the world, except Tantra, have created schizophrenia. They split you. They make something in you bad and something good. And they say the good has to be achieved and the bad denied, the Devil has to be denied and God accepted. They create a split within you and a fight. Then you continuously feel guilty, because how can you destroy the part that is organically one with you? You may call it bad, you may call it names; that doesn't make any difference. How can you destroy it? You never created it. You have simply found it — given. Anger is there, sex is there, greed is there — you have not created them; they are given facts of life, just like your eyes and your hands. You can call them names, you can call them ugly or beautiful or whatsoever you like, but you cannot kill them.

Nothing can be killed out of existence, nothing can be destroyed.

Tantra says a transformation is possible, but destruction? — no. And a transformation comes when you accept your total being. Then suddenly everything falls in line, then everything takes its own place; then anger is also absorbed, then greed is also absorbed. Then without trying to cut anything out of your being, your whole being re-arranges itself. If you accept and say yes, a rearrangement happens, and whereas before there was a noisy clamour inside, now a melody, a music is born, a harmony comes in.

Between noise and harmony, what is the difference? The same sound waves arranged in a different way. In a noise there is no center. If a madman is playing on a piano, the notes are the same, the sound is the same, but it has no center to it. If you can give a center to noise it becomes music, then it converges on a center and everything becomes organic. If a madman is playing on a piano, then every note is separate, individual; it is a crowd of notes, not a melody. And when a musician plays on the same piano with the same fingers, there comes an alchemical change: now the same notes have fallen into a pattern, the same notes have joined into an organic unity, now they have a center to them; now they are not a crowd, now they are a family; a subtle love joins them together — now they are one. And that is the whole art: to bring notes into a loving phenomenon, so they become harmonious.

Tantra says you are a noise right now as you are. Nothing is wrong in it — simply you don't have a center. Once you have a center, everything falls in line, and everything becomes beautiful.

When Gurdjieff gets angry it is beautiful. When you get angry it is ugly. Anger is neither ugly nor beautiful. When Jesus gets angry it is sheer music — even anger. When Jesus takes a whip in the temple and chases the traders out of the temple, there is a subtle beauty to it. Even Buddha lacks that beauty; Buddha seems to be one-sided. It seems there is nothing in him of the play of anger; the tension of anger, the salt of it is not there. Buddha doesn't taste so good as Jesus. Jesus has a little salt in him, he can get angry — even his anger has become part of his whole being; nothing has been denied, everything has been accepted.

But Tilopa is incomparable. Jesus is nothing. . . . The Tantric

Masters are simply wild flowers, they have everything in them. You must have seen pictures of Bodhidharma; if you have not seen, take a look — so ferocious that if you meditate on Bodhidharma's picture in the night, alone, you will not be able to sleep: he will haunt you. It is said of him that once he looked at anybody, that man would have nightmares continuously. He would haunt him; the very look was so ferocious. When Bodhidharma or Tilopa spoke, it is said their speaking was like a lion's roar, a thunder-cloud, a tremendous waterfall — wild, fiery.

But if you wait a little and don't judge them too soon, you will find within them the most loving of all hearts. Then you will feel the music, the melody in them. And then suddenly you will realize that they have not denied anything; they have absorbed everything, even ferociousness. A lion is beautiful, even its ferociousness has a beauty of its own. If you take the ferociousness out of a lion, then he is just a stuffed lion, dead.

Tantra says everything has to be absorbed, *everything*!—remember, without any condition. Sex has to be absorbed, then it becomes a tremendous force in you. A Buddha, a Tilopa, a Jesus, they have such a magnetic force around them — what is that? Sex absorbed. Sex is human magnetism. Suddenly you fall into their love. Once you come across their path, you are being pulled towards a different world altogether. You are torn from your old world, and you are being pulled towards something new, something that you never even dreamt about. What is this force? It is the same energy, sex, which has become transformed; now it has become a magnetism, a charisma. Buddha has anger absorbed; that very anger becomes compassion. And when Jesus takes the whip in his hand, it is because of compassion. When Jesus talks in fire, this is the same compassion.

Remember this, that Tantra accepts you in your totality. When *you* come to me, I accept you in your totality. I am not here to help you deny anything. I am here only to help you to rearrange, to get a center to all your energies, to converge them into a center. And I tell you that you will be richer if you have anger absorbed in it; you will be richer if you have sex absorbed in it; you will be richer if you have hatred, jealousy absorbed into it — they are the spices of life, and you will have a taste. You will not become *tasteless*, you will have an enrichment to your taste. You need a little salt. And anger comes exactly in the same amount as it is needed. When it overpowers you, then it becomes ugly. If you eat only salt then you will die. Salt comes in a certain proportion, and in that proportion it is needed, absolutely needed. Remember this.

On the path you will meet many people who would like to cripple you, to cut you, to dissect you. They will say, 'This hand is bad, cut it! This eye is bad, throw it out! Anger is bad, hate is bad, sex is bad.' They will go on cutting you, and by the time they have left you, you will be simply paralyzed, a crippled one. You will have no life left. That's how the whole of civilization has become paralyzed and crippled.

Unless Tantra becomes the foundation of the whole human mind, man will not be complete — because no other vision accepts man in his totality. But the acceptance, remember again, is of overflowing, it is not of impotence.

One lives one's life, one goes through it: each shade of it has to be lived, and each taste of it has to be tasted. Even the wandering, even going astray is meaningful, because if you never go astray you will not achieve an enriched Enlightenment, you will never be simple. You may be a simpleton, but you will never be simple — and a simpleton is not simple.

Simplicity needs a very deep and complex experience behind it. A simpleton is simply one without any experience. He may be a fool, but he cannot be a sage. A sage is one who has lived all the sins of life, who has not denied anything, who has not called anything a sin, who has simply accepted whatsoever has happened, who has allowed it to happen; who has moved with every wave, who has drifted, who went astray, who fell down to the very depths of hell.

Somewhere Nietzsche says, 'If a tree wants to reach the sky, its roots need to go to the very depths of hell.' He's right. If you want a real flowering into the sky, your roots will need to go to the deepest hell in the earth.

When a sinner becomes a sage, the sage has a beauty. When a sage is simply a sage, without having ever become a sinner, he is just a simpleton, he has missed life. And no virtue can arise unless there has been a wandering away, a going astray.

There is a beautiful parable Jesus goes on telling: One father had two sons. The younger son asked for his heritage, took it away, wasted it in the city on wine and women, and became a beggar. The other son remained with the father, worked hard on the farms and accumulated much wealth. And then one day, the beggar-son, the son who had gone astray, informed his father, 'I am coming back — I was a fool, I wasted your wealth. Forgive me. Now I have nowhere to go, accept me, I am coming back.' And the father said to his sons, 'Celebrate this occasion: kill the fattest sheep, make many delicious foods, distribute sweets to the whole town, find the oldest wine for him. This is going to be a feast — my son who had gone astray is coming back.'

Some people from the village went to the farm, and they said to the other son, 'Look — what injustice! You have been with your father, you served him like a servant, you never went astray, you never did anything against him, but never was a feast given in your honour, it was never celebrated. And now that vagabond, that beggar, who has wasted all your father's money and who has lived in sin, is coming back. And look at the injustice — your father is celebrating it. Come to the town! Sweets are being distributed, a great feast is being arranged.'

Of course, the elder son felt very very angry. He came back, he was very sad, and he said to his father, 'What type of justice is this? You never killed any sheep for me, you never gave me any gift. And now that son of yours is coming back, who has wasted all the wealth that you had given to him, and wasted it in wrong ways — and you are celebrating it.'

The father said, 'Yes, because you have always been with me, there is no need. But his coming back *has* to be celebrated: he had gone astray, he's the sheep lost and found again.'

This story has not been taken in its full significance by Christians. In fact, it says what I am saying, what Tantra means; it is a Tantric story. It means that if you remain always on the right path, you will not be celebrated by Existence. You will be a simpleton, you will not be enriched by life. You will not have any salt in you; you may be nutritious, but you will have no spices. You will be very simple, good, but your goodness will not have a complex harmony in it. You will be a single note, not millions of notes falling into a melody. You will be a straight line, with no curves and no corners. Those curves and corners give a beauty, they make life more mysterious, they give depth. You will be shallow in your saintliness, you will not have any depth in you.

That's why Tantra says everything is beautiful. Even sin is beautiful, because sin gives depth to your saintliness. Even going astray is beautiful, because coming back becomes more enriched. This world is needed for you in order to move into it deeply so that you forget yourself completely — and then a coming back.

People ask, 'Why does this world exist if God is against it; then why does He throw us into the world, into the world of *karmas*, sins,

102

wrongs? Why does He throw us? He can simply redeem us back.' That is not possible. Then you would be shallow, superficial. You have to be thrown to the farthest corner of the world, and you have to come back. That coming back has something in it — that something is the crystallization of your being.

Tantra accepts everything, *lives* everything. That's why Tantra could never become a very accepted ideology. It always remained a fringe ideology, just somewhere on the boundary, outside the society, civilization, because civilization has chosen to be shallow; good, but shallow. Civilization has chosen to deny, to say no to many things. Civilization is not courageous enough to accept all, to accept everything that life gives.

The greatest courage in the world is to accept all that life gives to you. And this is what I am trying to help you towards, to accept all that life gives you, and accept it in deep humbleness, as a gift. And when I say this, I mean even those things which society has conditioned you to call wrong and bad. Accept sex, and then there will come a flowering out of it; a *brahmacharya* will come, a purity, an innocence will come; a virginity will come out of it — but that will be a transcendence.

Through experience one transcends.

Moving in the dark alleys of life one's eyes become trained, and one starts seeing the light even in darkness. What beauty is there if you can see light while it is day! Beauty is there also when it is the darkest night, and your eyes are so trained for darkness that you can see the day hidden there.

When in the darkest night you can see the morning,
then there is beauty, then you have achieved.
When in the lowest you can see the highest,
when even in hell you can create a heaven,
then, then you have become an artist of the life.
And Tantra wants to make you artists of the life — not deniers, but great yea-sayers.

Accept, and, by and by, you will feel that the more you accept, the less desire is there. If you accept, how can desire stand there? Whatsoever the case is in this moment, you accept it. Then there is no movement for anything else. You live it moment to moment in deep acceptance; you grow without there being any goal, without there being any desire to go somewhere and be something else or be somebody else.

Tantra says, 'Be yourself' — and that is the only being you can

103

achieve ever. With acceptance desires fall. With acceptance, a desire-lessness comes into being by itself. You don't practise it, you don't force it upon yourself. You don't cut your desires — just by accepting, they disappear.

And when suddenly one moment happens that you accept totally and all desires have gone, there is a sudden Enlightenment. Suddenly, without doing anything on your part, it happens. That's the greatest gift this existence can give to you.

This is the Tantric attitude towards life. There is no other life than this, and there is no other world than this. This very *samsara* is the *nirvana*. You just have to be a little more understanding, more accepting, more childlike, less egoistic.

Now, the *sutras* of Tilopa.

The practice of mantra and paramita,
instruction in the sutras and precepts,
and teaching from the schools and scriptures,
will not bring realization of the Innate Truth.

No Vedas will help, no Bibles. The practice of *mantra* will not be of any help, rather, it can become a hindrance. What is a *mantra* in fact? What are you doing when you chant a *mantra*? What is Maharishi Mahesh Yogi teaching people when he teaches transcendental meditation? He is saying repeat a certain word or a certain *mantra* continuously inside: Ram, Ram, Ram; *AUM, AUM, AUM;* anything, even your own name will do; even if you repeat H_2O, H_2O, H_2O, that will do — because it is not a question of the sound or the word; it is a question of repeating something continuously, and then by the *very* repetition something happens. What is that?

When you repeat a certain word continuously, a rhythm is created inside: Ram, Ram, Ram — a rhythm is created, and the rhythm is monotonous. Whenever you repeat a certain word continuously, a monotony happens. It is monotonous repeating a certain word continuously, you start feeling sleepy. This is what hypnosis is, this is auto-hypnosis; repeating a mantra is auto-hypnotizing. You become drunk from your own monotonous sound-rhythm.

It is good! Nothing is bad in it; it gives you a good sleep, very refreshing. If you are tired, it is a good mental trick; you will feel fresh, even fresher than you can feel from ordinary sleep, because ordinary sleep cannot go so deep as a mantra sleep can go, for in ordinary sleep many thoughts continue, dreams continue, they continuously disturb. But if you repeat a certain mantra continuously, nothing else can be there, only the mantra. It takes you into a very very deep sleep.

In Yoga we have a special word for it; in Sanskrit sleep is called *nidra*, and a sleep created by mantra chanting is called *tandra*. That is a deeper sleep but still sleep, it is called *yoga-tandra*, sleep created by yoga, mantra, chanting.

If you are disturbed in your sleep, TM can be helpful. That's why in America it seems Maharishi's influence has been great, because America is the most disturbed country as far as sleep is concerned. So many tranquillizers are being used, so many sleeping pills are being used; people have lost the natural capacity to sleep — hence the influence. In India, nobody bothers about TM because people are already sleeping so deeply that it is difficult to wake them.

Mantra gives you a subtle sleep; as far as it goes it is good — but don't think that it is meditation, then you will become a victim. Don't think that it is a meditation, it is just a mental tranquillizer. And it is as chemical as any sleeping pill, because sound changes the chemistry of your body, sound is part of the chemistry of your body. That's why with a certain type of music you feel very very refreshed; the music falls on you, cleanses you, as if you have taken a bath. Sound changes the chemistry of your body. There are certain types of music which will make you very passionate and sexual; just their hitting sounds change the chemistry of your body.

Mantra is creating an inner music with a single note; monotonousness is basic to it. And there is no need to ask Maharishi Mahesh Yogi about it — every mother in the world knows about it. Whenever the child is restless, she hums a lullaby — a lullaby is a mantra: just two or three words, even meaningless, there is no need for any meaning. She sits by the side of the child, or takes the child near her heart — that too, the beating of the heart is a monotonous music — so whenever a child is restless, the mother puts his head on her heart and the beat of the heart becomes a mantra. And the child is befooled; he falls asleep. Or, if the child has grown a little and cannot be befooled so easily, then she chants a lullaby; just two or three words, monotonous, simple words, she goes on repeating. Monotonousness helps; the child falls into sleep — nothing bad in it. It is a better tranquillizer than any chemical pill, but still a tranquillizer, a pill — subtle, a sound-pill, but it affects the chemistry of the body.

So if you are disturbed in your sleep, if you have a certain degree of insomnia, a mantra is good, but don't think that it is meditation. It will make you more and more adjusted, but it will not transform you. And the whole society is always trying to make you more adjusted to itself. It has tried religion to make you adjusted to itself, it has tried morality, it has tried mantras, yogas. It has tried psychoanalysis, and many types of psychiatry, to bring you back to the adjusted society. The whole goal of the society is how to create an adjusted individual. But if the whole society is wrong, being adjusted to it cannot be good. If the whole society is mad, being adjusted to it means only becoming mad.

Somebody asked Sigmund Freud once, 'In fact, what exactly are you doing in psychoanalysis, and what is the goal of it?' He said, and he was a rarely authentic person, he said, 'At the most what we can do is this: we make hysterically unhappy people normally unhappy. That's all — hysterically unhappy people, normally unhappy; we bring them back to the normal unhappiness, like everybody else. They were going a little too far; they were creating too much unhappiness and they were becoming neurotic. We bring them back to the normal neurosis of humanity.' Freud says, 'Man can never be happy. Man can only be either neurotically unhappy or *normally* unhappy, but man can never be happy.'

As far as ordinary humanity is concerned, his diagnosis seems to be exactly right, but he is not aware of a Buddha or a Tilopa; he is not aware of those who have achieved a totally blissful state of being. And this is as it should be, because a Buddha will not go to be treated by Freud — for what? Only hysterical persons come to Freud, and then he treats them. And his whole knowledge, his whole experience, is of hysterically neurotic people. He has not known a single individual in his whole forty years' experience with patients who is happy. So he is right, empirically right. His experience shows that there are only two types of people: normally unhappy and hysterically unhappy. And at the most he can help this much: he can make you more adjusted.

Mantra, psychoanalysis, religion, morality, churches, prayers, they have all been used to make you adjusted. And real religion starts only when you start on a journey of transformation; not to be adjusted with the society, but to be in harmony with the cosmos. To be adjusted with the society you have to fall down.

It happens many times that a madman has nothing wrong with him; the madman is simply too much of an energy and he cannot

106

adjust himself to the society — he goes astray. A madman is too much of an individual; a madman is so talented in certain things that he cannot get adjusted to the society. You must remember that all geniuses always remain maladjusted to the society, and out of one hundred geniuses, almost eighty percent always have a trip to the madhouse. They have to, because they go beyond society. A genius has much more than ordinary society allows.

The ordinary society is like a paper-weight on you: it won't allow you to fly. A genius throws the paper-weight and would like to be on the wing and go to the farthest corner of the sky. The moment you go beyond the line of the society, the boundary, you are mad. And the whole society tries to readjust you.

Tantra says that readjustment or adjustment is not the goal, it is not worth anything — transformation is the goal. What to do? Don't try tricks to become readjusted — mantra is a trick. If you are feeling that you cannot sleep, then don't try through mantra to find sleep. Rather, on the contrary, try to find what the restlessness is that is causing you sleeplessness. You may be desiring too much, you may be too ambitious. Your ambition won't allow you to sleep, your restlessness continues, your desiring mind goes on and on and on, and the thinking process continues. That's why you cannot sleep. Now there are two ways: one is of mantra and the other is of Tantra.

Mantra says: Don't bother about the causes; simply repeat a mantra and fall asleep. This is so superficial: don't bother about the causes, just repeat a mantra — fifteen minutes in the morning and fifteen in the evening — and you will be able to sleep; you will feel good and you will feel healthy. But even if you feel good and healthy, what will happen out of it? There are many healthy people who sleep beautifully, but nothing has happened to them — the ultimate blooming has not come. Health is good in itself, but it cannot be the goal. To sleep is good, but it cannot be the goal. Tantra says find out the causes of why you are restless.

A minister in the Indian government used to come to me. He was always worried about his sleep, and he would say, 'Just give me some technique so that I can sleep.' But I told him, 'A politician cannot sleep — that is not possible. A politician is not *meant* to sleep, he is not expected to sleep. And that is good, and I am not going to give you any technique. You go to Maharishi Mahesh Yogi, he will give you a technique without asking *why*.' And in fact he went.

Then he came after three months. He said, 'You made a suggestion and it worked! Now it is beautiful, now I can sleep.' Then I told him, 'Whenever you are in need and you feel that sleep is not enough, that awakening is needed, then come to me.' Because you can sleep, but what will happen out of it? You will remain the same; in the morning you will again be on the same ambitious trip. You may think something good has happened, but only one thing has happened: now you will not be aware of the causes; they will have been forced into the deeper unconscious by the mantra, and the possibility of transformation will have been postponed.

I cannot give you better sleep. I would like to give you better awakening, better awareness.

A politician is continuously desiring, fighting, competing, jealous, trying to reach higher and higher in the hierarchy. In the end nothing is achieved.

Mulla Nasrudin worked his whole life in politics and went to the highest post possible. Then I asked him, 'What have you attained?' He said, 'To be frank, I'm the greatest ladder climber in the world. That is my achievement: the greatest ladder climber.'

But even if you reach the highest rung of the ladder, what then? Your presidents and prime ministers have reached, they are the greatest ladder climbers — *but ladder climbing is not life.* And just going on and on climbing bigger and bigger ladders, what is the point of it?

Ambition creates restlessness. I would like you to understand your ambition. Desiring creates restlessness. I would like you to be aware of your desiring. This is the way of Tantra. And when the cause disappears, the disease disappears. And if the *cause* disappears, then you are transformed. The disease is just a symptom — don't try to hide the symptom; let it be there, it is good, because it goes on poking, goes on hitting you and saying that something is wrong. If you cannot sleep, it is good because it shows that something is wrong in your very style of life.

I am not going to help you to attain better sleep. I will say: Try to understand, this is a symptom. This symptom is a friend, it is not an enemy. It is simply showing that deep down in your unconscious there are undercurrents which won't allow you to sleep. Understand them, absorb them, go through them, transcend them — and then there will be a deep sleep; not because you have forced the symptom underground, but because the disease has disappeared. And in that 'sleepness' a totally different quality of consciousness comes into existence. Then you can be deep asleep and still alert. It is not hypnosis then, it is not like a drunken state, it is not through a drug. And all mantras are drugs; very subtle, but still drugs. Don't become a drug-addict.

Says Tilopa:

The practice of mantra and paramita,
instruction in the sutras and precepts,
and teaching from the schools and scriptures,
will not bring realization of the Innate Truth.

Paramita is a Buddhist word; it means compassion, serving the people. Whatsoever the Christian missionaries are doing all over the world is *paramita* — Serve! Help! Sympathize! Be compassionate! But Tilopa says that will not help either.

I have also observed — I know many people who are social re-formers, great servants of society; their whole life they have devoted and sacrificed for the uplift of people — but no transformation has happened to them. It cannot happen, because serving the people, serving the society, becomes an occupation; they become occupied.

In fact, if the society is suddenly transformed by a Divine miracle, and there is no beggar to be served, no poor man to be served, no ill person, no hospitals, no mad people — if this suddenly happens, can you conceive what will happen to your great servants of the society? They will commit suicide! Not finding anybody to serve, what will they do? They will simply be at a loss. What will happen to Christian missionaries? If there is nobody to be converted and forced and led and seduced to their path, converted; if everybody becomes Christian, what will they do? Where will they go on their great missions? They will have to commit suicide. If the revolution really happens, what will the fate of your revolutionaries be? What will they do? Suddenly out of a job, unemployed, they will start praying to God: 'Bring back the old society — we need lepers to serve, we need beggars to help.'

You can be occupied either in your own business, or you can be occupied with other people, but the mind needs occupation. The mind needs you to forget yourself and be occupied with something. This is an escape from the Innate Truth. And Tilopa says these are not the ways.

Tantra has a very very beautiful thing to say to you, and that is: First, before you start serving anybody else, be absolutely selfish. How can you serve anybody else unless you have attained your inner being first? *Be absolutely selfish!* If your own inner light is burning you may be able to help others — otherwise your service will be a mischief. And the world is in so much mischief because of so many revolutionaries, so many social reformers, so many self-appointed servants. They create mischief, they create chaos; it is natural because they have not attained to their own truth and they have started helping others. If you have a light within, you may share your light with somebody else, but if you don't have it how can you share it? How can you share that which you don't have?

A man came to Buddha — he must have been a very very great revolutionary, like Marcuse or others — and he asked Buddha, 'Tell me how I can serve others? I have a deep compassion in me and I would like to make everybody happy.' Buddha looked at him. It is said he became sad; Buddha became sad looking at him. The man said, 'Why have you become so sad?' Buddha said, 'It is difficult because you yourself don't seem to be happy and you are on a mission to make everybody happy. How can you share that which you don't have?'

First you be, and once you are then it is not a mission. Once you are blissful, then you don't go out of your way to help others — your very being is a help wherever you are; you don't make it a profession. The way you are, wherever you are, you help. If you sit near a tree, you help the tree. Not consciously, not with any effort on your part, just being near the tree, the tree responds and your inner being flows into the tree, and the tree flows into you — and you have awakened a tree. Some day this tree will become a Buddha and you will be a part in it, you participated in it; and when this tree becomes a Buddha and the whole universe celebrates, you will also celebrate — you have given a part of yourself to the tree, you have shared.

You sit by a river and you share; you move, your very movement becomes your compassion — it is nothing to be done. If you *do*, something is wrong. How can you 'do' love? It is not an act, it is a state of being. You are in love, you have the light, and your doors are open, then whosoever wants to come in, into the inner shrine of your being, is invited. And whosoever wants to light his own light from your source of light, you are ready.

Never go and seek somebody to help. When you go, one thing is certain, you are not the right person. When you start doing something, one thing is certain, you are creating mischief. You will simply poke your nose into others' affairs. Let them be themselves. It is enough compassion on your side that you don't disturb them. Don't try to change them. You don't know what you are doing.

Only one who is Enlightened can help: the help flows spontaneously. It is just like a flower that has bloomed — the winds take the fragrance and they spread it all over the earth. It is very subtle and indirect; it never hits anybody directly. A real Master never tries to change anybody directly; he is like a subtle fragrance, he surrounds you. If you are open, a little whiff will enter into you. If you are not open, he will wait at the door; he will not even knock, because that may also disturb your sleep. It is *your* sleep, you have every right to sleep as long as you want; it is nobody's business to awaken you.

I may have become awakened; I may like you to be awakened, but that is my thing, not your thing. If you are fast asleep and dreaming beautiful dreams, who am I to disturb you? I will wait. I will surround you like a fragrance. And if that fragrance catches you, and if that fragrance brings you out of your sleep, it is okay. But it is not a direct effort, it is very very indirect. And always remember: only those people who are absolutely indirect can be of any help. Direct help is from the politician, indirect help is from the sage.

Instruction in the sutras and precepts,
and teaching from the schools and scriptures,
will not bring the realization of the Innate Truth.

Why? Because it is already there. It does not have to be brought in. You are seeking something which you have already there inside you in its total beauty and perfection. Nothing has to be done. Doing is absolutely irrelevant. You just have to come back home. The guest is already there, but the host is out — you are not inside. Through your desires you are moving further out and further out and further out. You would like to have a big house and big car, and this and that, and you are moving out and out. You have no time to come back home.

Meditation is nothing but coming back home, just to have a little rest inside. It is not the chanting of a mantra, it is not even a prayer; it is just coming back home and having a little rest. Not going anywhere is meditation, just being where you are; there is no other 'where' — just being there where you are, just occupying only that space where you are. Desire takes you on long journeys in time and space — and desire never brings you to your home; it always takes you somewhere else.

111

For if the mind when filled with some desire
should seek a goal,
it only hides the Light.

That's how you are missing — by going out you are missing, by seeking you are missing, by searching you are missing, by trying to get it you are missing. Nothing is needed on your part — the Divine has given all that can be given to you. You are not sent as beggars into the world, you are sent as emperors. Just have a look inside. In some moments just don't go anywhere, desireless, not thinking of the future, not thinking of the past, just remaining here and now, and suddenly it is there — it has always been there — and you start laughing.

When Lin Chi was asked what he did when he attained Enlightenment, what was the first thing he did, he said, 'What can one do? I laughed and asked for a cup of tea. I laughed! What had I been doing? — seeking something which was already there.' All the Buddhas have laughed, and all the Buddhas have asked for a cup of tea — because what else to do? It is already there. You were unnecessarily running here and there; tired, you have come back home. A cup of tea is exactly the right thing.

For if the mind when filled with some desire
should seek a goal,
it only hides the Light.

Your seeking creates smoke around the flame. You go on running around and around, you stir up much dust, and you create much smoke, and it is your own effort that stirs the dust and creates the smoke, and the flame becomes hidden. Rest a little, let the dust settle back to the earth. And if you are not running very fast, not in a hurry, you will not create smoke. By and by, things settle and the inner light is revealed.

This is the most fundamental thing in Tantra, that it says you are already perfect. No other vision says that. They say you have to achieve it, they say you have to go, you have to struggle, and you have to do many things and the path is arduous; and it is very very rarely that somebody reaches because the goal is very very distant; for millions of lives one has to try, and then one reaches; perfection has to be achieved. Tantra says this is the reason why you are not achieving. Perfection does not have to be achieved. It simply has to be realized that it is there.

Tantra offers you Enlightenment right here and now — no time, no postponement. Tantra says if you rest, just resting will help, because by your restlessness you are creating the smoke all around, and you are in such a hurry that you cannot listen. If somebody says, 'Rest,' you will say, 'There is no time to rest. I have to achieve a goal and the goal is very far. And if I rest I will miss.' Tantra says you are missing because you are running. Tantra says you are missing because you are in such a hurry.

> *He who keeps Tantric precepts, yet discriminates,*
> *betrays the spirit of samaya.*
> *Cease all activity, abandon all desire,*
> *let thoughts rise and fall*
> *as they will like ocean waves.*
> *He who never harms the non-abiding,*
> *nor the principle of non-distinction,*
> *upholds the Tantric precepts.*

Very, very simple. But you are too complex, you are too puzzled inside, otherwise everything is very very easy.

> *Cease all activity, abandon all desire,*
> *let thoughts rise and fall*
> *as they will like ocean waves.*

What does one do? If you go to the ocean you simply sit on the shore, on the beach, and you watch. The waves rise and fall, and there is an ebb and there is a flow; the ocean passes through many moods. What do you do? You simply sit and watch. Exactly the same is the case with the mind; it is also like an ocean — waves arise and fall. Sometimes there is a flow and much turmoil, and sometimes there is an ebb, and you feel a little silent.

And this is in fact the case: the whole consciousness is like an ocean. And your mind is not only yours: your mind is part of the collective mind; all around you is the ocean of consciousness. Just like fishes in the ocean, you are fishes in the consciousness — in and out, this side and that, above and below, is the ocean and the ocean waves. Who are you to disturb it? And who are you to make it quiet and silent? And how can you do it?

So whenever a person becomes too interested and eager to calm down the mind, he creates many troubles for himself. It is not possible! And when you try some impossibility, you get frustrated. Then you think of a thousand and one causes why it is not happening. The simple fact is that it cannot happen! Tantra says, 'Watch it! It is none of your business that thoughts come and go. They come of their own accord, they go of their accord. Why do you get involved in them? Who are you to calm them down? They don't belong to you; they belong to the vast ocean that surrounds you. You were not there, and they were. You will not be one day, and they will remain.'

Now science accords with this: every thought is a wave. That's why a radio can broadcast thoughts. They pass through walls and hills and your bodies, and nothing hinders them. Something is broadcast in New York and you hear it here. Now scientists suspect that the possibility is there that soon we may be able to catch thoughts from the past, because thoughts never die. It may be possible some day to catch Tilopa saying to Naropa, 'Because of you, because of your trust, that which cannot be uttered, I will say it.' It is possible because thoughts never die. This thought of Tilopa's must be somewhere near some star. If we can catch it — science may be able to some day, because when from New York a thought is broadcast, it takes time to reach Poona; it takes a few seconds, but it takes time; it travels, it will go on travelling; it will leave this earth, it will go on travelling; in a few million years it will reach some star — if we can catch it there, you will be able to hear it again.

Thoughts are an ocean all around you, they exist without you — just be a witness. So Tantra says:

Accept them!
The high-tide comes, it is beautiful;
the ebb-tide comes, it is beautiful.
Big, strong waves trying to reach the sky;
tremendous energy — watch it!
Then comes a calm ocean, everything subsided,
and the moon reflects in it, beautiful — watch it.
And if you can watch you will become absolutely silent.
The thoughts may go on coming to the beach,
scattering on the rocks,
you will remain calm and quiet,
they will not affect you.

So the real problem is not thoughts, but being affected. Don't fight with thoughts, simply become a witness and you are not affected. And it is a richer silence, remember, and Tantra is always for richer experiences. It is possible to create a dead silence, a silence that you find in the cemetery. You can force your mind so much that the whole nervous system becomes paralyzed. Then there will be no thoughts, because a very delicate nerve system is needed to receive them. The ocean will be there but you will not be receptive, your receptivity will be lost.

That is what is happening to many yogis, so-called yogis. They go on dulling their nervous systems. They eat less so that no energy moves to the brain. In fasting the energy cannot move to the brain, the body needs it first. They live in such a way that, by and by, their whole brain system becomes paralyzed, numb: sitting in one posture, monotonous; repeating a mantra, monotonous. If you continuously repeat a mantra for a few years, of course the system becomes dull, because no new sensations enter, the vitality is lost.

In fact this man has not become silent — this man has become more stupid. And he will have the stupid look that exists on many yogis' faces. You will not see intelligence, you will see something dull, dead; a stone-like thing has happened. These yogis have not attained to silence — they have lost their brains, they have lost their receptivity, they have dulled themselves completely, they are dead. Nothing happens to them inside because for anything to happen a very delicate nervous system is needed — very delicate, very receptive, sensitive.

So this should be the criterion: if you see on the face of a yogi radiance, intelligence, awareness, sensitivity, as if something has flowered within, he is fulfilled — then only has silence happened. Otherwise, one can be silent; stupid people are; idiots are perfectly silent, because they cannot think — but what type of silence is this?

An idiot is not a yogi. An idiot is simply born in such a way that his brain system is not functioning. You can do it with your own brain system by fasting, by yoga postures; you can stand on your head for hours — that will do. *Shirshasan* is perfect: you stand on your head for hours — that will make your nervous system dead, because your brain exists only if very very minute amounts of energy and blood reach it, because the nerves are so delicate, so small, fragile. You cannot conceive it because with the naked eye they cannot be seen. Your hair seems to be very thin, it is nothing; if you put ten thousand nerves one on top of the other, then they will be of the thickness of a hair. So if blood goes fast, it simply destroys them; it is like a flood.

Man attained to this brain, and no animal has attained, because man stood on the feet — that's why the blood cannot go to the head, it is against gravitation. Gravitation goes on pulling the blood downwards, and a very very minute part of the blood reaches the head. That's why that subtle system can exist. Animals cannot have it because they move on all fours and their brains remain on the same level as their bodies. If you stand on your head, you do *shirshasan,* for a single minute it may be good, or even for a single second it may be good, because it just gives a bath; the blood just reaches, and by the time it reaches you are back to your normal posture: it cleanses. But if you do *shirshasan* for minutes together or hours together, it will kill your whole brain-system. The flood is too much, the brain cannot exist.

And yogis have found many ways to destroy the brain. Once it is destroyed you cannot see the ocean — but the ocean is there, thoughts are there. It is just as if your radio has gone out of order. Don't think that broadcasts are not passing through this room, they are passing, but your receiving mechanism is not functioning. Start the radio, put it on — immediately it starts catching them.

The brain is just like a receiving center; if you destroy it you will be silent, but that silence is not of Tantra. And I don't teach that silence — that is death. It is good in the cemetery, you are not going anywhere through it — you are wasting your life. And a very subtle instrument which can make you perfectly intelligent, an instrument which can become so perceptive that you can enjoy the whole celebration of existence, you have destroyed.

More sensitivity is needed, more poetry is needed.

More life, more beauty, everything more is needed.

What will you do then? Attain to Tantric silence. Watch the waves, and the more you watch, the more you will be able to see the beauty of them. The more you watch, the more subtle nuances of thought will be revealed to you. And it is beautiful — but you remain the witness, you remain on the beach; you just sit on the beach, or lie down in the sun, and just let the ocean do its own work — you don't interfere.

If you don't interfere, by and by, by and by, the ocean doesn't affect you. It goes on roaring all around, but it doesn't penetrate you. It is beautiful in itself, but it is separate, a distance exists. That distance is real meditation, the real silence.

The world goes on and on, you are not affected; you remain in the world, but you are not in the world; you remain in the world, but the world is not in you. You pass through the world, untouched, unscarred. You remain virgin. Whatsoever you do, whatsoever happens to you, makes no difference:

your virginity remains perfect,
your innocence remains absolute,
your purity is not destroyed.

He who keeps Tantric precepts, yet discriminates,
betrays the spirit of samuya.

And says Tilopa, that if you are trying to keep the Tantric path, the Tantric precepts, then remember, don't discriminate. If you discriminate you may be a Tantric philosopher, but not a Tantric follower. Don't discriminate. Don't say this is good and that is bad. Drop all discrimination. Accept everything as it is.

Cease all activity, abandon all desire,
rest in yourself, come back home;
let thoughts rise and fall
as they will like ocean waves.
He who never harms the non-abiding,
nor the principle of non-distinction,
upholds the Tantric precepts.

One who never harms the principle of non-distinction, who never discriminates, he follows the right path.

And . . . *who never harms the non-abiding.*

This is one of the most beautiful things in Tantra. Tantra says remain homeless, don't abide anywhere, don't get identified, and don't cling to anything. Remain homeless, because in homelessness you will attain to your real home. If you start abiding in this and that, you will miss the home. Don't cling to anybody, to anything, to any relationship. Enjoy, but don't cling. Enjoyment is not a problem, but once you start clinging, once the clinging mind comes in, then you are not flowing, then a block has come in. Don't abide anywhere, then you will abide in yourself. Don't cling to anything, only then will you be able to rest in yourself.

So two principles are very basic: don't harm the principle of non-abiding, and don't harm the principle of non-distinction.

He who abandons craving
and clings not to this or that,
perceives the real meaning given in the scriptures.

Through scriptures you cannot attain to Truth. But if you attain to Truth, you will understand the scriptures. Scriptures are nothing but witnesses, they bear witness. You cannot learn the Truth from them, but once you know the Truth, they will bear witness. All the scriptures of the world will say, 'Yes, you have attained.' This is what Truth is. Scriptures come from persons who have attained. Whatsoever their language and symbology, whatsoever their metaphors, once you attain you penetrate through all metaphors, symbology, all languages.

People ask me, 'What are you doing here? Sometimes you talk on Tantra and Tilopa, and sometimes you talk on Yoga and Patanjali, and sometimes you talk on Lao Tzu and Chuang Tzu, the Taoists and the Tao, and sometimes you jump to Heraclitus and Jesus — what are you doing here?' I am talking about the same thing. I am not talking about anything else. Heraclitus or Tilopa or Buddha or Jesus, it makes no difference to me. I myself am talking. They are just excuses — because once you attain, you fulfill all the scriptures of the world. Then there is no Hindu scripture, Jewish scripture, Christian scripture; then suddenly you become the culmination of all the scriptures.

I am a Christian, a Hindu, a Jew, a Mohammedan, because I am no one. And the Truth, once known, is beyond all scriptures. All scriptures indicate towards it, scriptures are nothing but fingers pointing to the moon; the fingers may be millions — the moon is the same. Once you know, you have known all.

Through scriptures you will become sectarians: you will be a Christian because you cling to the Bible; you will be a Mohammedan if you cling to the Koran; you will be a Hindu if you cling to the Gita — but you will not be religious. Religiousness happens only when the Truth has happened to you. Then you don't cling to anything, and all the scriptures start clinging to you. Then you don't follow anybody, and all the scriptures follow you, they become like your shadows. And all the scriptures are the same because they talk about the same. Their metaphors, of course, are different, their languages are different, but the experience is the same.

Says Buddha, 'You taste the ocean from anywhere, you will always

118

find it salty.' You taste it from the Koran, or from the Bible, or from the Torah, or the Talmud, the taste is always the same. Scriptures cannot lead *you*. In fact, they are dead without you. When you achieve the Truth, life suddenly comes to all the scriptures. Through you they become again alive, through you they are reborn.

That is what I am doing, giving rebirth to Tilopa. He has been dead for many hundreds of years. Nobody has talked about him, nobody has given him again a birth. I am giving him a rebirth. While I am here, he will be again alive. You can meet him if you are capable. He is again near here. If you are receptive, you can feel his footsteps. He has again materialized.

Through me, I will give birth to all the scriptures. Through me, they can again come to this world, I can become an anchor. That's what I am doing. And that's what I would like you to do in your own life, some day.

When you realize, when you come to know,
then bring all that is beautiful in the past back
and give it a rebirth, renew it,
so that all those who have known
can be again on the earth
and travel here, and help people.

The Song of Mahamudra continues:

In Mahamudra all one's sins are burned;
in Mahamudra one is released
from the prison of this world.
This is the Dharma's supreme torch.
Those who disbelieve it are fools,
who ever wallow in misery and sorrow.

To strive for liberation
one should rely on a Guru.
When your mind receives his blessing
emancipation is at hand.

Alas, all things in this world are meaningless,
they are but sorrow's seeds.
Small teachings lead to acts—
one should only follow teachings that are great.

VI   THE GREAT TEACHING
16th February 1975

TANTRA BELIEVES, not in the gradual development of the soul, but in sudden Enlightenment. Yoga believes in gradual development: inch by inch, step by step, you progress towards the Final.

Yoga is very arithmetical: each sin that you have committed you have to balance by a virtuous act; your account has to be closed completely. Without completing the account with this world, you cannot become Enlightened. It is a mathematical conception, scientific, and the mind will say, 'Of course, it has to be so. You committed sins — who is going to suffer for them? You committed sins, you have to suffer for them. And only through suffering can you become liberated. Evil have been your acts; you have to balance them, you have to pay for them, and you have to move in good acts. When the balance is complete, then only is liberation possible. Otherwise, you will have to be thrown again and again to the earth, to be reborn, to move, to grow.' That is the whole philosophy of transmigration, rebirth.

Tantra says just the opposite. Tantra is a very very poetic approach, not arithmetical. And Tantra believes in love, not in mathematics; it believes in sudden Enlightenment. It says that small teachings teach you about action; great teachings don't teach you about how to act, they teach you what to be, how to be.

Actions are millions, and if you have to pay for all your actions, it seems almost impossible that you are ever going to be liberated. Millions of lives you have lived; in each life, millions of acts you have committed. If you are going to pay for all those acts, suffer, and have to balance each bad act with a good one, it will take again millions of lives for you. And meanwhile, in the complex relationships of life, you will be committing many more actions. So where will this chain

123

end? It seems impossible. Liberation becomes almost impossible — it cannot happen. If this is the way, that inch by inch one has to grow, then growth seems an impossible dream.

If you understand the attitude of Yoga, you will feel very very hopeless. Tantra is a great hope. Tantra is like an oasis in a world of deserts.

Tantra says this is not the point at all: acts are not the question; you committed them because you were ignorant, they came out of your ignorance. In fact, Tantra says you are not responsible for them. If somebody is responsible, then it is the Whole — you may call it God — God may be responsible, but you cannot be responsible. Tantra says that even to take this responsibility is very egoistic. To say, 'I will have to balance, I will have to do good acts, I will have to liberate myself inch by inch and step by step,' this too is a very egoistic, ego-centered attitude.

Why do you think you are responsible? Even if responsibility has to be somewhere, then it has to be with the Divine Himself, with the Whole. You have not created yourself, you have not given birth to yourself — you have been given birth to, you have been created. Then the Creator must be responsible, not you.

And you committed all your actions in ignorance, you were not aware of what you were doing, you were completely drunk with ignorance; in darkness you were groping, in darkness you came in conflict with others, in darkness you stumbled upon things and something happened. Tantra says the only thing that is needed is light, awareness. It is not that millions of acts have to be answered; only one thing has to be done and that is: don't remain ignorant, become aware.

Once you become aware, all that belongs to the world of darkness disappears. It will look like a dream, a nightmare. It will not look like a reality. And it has not been a reality, because when you are deeply unconscious, only dreams can exist, not reality. You have been dreaming that you loved. You cannot love. *You are not there to love.* You still don't exist, you don't have any center. How can you love? You only believe that you love, and then your love-life and the acts concerned with it become a dream. When you awaken out of this dreaming, you will simply say, 'How could I have loved? Impossible! I was not there in the first place. I was non-existential in fact.' Without awareness, what does it mean to say, 'You are'? It means nothing.

You are fast asleep, so deeply asleep, as if you are not there. A person fast asleep, in a coma in the house—is he really there? There is no distinction to be made. Whether he is there or not makes no difference—he is in a coma. If thieves come and rob the whole house, will you call that man responsible who is lying down in a coma, unconscious? Will he be responsible? Will he be asked and judged: 'Thieves came! What were you doing here?' How can you make a man responsible who is in a coma, unconscious?

Tantra says that in all your lives you have remained in a coma—you are not responsible. This is the first liberation that Tantra gives you. And on the base of it, many things immediately become possible. Then you need not wait for millions of lives—this very moment the door can open. It is not a gradual process, it is a sudden awakening—and it has to be so.

When you are fast asleep and somebody tries to wake you up, is it a gradual process? Or a sudden thing? Even in ordinary sleep, is it a gradual process? Is it like this, that first you become a little awake, then a little more, then a little more; ten percent, twenty percent, thirty percent, fifty percent; does it happen that way? No. Either you are awake or you are asleep; there are no gradual steps in it. If you have heard the man who is calling your name, you are awake, not ten percent awake. Eyes may be closed, but if you have become aware that somebody is calling, you are already awake.

It is not a gradual process, it is a sudden jump. At one hundred degrees heat, the water jumps and become vapour. Is there any gradual transformation? Does the water first become ten percent, twenty percent, thirty percent vapour? No. Either it is water or it is vapour, there is no middle ground to be divided.

When a person dies, is he dead by and by, in a gradual process? Can you say that he is half-alive and half-dead? What will it mean? How can a person be half-alive? Either he is dead or he is not dead. Half-alive means he is not dead.

When you love a person, do you love ten percent, twenty percent, thirty percent? Either you love or you don't love. Is there any possibility of dividing your love? There is no possibility.

Love, life, death, they all happen suddenly.

When a child is born, he is either born or not born. And the same is true about Enlightenment, because that is the ultimate birth, ultimate death, ultimate life, ultimate love—everything comes to its ultimate peak in Enlightenment. It is a sudden thing.

Tantra says don't focus your attention on the acts, focus your attention on the person who has done the acts. Yoga focuses on the acts. Tantra focuses on the person, on the consciousness, on you.

If you are ignorant, Tantra says you are bound to commit sins. Even if you try to be virtuous, your virtue will be a sort of sin—because how can an ignorant man, fast asleep, be virtuous? How can virtue arise out of ignorance, unconsciousness? Impossible! Your virtue must be just a mask; behind it will be the real face, the real face of sin.

You may talk about love, but you cannot love—you will hate. You can talk about compassion, but compassion must be just a covering for your anger, greed, jealousy. Your love is poisonous. Deep inside your love is the worm of hate, eating it continuously. Your love is like a wound, it hurts. It is not like a flower, it cannot be. And those who expect love from you are fools, they are asking the impossible. Those who ask morality from you are fools, they are asking the impossible. Your morality is bound to be a sort of immorality.

Look at your moral persons, your so-called saints. Watch and observe them and you will find their faces are just the faces of hypocrisy, deception. They say one thing, they do something else. They do something, and they not only hide it from you, they have become so clever in hiding that they hide it from themselves.

In ignorance, sin is natural.

In Enlightenment, virtue is natural.

A Buddha cannot sin;

you cannot do otherwise—you can only sin.

Sin and virtue are not your decisions,

they are not your acts,

they are shadows of your being.

If you are Awakened, then the shadow falls and the shadow is full of light. Then the shadow never harms anybody, it cannot; it has a flavour of the Unknown, of the Immortal. It can only shower on you like a blessing, otherwise is not possible. Even if a Buddha gets angry with you, it is compassion—it cannot be otherwise. Your compassion is not true; Buddha's anger cannot be true. Your sin, your natural shadow, whatsoever you do—you can decorate it, you can make a temple on top of it, you can hide it, you can beautify it, but that won't help—deep inside you will find it there. Because it is not a question of what you do, it is a question of what you *are*.

Look at the emphasis. If you understand this change of emphasis, and this change of emphasis is a great point, only then will you be able to understand Tantra.

Tantra is a great teaching. It doesn't teach about acts, it teaches only about your being. Who you are is the point — fast asleep, snoring, or awake? Who you are — alert, conscious, or moving in a hypnosis? Are you a sleep-walker? Or are you awake, alert, whatsoever you do? Do you do it with self-remembrance? No. It happens, you don't know why, from where it comes, from what part of the unconscious an urge comes — but it possesses you, and you have to act.

This act, whatsoever the society says about it — moral or immoral, sin or virtue — Tantra doesn't bother about it. Tantra looks at *you*, at the very center of your being from where it comes. Out of the poison of your ignorance, life cannot come, only death. Out of your darkness only darkness is born. And that seems to be absolutely natural. So what to do? Should we try to change the acts? Should we try to become more moral, virtuous, respectable? Or should we try to change the being?

The being can be changed. There is no need to wait for infinite lives for it. If you have an intensity of understanding, if you bring your total effort, energy, being, to understand it, in that very intensity, a light suddenly burns in you; a flame comes up from your being like lightning, and your whole past and your whole future is suddenly in your vision — you understand what has happened, you understand what is happening, you understand what is going to happen. Suddenly everything has become clear. It is as if it was dark and somebody brought a light, and suddenly everything is clear.

Tantra believes in burning your inner light. And Tantra says that with that light, the past becomes simply irrelevant. It never belonged to you. Of course, it happened, but it happened as if in a dream and you were fast asleep. It happened — you did many things, good and bad, but they all happened in unconsciousness, you were not responsible. And suddenly everything of the past is burned down, a fresh and virgin being comes up — this is sudden Enlightenment.

Yoga appeals to people because it looks very business-like. You can understand Patanjali very easily because he fits with your own mind, the logical mind, the mathematical thinking. Tilopa is difficult to comprehend, but Tilopa is rare. Patanjali's understanding is common. That's why Patanjali's influence was so great and spread all over history.

People like Tilopa have simply disappeared without leaving any trace on the human mind, because you couldn't find in him any affinity with yourself. Patanjali may be very very great, but still he belongs to the same dimension. You may be a very, very small thinker, and Patanjali may be a great, great thinker, but you belong to the same dimension. If you make a little effort you can understand Patanjali; if you make a little effort you can practise Patanjali. Only a little effort is needed, nothing more.

But to understand Tilopa you have to enter into a completely unknown dimension. To understand Tilopa you have to move through a chaos. He will destroy all your conceptions, all your mathematics, all your logic, all your philosophy. He will simply destroy you completely. He will not be satisfied unless you are completely destroyed and a new being arises.

With Patanjali you will be modified, you will become better and better and better — and the process is infinite, you can go on for many lives becoming better and better and better. With Tilopa, in a second, you can reach the Ultimate. 'Better' is not the question because he doesn't think in terms of degrees.

It is just as if you are standing on top of a hill: you can take the path of the steps and one by one you go downwards to the valley, or from the valley you go up to the hill, but by steps. With Tilopa you simply jump into the abyss, there are no steps; or you simply spread your wings and you start flying. With Patanjali you move in a bullock-cart, very slowly, safe, secure, no fear of any accident, the bullock-cart always in control. You can step down any moment, you can stop at any moment. Nothing is beyond you, you remain the master. And the dimension is horizontal: a bullock-cart moves from A to B, from B to C, from C to D, but the dimension is the same, the same plane. With Tilopa, the dimension changes: it becomes vertical; it is not from A to B, from B to C; no, it is just like an aircraft, not like a bullock-cart; not moving forward but moving upward.

With Tilopa you can transcend time.
With Patanjali you move in time.
With Tilopa eternity is the dimension.

You may not be aware of it, but within these few ten or twelve years, a miracle has happened, and that is that new spaceships have destroyed the old time concept completely — because a new spaceship can move around the earth, within seconds it can make one circle. You may not be aware of the theoretical problem. It means that a spaceship takes off from Poona, it is Sunday; then it moves around the earth — somewhere it must be Monday, somewhere it may still be Saturday; so the spaceship moves from Sunday, goes back into Saturday, jumps forward into Monday, comes back to Poona on Sunday. The whole time concept is lost. It looks absurd! You start on the sixteenth, you move into the seventeenth, and you come back on the same date, the sixteenth. And this can be done in twenty-four hours many times now. What does it mean? It means you can go backward in time, from Sunday to Saturday, from the sixteenth to the fifteenth. You can go forward into the seventeenth, into Monday, and you can come back on the same date.

With speed and a different dimension, the vertical, time becomes irrelevant. Time is relevant with a bullock-cart, it is a bullock-cart world. Tilopa is a vertical mind, a vertical consciousness. That is the difference between Tantra and Yoga: Yoga is horizontal, Tantra is vertical; Yoga takes millions of lives to reach, Tantra, within a second. Tantra says time is irrelevant, don't bother about time. Tantra has a technique, a method, which Tantra says is a no-method, a no-technique, through which you can suddenly surrender everything and take a jump into the abyss.

Yoga is effort, Tantra is effortlessness. With effort, with your tiny energy, and your tiny ego, you fight with the Whole. It will take millions of lives. Then too it doesn't seem possible that you will ever become Enlightened. Fighting with the Whole is stupid, you are just a part.

It is as if a wave is fighting with the ocean,
a leaf is fighting with the tree,
or your own hand fighting with your body.
With whom are you fighting?

Yoga is effort, intense effort. And Yoga is a way to fight the current, to move against the current. So whatsoever is natural, Yoga has to drop it; and whatsoever is unnatural, Yoga has to strive for it. Yoga is the unnatural way: fight with the river and move against the current! Of course, there is challenge and the challenge may be enjoyed. But who enjoys the challenge? Your ego.

It is very difficult to find a yogi who is not an egoist; very difficult, rare. If you can find a yogi who is not an egoist, it is a miracle. It is difficult because the whole effort, the fight, creates the ego. You may find humble yogis, but if you look a little deeper, in their humbleness you will find the most subtle ego hidden, the *most* subtle ego. They will say, 'We are just dirt on the ground.' But look into their eyes — they are bragging about their humility. They are saying, 'There is nobody more humble than us. We are the humblest people.' But this is what ego means.

If you move against nature you will be strengthened in your ego—

that is the challenge, that's why people like challenges. A life without challenges becomes dull because the ego feels hungry. Ego needs food, challenge gives food — so people seek challenges. If there are no challenges, they create them; they create hurdles so that they can fight with the hurdles.

Tantra is the natural way; the loose and the natural is the goal. You need not fight with the current; simply move with it, float with it. The river is going to the sea so why fight? Move with the river, become one with the river, surrender. 'Surrender' is the key-word for Tantra; 'will' is the key-word for Yoga. Yoga is the path of will; Tantra is the path of surrender.

That's why Tantra is the path of love — love is surrender. This is the first thing to understand, then Tilopa's words will become very very crystal-clear. The different dimension of Tantra has to be understood, the vertical dimension, the dimension of surrender, of not fighting, of being loose and natural, relaxed. Like Chuang Tzu says, 'Easy is right.' With Yoga, *difficult* is right; with Tantra, easy is right.

Relax and be at ease, there is no hurry. The Whole itself is taking you of its own accord. You need not make an individual striving, you are not asked to reach before your time, you will reach when the time is ripe — you simply wait. The Whole is moving — why are you in a hurry? Why do you want to reach before others?

There is a beautiful story about Buddha: He reached the gate of Heaven. Of course, the people there were waiting. They opened the door, they welcomed him, but he turned his back towards the door, looked at the *samsara*, the world — millions of souls on the same path, struggling, in misery, in anguish, striving to reach this gate of Heaven and bliss. The door-keeper said, 'You come in please! We have been waiting for you.' And Buddha said, 'How can I come when others have not reached? It doesn't seem to be the right time. How can I enter when the whole has not entered into it? I will have to wait. It is just as if my hand has reached into the door, and my feet have not reached yet. I will have to wait. Just the hand cannot enter alone.'

This is one of the most profound insights of Tantra. Tantra says nobody can in fact become Enlightened alone. We are parts of each other, we are members of each other, we are a whole! One person may become the peak, may become a very great wave — but he remains connected with the small waves all around. The wave is not alone, it remains one with the ocean and all the waves there. How can a wave become Enlightened alone?

It is said in this beautiful story that Buddha is still waiting. He has to wait, nobody is an island, we make a continent, we are together. I may have stepped a little further than you, but I cannot be separate. And now I know it deeply, now it is not a story for me — I am waiting for you. Now it is not just a parable, now I know that there is no individual Enlightenment. Individuals can step a little ahead, that's all, but they remain joined together with the whole.

And if an Enlightened person is not aware that he is part of others, one with others, then who will know this? We move as one being, and Tantra says, 'So don't be in a hurry, and don't try, and don't push others, and don't try to be first in the queue — be loose and natural. Everything is going towards Enlightenment. It is going to happen. Don't you create an anguish about it.' If you can understand this, already you are near it, one relaxes. Otherwise, religious people become very very tense; even ordinary worldly people are not as tense as religious people become.

Ordinary worldly people are for worldly goals; of course they are tense, but not so much as religious people because they are tense for the other world, and their world is very far away, invisible, and they are always in doubt whether it is there or not. And then a new misery arises: maybe they are losing this world and the other doesn't exist. They are always in anguish, mentally very much disturbed. Don't become that type of religious man.

To me a religious man is loose and natural. He's not worried about this world or the other world. He is not worried at all, he simply lives and enjoys. This moment is the only moment for him, the next moment will take care of itself. When the next moment comes, he will receive it also enjoying, blissful. A religious man is not goal-oriented. To be goal-oriented is to be worldly. Your goal may be God — it makes no difference.

Tantra is really beautiful. Tantra is the highest understanding, and the greatest principle. If you cannot understand Tantra, then Yoga is for you. If you can understand Tantra, then don't bother about small teachings. When the great vehicle is there, why bother about small boats?

In Buddhism, there are two sects. The names of the sects are very very significant. One sect is known as *Hinayana*, the small vehicle; it is the path of Yoga, a small boat: you alone can sit in it, you cannot have anybody else in it, it is so small. The yogi moves alone. *Hinayana* means the very small boat. And then there is another sect of Buddhists that is called *Mahayana*, the great boat, the great vehicle. Millions can enter into it, the whole world can be absorbed into it.

Mahayana is the path of Tantra and *Hinayana* is the path of yoga. Tilopa is a *Mahayanist*, a man who believes in the great vehicle, the great principle.

Small boats are for egoistic people who cannot tolerate anybody else in the boat, who can only be alone, who are great condemners, who always look at the other with condemnation: 'You — and trying to reach there? You cannot reach, it is very difficult, only rare persons reach.' They will not allow you to enter into the boat. *Mahayana* has a deep love for all. Everybody can enter. In fact, no conditions exist.

People come to me and they say, 'You give *sannyas* to everybody and anybody?' *Sannyas* has not been given that way ever. It is for the first time in the whole history of the world that I give *sannyas* without any conditions. *Sannyas* has always been for very egoistic people, the other-worldly, the condemners, the poisoners, who say everything is wrong, everybody is wrong, this whole life is a sin, who always have a look in their eyes of holier-than-you; you are always condemned, Hell is for you. They are great *sannyasins*; they have renounced the world, the world of sin and dirt and poison, and you are still in it. The great egoists have been the *sannyasins*.

For the first time I have allowed everybody, I have opened the door. In fact I have thrown the door completely, now it cannot be closed, now anybody and everybody is welcome. Why? Because my attitude is that of Tantra, it is not of Yoga. I also talk on Patanjali for those who are not able to comprehend Tantra; otherwise, my attitude is that of Tantra — everybody is welcome. When God welcomes you, who am I . . . ? When the whole world supports you and the Existence tolerates you, not only tolerates, but gives you energy and life, who am I . . . ? Even if you are committing sin the Existence never says, 'No, no more energy for you. Now you cannot get any more gas. Stop! You are doing too much nonsense.' No. The energy goes on being given. There is never any gas-crisis; the Existence goes on supporting you.

It happened: A Mohammedan mystic, Junnaid, once asked God about one of his neighbours: 'This man is so evil and he is creating so much mischief for the whole village, and people come to me and they say, "You ask your God, pray to God, if He can get rid of this man."' And Junnaid heard the voice in his prayer saying, 'When I am accepting him, who are you to reject him?' And Junnaid has written in his autobiography: 'Never again did I ask Him such a thing like that, because it was really foolish of me. If He has given birth to this man, if He is still helping him to be alive, not only alive but flourishing, blooming, then who am I . . . ?'

The Existence gives you life unconditionally.

I give you *sannyas* unconditionally.

If the Existence hopes about you so infinitely
that you cannot destroy its hope,
who am I . . . ?

Tantra is for all. It is not for the chosen few. It became a path for the chosen few because they wouldn't all understand it, but it is not for the chosen few — it is for all; it is for everybody who is ready to take the jump.

Now try to understand:

In Mahamudra all one's sins are burned.

They are not to be balanced by good acts.

In Mahamudra all one's sins are burned.

What is this Mahamudra again and again? What happens? Mahamudra is a state of your being when you are not separate from the Total. Mahamudra is like a deep sexual orgasm with the Whole.

When two lovers are in deep sexual orgasm, they melt into each other; then the woman is no more the woman, the man is no more the man. They become just like the circle of *yin* and *yang*, reaching into each other, meeting into each other, melting, forgetting their own identities. That's why love is so beautiful. This state is called *mudra*, this state of deep orgasmic intercourse is called *mudra*. And the final state of orgasm with the Whole is called Mahamudra, the great orgasm.

What happens in orgasm, in sexual orgasm? You have to understand it because only that will give you the key for the final orgasm. What happens? When two lovers are there . . . and always remember: two lovers, not wife and husband, because with a wife and husband it almost never happens. Because wives and husbands develop more and more fixed roles, they are not melting and flowing. 'Husband' has become a role, 'wife' has become a role: they act; the wife has to act as a wife whether she likes it or not; the husband has to act as a husband. It has become a legal thing.

Once I asked Mulla Nasrudin, 'How many years have you been married, Nasrudin?'

He said, 'Twenty odd years.'

So I asked, 'Why do you call them "odd"?'

He said, 'When you see my wife you will understand.'

Wives and husbands are social phenomena, marriage is an institution, it is not a relationship; it is an institution, it is a forced phenomenon — not for love, but other reasons: economic, security, safety, children, society, culture, religion, everything else except love.

Orgasm almost never happens between a wife and a husband — unless they are lovers also. That is possible: you can be a wife or a husband and a lover; you can love your wife. Then it is totally different, but then it is not a marriage at all, it is no longer an institution.

In the East, because marriage has existed for thousands of years, people have completely forgotten what orgasm is. I have not come across a single Indian woman who knows what orgasm is. Some Western women, just within the last few years, twenty-five years, have become aware that orgasm is something worth achieving. Otherwise, women have completely forgotten that they have any possibility of orgasm within their bodies.

This is one of the most unfortunate things that could have happened to humanity. And when the woman cannot have orgasm, the man cannot have it really either, because orgasm is a meeting of the two. Only two, when they melt into each other, can have it. It is not that one can have it and the other may not have it — it is not possible. Release is possible, ejaculation is possible; relief is possible, but not orgasm. What is orgasm?

Orgasm is a state where your body is no longer felt as matter; it vibrates like energy, electricity. It vibrates so deeply, from the very foundation, that you completely forget that it is a material thing. It becomes an electric phenomenon — and it is an electric phenomenon.

Now physicists say that there is no matter, that all matter is only appearance; deep down, that which exists is electricity, not matter. In orgasm, you come to this deepest layer of your body where matter no longer exists, just energy waves; you become a dancing energy, vibrating. There are no longer any boundaries to you — pulsating, but no longer substantial. And your beloved also pulsates.

And, by and by, if they love each other and they surrender to each other, they surrender to this moment of pulsation, of vibration, of being energy, and they are not scared — because it is death-like.

When the body loses boundaries,

when the body becomes like a vaporous thing,

when the body evaporates substantially
and only energy is left, a very subtle rhythm,
you find that it is as if you are not.
Only in deep love can one move into it. Love is like death:
you die as far as your material *image* is concerned,
you die as far as you think you are a body;
you die as a body
and you evolve as energy, vital energy.

And when the wife and the husband, or the lovers, or the partners, start vibrating in a rhythm, the beats of their hearts and bodies come together, it becomes a harmony — then orgasm happens, then they are two no more. That is the symbol of *yin* and *yang*: *yin* moving into *yang*, *yang* moving into *yin*; the man moving into the woman, the woman moving into the man.

Now they are a circle and they vibrate together,
they pulsate together.
Their hearts are no longer separate,
their beats are no longer separate;
they have become a melody, a harmony.
It is the greatest music possible;
all other musics are just faint things compared to it,
shadow things compared to it.

This vibration of two as one is orgasm. When the same thing happens, not with another person, but with the whole Existence, then it is Mahamudra, then it is the great orgasm. It happens. I would like to tell you how you can try it, so that the Mahamudra becomes possible, the great orgasm.

In Indonesia, there is a very rare man, Bapak Subuh. He has come unknowingly to a method known as *latihan*. He stumbled upon it, but *latihan* is one of the oldest Tantra methods. It is not a new phenomenon; *latihan* is the first step towards Mahamudra. It is allowing the body to vibrate, allowing the body to become energy, non-substantial, non-material; allowing the body to melt and dissolve the boundaries.

Bapak Subuh is a Mohammedan but his movement is known as 'Subud'. That word is Buddhist: 'Subud' comes from three words: 'su', 'bu', 'dha' — 'su' means *sushila*, 'bu' means Buddha, 'dha' means *Dharma*; Subud means sushila-Buddha-Dharma. The meaning is: the law of great virtue derived from Buddha, Buddha's law of great virtue. This is what Tilopa calls the Great Teaching.

Latihan is simple. It is the first step. One has to stand relaxed, loose and natural. It is good if you stand alone and nobody is there to disturb you. Close your room, stand alone. If you can find someone who has already stepped into *latihan*, his presence can be helpful, his very presence works like a catalytic agent, he becomes the opener. So if somebody is advanced a little already, he can open you very easily. Otherwise, you can also open yourself, a little more time will be needed, that's all. Otherwise an opener is good.

If an opener is standing just by your side and he starts his *latihan*, you simply stand and his energy starts pulsating with you, his energy starts moving around you, like a fragrance he surrounds you — suddenly you feel the music. Just like when there is a good singer, or somebody is playing on an instrument, you start beating your feet, or you start tapping the chair, or you start pulsating with it. Just like that, a deep energy inside him moves and the whole room and the quality of the room is changed immediately.

You are not to do anything; you are to simply be there, loose and natural, just waiting for something to happen. And if your body starts moving, you have to allow it, you just have to cooperate and allow. The cooperation should not become too direct, it should not become a pushing; it should remain just an allowing. Your body starts moving suddenly, as if you are possessed, as if a great energy from the above has descended on you, as if a cloud has come and has surrounded you — and now you are possessed by that cloud, and the cloud is penetrating within your body, and your body starts taking movements. Your hands are raised, you make subtle movements, you start a small dance, soft gestures; your body is taken up.

If you know anything about automatic writing it will be easy to follow what happens in *latihan*. In automatic writing you take a pencil in your hand, you close your eyes, you wait — suddenly you feel a jerk in the hand: your hand is possessed, as if something has entered. You are not to do anything, because if you do then it will not be from the beyond; it will be your doing. You simply have to allow. Loose and natural: Tilopa's words are wonderful; they cannot be improved upon. Loose and natural, you wait with the pencil, with closed eyes; when the jerk comes and the hand starts moving, you have to allow it, that's all. You must not resist it, because you can resist. The energy is very subtle, and, in the beginning, not very powerful. If you just stop it, it can be stopped easily and the energy is not aggressive; if you don't allow, it will not come. If you doubt, it will not happen, because with

136

doubt, your hand will be resisting. With doubt, you will not allow, you will fight. So that's why trust is so meaningful, *shraddha*. You simply trust and leave your hand loose; by and by the hand starts moving, now the hand starts making wriggles on the paper — allow it. Then somebody simply asks a question, or you yourself ask a question; let the question be there, loose in the mind, not very persistent, not forcing; just raise the question and wait. And suddenly the answer is written.

If ten persons try, at least three persons will be absolutely capable of automatic writing. Thirty percent of people are not aware that they can become so receptive. And this can become a great force in your life. Explanations differ as to what happens — that is not important. The deepest explanation that I find true is that your own highest center possesses your lowest center; your own highest peak of consciousness catches hold of your lowest unconscious mind. You ask and your own inner being answers. Nobody else is there, but your inner being, which you don't know, is very superior to you. Your own innermost being is your ultimate flowering possibility.

It is as if the flower takes possession of the seed and answers.
The seed doesn't know —
but it is as if the flower, your possibility,
takes possession of your actuality and answers;
as if your ultimate potentiality
takes possession of whatsoever you are, and answers,
or, the future takes possession of the past,
the unknown takes possession of the known,
the formless takes possession of the form
— all metaphors, but I feel you will understand the significance —
as if your old age takes possession of your childhood,
and answers.

The same happens in *latihan* with the whole body. In automatic writing you only leave your hand loose and natural. In *latihan* you leave your whole body loose and you wait, and you cooperate, and suddenly you feel an urge: the hand is rising by itself, as if somebody is pulling it by some invisible strings — allow it. And the leg starts moving; you take a turn, you start a small dance; very chaotic, to no rhythm, with no manipulation, but by and by, as you get deeper, it takes its own rhythm. Then it is no longer chaotic, it takes its own order, it becomes a discipline, but not forced by you. This is your highest possibility taking possession of your lowest body and moving it.

Latihan is the first step. And, by and by, you will feel so beautiful doing it, that you will feel a meeting is happening between you and the cosmos. But this is only the first step. That's why in Subud something is missing. The first step in itself is very beautiful, but it is not the last step. I would like you to complete it. For thirty minutes at least — sixty will be wonderful; by and by from thirty reach to sixty minutes of *latihan* dancing.

In sixty minutes your body, from pore to pore, from cell to cell, is cleansed; it is a catharsis, you are completely renewed, all the dirt is burned. That's what Tilopa says: 'In Mahamudra all one's sins are burned.' The past is thrown into fire. It is a new birth, a rebirth. And you feel an energy showering all over you, in and out. And the dance is not only outside; soon, when you get attuned to it, you will feel an inner dance also, not only that your body is dancing, inside the energy is also dancing; they both cooperate with each other. And then a pulsation happens, and you feel as if you are pulsating with the universe — you have found the universal rhythm.

Thirty to sixty minutes is the time: start with thirty, end with sixty. Somewhere in between you will have the right time. And you will come to know: if you feel attuned at around about forty minutes, then that is your right time; if you feel attuned at twenty minutes, then that is your right time. Then your meditation must go beyond that: if you feel tuned at ten minutes, twenty minutes will do; if you feel tuned at fifteen minutes, thirty minutes will do. Do it double, don't take any chances, so you are really completely cleaned. And end it with a prayer.

When you are completely cleaned and feeling that your body is refreshed — you have been under a shower of energy, and your whole body is feeling one, undivided; and the substantiality of body is lost, you feel it more like an energy, a movement, a process, not material — now you are ready. Then kneel down on the earth.

Kneeling down is beautiful; just like Sufis kneel down, or Mohammedans do their prayer in the mosque, kneel down like them because that is the best posture for prayer. Then raise both your hands towards the sky with closed eyes, and feel yourself like a hollow vessel, a hollow bamboo; inside, hollow, just like an earthen pot. Your head is the mouth of the pot, and the energy is falling tremendously on your head as if you are standing under a waterfall. And you will actually be standing under a waterfall. After the *latihan* you will feel it; it is like a waterfall, not like a shower. When you are ready it falls in greater strength, strongly, and your body will start trembling, shaking, like a leaf in a strong wind; or, if you have stood under a waterfall sometime, then you will know. If you have never stood under a waterfall, go to one and stand under it and feel how it feels. That same feeling will come to you after *latihan*. Feel yourself hollow inside, nothing inside, just emptiness — and the energy is filling you, filling you completely.

Allow it to fall into you as deeply as possible, so it can reach to the farthest corner of your body and mind and soul. And when you feel that you are so filled, and the whole body is shaking, bow down, put your head down on the earth, and pour the energy into the earth. When you feel the energy is overflowing, pour it down into the earth. Take from the sky, give it back to the earth, and be just a hollow bamboo in between.

This has to be done seven times. Take from the sky and pour down into the earth and kiss the earth, and pour down — be empty completely. Pour down as completely as you did for filling, empty yourself completely. Then raise your hands again, fill again, pour down again. Seven times it has to be done, because each time it penetrates one *chakra* of the body, one center of the body; each time it goes deeper in you. And if you do less than seven times, then you will feel restless after it because the energy will be hanging somewhere in between.

No, it has to penetrate all the seven *chakras* of your body so that you become completely hollow, a passage. The energy falls from the sky and goes into the earth, you are earthed; you simply pass the energy to the earth. Just like electricity: for electricity we have to put an earth wire. The energy comes from the sky and goes into the earth, you become earthed — just a vessel, a hollow bamboo passing the energy. Seven times — more you can do, but not less. And this will be a complete Mahamudra.

If you do it every day, soon, within three months somewhere, one day you will feel you are not there. Just the energy will be pulsating with the universe — nobody is there, the ego is completely lost, the doer is not. The universe is there, and you are there, the wave pulsating with the ocean — that is Mahamudra. That is the final orgasm, the *most* blissful state of consciousness that is possible.

This is just like two lovers making love, but a millionfold, the same phenomenon multiplied by millions — because now you are making love with the whole universe. That's why Tantra is known as the Yoga of Sex; Tantra is known as the Path of Love.

In Mahamudra all one's sins are burned:
in Mahamudra one is released
from the prison of this world.
This is the Dharma's supreme torch.
Those who disbelieve it are fools
who ever wallow in misery and sorrow.

And Tilopa is perfectly clear. He's absolutely frank. He says,
'Those who disbelieve it are fools.'

Why call them fools? He does not call them sinners, he does not
call them irreligious, he simply calls them fools — because not believing it they are missing the greatest bliss that life can give them. They
are simply fools! And it cannot happen unless you trust. Unless you
trust so much that you can surrender completely, it cannot happen.
All bliss, all moments of bliss, happen only when you surrender. Even
death becomes beautiful if you can surrender to it, then what to say
about life? If you surrender, of course, life is the greatest blessing, it is
a benediction. You are missing the ultimate gift because you cannot
trust.

If you want to learn anything,
learn trust — nothing else is needed.
If you are miserable,
nothing else will help — learn trust.
If you don't feel any meaning in life
and you feel meaninglessness,
nothing will help — learn trust.
Trust gives meaning because trust
makes you capable of allowing the Whole to descend upon you.

Those who disbelieve it are fools
who ever wallow in misery and sorrow.

To strive for liberation,
one should rely on a Guru.
When your mind receives his blessing,
emancipation is at hand.

Why believe in a Guru? Why believe in a Master? Because the
Unknown is very far from you. It is just a dream, a hope at the
most, a wish-fulfillment.

You listen to me; I may talk about the bliss, but that bliss remains
a word. You may desire it, but you don't know what it is, you don't

140

know the taste of it. It is very very far away from you. You are deep in misery, in anguish. In your misery and anguish you may start hoping, expecting, desiring bliss, but that will not help — you need a real taste of it. Who will give it to you? Only one who has tasted it can become the opener. He can act like a catalytic agent. He will not do anything; just his presence and from him the Unknown flows towards you. He is just like a window. Your doors are closed? — his doors are not closed. Your windows are closed and you have forgotten how to open them? — his windows are not closed. Through his window you can have a look at the sky; through him you can have a glimpse.

A Master, a Guru, is nothing but a window. One has to pass through him, one has to have a little taste — then you can also open your own windows; otherwise the whole thing remains verbal. You can read Tilopa, but unless you find Tilopa nothing will happen to you. Your mind may go on saying, 'Maybe this man is mad, in some hallucination, dreaming, a philosopher, thinking, a poet. But how can this happen? How is it possible for you to be blissful? You have known only misery and suffering, you have known only poison. You cannot believe in elixir; you have not known it so how can you believe it?

A Master is nothing but a personified phenomenon of the total bliss. In him it is there vibrating. If you trust him, his vibrations can reach you. A Master is not a teacher, he doesn't teach you. A Master is not concerned with doctrines and principles — a Master is a presence. If you trust him, he's available. A Master is an availability. Through him you will have the first glimpse of the Divine. Then you can go on your own.

> *To strive for liberation*
> *one should rely* on a Master, *on a Guru.*
> *When your mind receives his blessing,*
> *emancipation is at hand.*

A Master cannot give you emancipation, but he can bring you to the very brink of it. He cannot give you the emancipation; that has to be achieved by you, because a thing given by someone can be taken by someone else. Only that which is yours can be yours. A Master cannot give you it. He can only bless you — but his blessing is a vital phenomenon.

Through him you can look into your own future.

Through him you can be aware of your own destiny.

Through him the farthest peaks come nearer, closer.

Through him you start coming up,
like a seed trying to sprout towards the sky.
His blessing can water your seed.

In the East, the blessing of the Master is very very significant. The West has remained completely unaware of the phenomenon. The West knows teachers, not Masters. Teachers are those who teach you about Truth. A Master is one who gives you the taste of it. A teacher may be someone who does not know himself, he may have learned from other teachers. Seek a Master — teachers are many, Masters are few.

And how will you seek a Master? Just move. Whenever you hear a rumour that somebody has become Enlightened, go and remain available. Don't be much of a thinker, be more of a lover — because a Master is found through feeling. A teacher is found through thinking: listen to the teacher, his logical appeal will be there, his arguments. Eat the Master, drink the Master. Listening won't help because he is a living phenomenon; the energy is there. If you drink and eat him, then only will you become aware of a different quality of being.

A great receptivity is needed, a great feminine receptivity is needed to find the Master. And if you are available and a living Master is there, suddenly something clicks. There is nothing to do on your part — you simply be there. It is such a vital energy phenomenon that if you are available something simply clicks, you are caught. It is a love phenomenon. You cannot prove to anybody else that 'I have found the Master.' There is no proof. Don't try that because anybody can prove against it. You have found it and you know it; you have tasted it and you know it. This knowledge is of the heart, of the feeling.

Says Tilopa:

To strive for liberation,
one should rely on a Guru.
When your mind receives his blessing,
emancipation is at hand.

The very word 'guru' is meaningful. The word 'master' doesn't carry that significance. The Master seems to be like someone who has mastered a thing, undergone a long training, has become disciplined, has become a Master. A Guru is totally different.

The word 'guru' means one who is very very heavy, a heavy cloud just waiting for your thirst to pour down; a flower heavy with perfume just waiting for your nostrils to be there and it will penetrate. The word 'guru' means heavy, very heavy, heavy with energy and the Unknown, heavy with the Divine, heavy like a woman who is pregnant.

A Master is pregnant with God. That's why in the East we call the Guru God Himself. The West cannot understand it because they think 'God' means the Creator of the world. We don't bother much about the Creator here. We call the Guru God. Why? Because he is pregnant with the Divine, he's heavy with the Divine — he is ready to pour down. Only your thirst, a thirsty earth is needed.

He has not mastered anything in fact, he has not gone through any training, he has not disciplined himself; there is no art of which he has become a master — no. He has lived life in its totality; not as a discipline, but naturally and loose. He has not forced himself. He has been moving with the winds, he has allowed nature to take its own course. And through millions of experiences of suffering and pain and bliss and happiness he has become mature, he has become ripe.

A Guru is a ripe fruit just waiting to fall, heavy.

If you are ready to receive, he can fall into you.

A Guru is a totally Eastern phenomenon. The West is not yet aware of it. In the West it is difficult to feel: 'Why go and bow down to a Guru? Why put your head at his feet? Looks humiliating.' But if you want to receive, you have to bow down. He is heavy, he can pour, but then you have to bow down, otherwise you won't receive it.

When a disciple with total trust bows down at the feet of his Master, something is happening there which is not visible to the eyes. An energy is falling from the Master, entering the disciple. Something invisible to the eyes is happening there. If you become aware you can see it also, the aura of the Master, his rainbow, pouring himself down into the disciple; you will in fact see it happening.

The Master is heavy with Divine energy. And he has infinite energy now, he can pour it down to infinite disciples. He can work alone with millions of disciples. He is never exhausted because now he is connected with the Whole, he has found the source of all. Through him you can also take the jump into that abyss. Surrender towards God is difficult because you don't know where God is. He has never given his address to anybody ever. But a Guru can be found. If you ask me what a Guru is, I will tell you that a Guru is the address of God.

> *When your mind receives his blessings,*
> *emancipation is at hand.*

Then you can be certain that you have been accepted. When you can feel the Master's blessings pouring on you, showering on you like flowers, you can be certain emancipation is at hand.

It happened: One of Buddha's disciples, Sariputta, one day bowed down at Buddha's feet. Suddenly he felt the energy falling on him. He felt a sudden transformation, a mutation of his whole mind, as if he was being destroyed and created again. He cried, 'No! Wait a little.' The whole assembly of Buddha's disciples could not understand what was happening. He said, 'Wait a little — not so soon.'

Buddha said, 'But why?'

He said, 'Then these feet will be lost to me. Wait a little. Emancipation is at hand and I would like to be with you a little longer. Don't push me away so soon' — because once the Master has blessed and the emancipation is at hand, this is the last thing. One has to say goodbye to the Master. Says Sariputta, 'Wait!'

Sariputta became Enlightened later on. Buddha told him, 'Now you go. I waited enough. Now you go and spread whatsoever I have given to you, go and give it to others.'

Sariputta had to go, weeping and crying. Somebody asked, 'You have become Enlightened and you weep and cry?'

He said, 'Yes, I have become Enlightened — but I can throw the bliss of Enlightenment if Buddha allows me to live at his feet.'

Such deep gratitude — and then Sariputta continued: every day in the morning he would bow down to the direction where he knew Buddha was moving. And people would ask him again and again, 'Why do you do this? To whom do you bow down?' He said, 'Buddha is moving in the south.'

When the last days of Sariputta came, he enquired, 'Where is Buddha right now? Because I would like to die bowing down in that direction.' And he died bowing down in the direction where Buddha was.

When the energy is received, when the final benediction comes from the Master, emancipation is at hand, one has to say goodbye.

In Zen, in Japan, when a disciple comes to a Master, he brings his mat. He unrolls his mat before the Master, sits on the mat, listens to the Master, comes every day, follows whatsoever he says, leaves the mat there — for years together. Then the day he receives the final blessing, he rolls the mat up again, takes the mat back, bows down, leaves the Master. That mat is symbolic. Whenever a disciple rolls the mat up again, others know he has received the benediction. Now this is the final goodbye.

144

Alas, all things in this world are meaningless,
they are but sorrow's seeds.
Small teachings lead to acts —
one should only follow teachings that are great.

Tantra is the Great Teaching. Small teachings tell you what to do, what not to do. They give you 'ten commandments': 'Do this, don't do that' — small teachings. A great teaching doesn't give you any commandment. It is not concerned with what you do. It is concerned with what you are — your being, your center, your consciousness, that is the only significant thing.

Says Tilopa:

Alas, all things in this world are meaningless,
they are but sorrow's seeds.
Small teachings lead to acts —.
one should follow teachings that are great.

In this world, everything is the seed of sorrow. But a ray of light enters into the world whenever a person becomes Enlightened. In this world everything is a seed of sorrow, but a light-ray comes from the above whenever a person becomes Enlightened. Follow that ray of light and you can reach to the very source of the light, the sun.

And remember, says Tilopa, 'Don't become a victim of small teachings.' Many are. People come to me, they say, 'We are vegetarians. Will it lead us to Enlightenment?' A very small teaching. They say, 'We don't eat in the night. Will it lead us to Enlightenment?' A very small teaching. They say, 'We believe in celibacy.' A very small teaching. They do many things, but one thing they never touch — that is their being. They manage their character, they try to be as sagely as possible, but the whole thing remains a decoration.

A discipline from the without is a decoration. It should come from the within; it should spread towards the periphery from the center. It should not be forced from the periphery towards the center. The Great Teaching is:

You are already that which you can be, realize this.
You are already the goal, be aware of this.
This very moment your destiny can be fulfilled.
For what are you waiting?
Don't believe in gradual steps —
take the jump, be courageous.

Only one who is courageous can follow the Great Teaching of Tantra.

Afraid, scared; afraid of dying, scared of losing yourself, fearful of surrender, you will become a victim of small teachings. Because you can manage small teachings: not to eat this, not to do this, you can manage, you remain in control.

The Great Teaching is to surrender,
to surrender your control and let the Whole take you away
wherever it would like to take you.
Don't swim against the current.
Leave yourself into the river,
become the river —
and the river is already going to the sea.
This is the Great Teaching.

The Song continues:

To transcend duality is the kingly view.
To conquer distractions is the royal practice.
The path of no-practice is the way of all Buddhas.
He who treads that Path reaches Buddhahood.

Transient is this world,
like phantoms and dreams, substance it has none.
Renounce it and forsake your kin,
cut the strings of lust and hatred,
and meditate in woods and mountains.

If without effort
you remain loosely in the natural state,
soon Mahamudra you will win
and attain the Non-attainment.

VII   THE PATHLESS PATH
17th February 1975

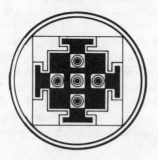

THERE ARE TWO PATHS. One is the path of the warrior, the soldier; the other is the path of the king, the Royal Path. Yoga is the first, Tantra is the second. So first you will have to understand what the path of a soldier, a warrior is, only then will you be able to understand what Tilopa means by the Royal Path.

A soldier has to fight inch by inch; a soldier has to be aggressive, a soldier has to be violent; the enemy has to be destroyed, or conquered.

Yoga tries to create a conflict within you. It gives you a clear-cut distinction between what is wrong and what is right, what is good and what is bad, what belongs to God and what belongs to the Devil. And almost all the religions, except Tantra, follow the path of Yoga. They divide reality and they create an inner conflict; through conflict they proceed.

For example: you have hate in you; the path of the warrior is to destroy hate within. You have anger and greed and sex, and millions of things — the path of the warrior is to destroy all that is wrong, negative, and develop all that is positive and right. Hate has to be destroyed and love evolved. Anger has to be completely destroyed and compassion created. Sex has to go and give place to *brahmacharya*, to pure celibacy. Yoga immediately cuts you with a sword in two parts: the right and wrong; the right has to win over the wrong.

What will you do? Anger is there — what does Yoga suggest to do? It suggests you should create the habit of compassion, create the opposite; make it so habitual that you start functioning like a robot — hence it is called the way of the soldier. All over the world, throughout history, the soldier has been trained in a robot-like existence; he has to create habits.

151

Habits function without consciousness, they do not need any awareness, they can move without you. If you have habits — and everybody has habits — you can watch this. A man takes out his packet of cigarettes from his pocket, watch him — he may not be at all aware of what he is doing. Just robot-like he reaches into the pocket. If there is some inner restlessness, immediately his hand goes to the pocket; he takes the cigarette and starts smoking. He may throw away the remaining part, the last part of the cigarette; he may have moved through all the gestures without even being aware of what he was doing.

A robot-like existence we teach to the soldier. The soldier has to do and follow, he has not to be aware. When he is commanded to turn to the right, he has to turn; he has not to think about whether to turn or not — because if he starts thinking then it is impossible, then wars cannot continue in the world. Thinking is not needed, neither is awareness needed. He should simply be this much aware that he can understand the order, that's all. The minimum of awareness: here the order is given and there, immediately, like a mechanism, he starts following. It is not that he turns to the left when he is ordered to turn left — he hears and turns. He is not turning, he has cultivated the habit. It is just like putting the light off or on: the light is not going to think about whether to be on or off — you push the button and the light is on. You say, 'Left turn!' and the button is pushed and the man moves left.

William James has reported that once he was sitting in a coffee-house and an old retired soldier, retired for almost twenty years, was passing with a bucket of eggs. Suddenly William James played a joke. He loudly called 'Attention!' and the poor old man stood to attention. The eggs fell from his hands, they were destroyed. He was very angry; he came running and said, 'What type of joke is this?'

But William James said, 'You need not follow it. Everybody is free to call "attention". You are not forced to follow it. Who told you to follow it? You should have gone on your way.'

The man said, 'That is not possible — it is automatic. Of course twenty years have passed since I was in the military, but the habit is deep-rooted.' Many years of training — a conditioned reflex is created.

This term 'conditioned reflex' is good. It was coined by a Russian psychologist, Pavlov. It says you simply reflect; somebody throws something in your eye — you don't think of blinking it or closing it, the eye simply closes. A fly comes flying and you close the eye: you

152

need not think, there is no need, it is a conditioned reflex — it simply happens. It is in your body-habit, it is in your blood, in your bones. It simply happens! Nothing has to be done for it.

The soldier is trained to exist in a completely robot-like way. He has to exist in conditioned reflexes. The same is done by Yoga. You get angry — Yoga says, 'Don't get angry, rather cultivate the opposite: compassion.' By and by, your energy will start moving in the habit of compassion. If you perservere for a long time, anger will disappear completely, you will feel compassion. But you will be dead, not alive. You will be a robot, not a human being. You will have compassion, not because you have compassion, but only because you have cultivated a habit.

You can cultivate a bad habit, you can cultivate a good habit. Somebody can cultivate smoking, somebody else can cultivate no-smoking; somebody can cultivate non-vegetarian styles of food, somebody can cultivate a vegetarian style — but both are cultivating, and in the final judgment both are the same because both live through habits.

This point has to be pondered very deeply because it is very easy to cultivate a good habit — it is very difficult to become good. And the substitute of a good habit is cheap, it can be done very easily.

Now, particularly in Russia, they are developing a therapy: conditioned reflex therapy. They say people cannot leave their habits. Somebody has been smoking for twenty years — how can you expect him to leave it? You may try to explain to him that it is bad, the doctors may say he is even in a dangerous situation, cancer may be developing, but twenty years of long habit — now it is engrained, now it has moved into the deepest core of his body, now it is in his metabolism. Even if he wants, even if he desires, even if he desires sincerely to stop, it is difficult — because it is not a question of sincere desire: twenty years of continuous practice — it is almost impossible. So what to do?

In Russia they say there is no need to do anything, and no need to explain to him. They have developed a therapy: the man starts smoking and they give him an electric shock. The shock, the pain of it, and the smoking, become joined together, become associated. For seven days he is hospitalized and whenever he starts smoking, immediately, automatically, he gets an electric shock. After seven days the habit is broken. Even if you persuade him to smoke he will start trembling. The moment he takes the cigarette in the hand the whole body will tremble because of the idea of the shock.

They say that now he will never smoke; they have broken the habit by a very sharp shock treatment. But now he cannot become a Buddha just by shock treatment because he has lost an old habit. All the habits can be changed through shock treatment. Will he become a Buddha? Enlightened? Because he has no bad habits any more? No. He will not even be a human being now — he will be a mechanism. He will be afraid of things, he will not be able to do them because you have given him *new* habits of fear.

That is the whole meaning of 'Hell': all the religions have used it as a shock treatment. Hell is nowhere, neither is there any 'Heaven'. Both are tricks, old psychotherapeutic concepts. They have painted Hell so horrible that a child can become afraid from his very childhood onwards. Just mention the name of Hell and the fear arises and he trembles. This is just a trick to prevent bad habits. And Heaven is also a trick to help good habits; so, much pleasure, happiness, beauty, eternal life is promised in Heaven if you follow good patterns. Whatsoever the society says is good you have to follow. Heaven is to help you towards positivity, and Hell is to prevent you from going in the negative direction.

Tantra is the only religion which has not used any such conditioned reflexes — because Tantra says you have to flower into a perfectly awakened being, not a robot-like mechanism. So if you understand Tantra, *habit* is bad; there are no bad habits, there are no good habits — *habit* is bad. And one should be awake so there are no habits. You simply live moment to moment with full awareness, not through habits. If you can live without habits that is the Royal Path.

Why is it Royal? Because a soldier has to follow, a king need not. The king is above, he gives orders, he receives no orders from anybody. A king never goes to fight, only soldiers go. A king is not a fighter. A king lives the most relaxed of all lives. This is just a metaphor. A soldier has to follow, a king simply lives loose and natural; there is nobody above him. Tantra says there is *nobody* above you. Whom do you have to follow, through whom do you have to get your pattern of life, through whom do you have to become imitators? — there is nobody. Live a loose and natural and flowing life — the only thing is: just be aware.

Through fighting you can cultivate good habits, but they will be habits, not natural. People say a habit is second nature; maybe —

but remember the word 'second'. It is not natural; it may look almost natural, but is not.

What will the difference be between real compassion and a cultivated compassion? A real compassion is a response — the situation and the response. A real compassion is always fresh; something has happened and your heart flows towards it. A child has fallen and you run and help the child to stand up, but this is a response. A false compassion, a cultivated compassion, is a reaction.

These two words are very very meaningful: 'response' and 'reaction'. Response is alive to the situation; reaction is just an engrained habit — because in the past you have been training yourself to help somebody if he has fallen, you simply go and help, but there is no heart in it. Somebody is drowning in the river, you run and help the person just because you have been taught to do so. You have cultivated the habit of helping, but you are not involved. You remain out of it, your heart is not there — you have not responded. You have not responded to *this* man, to *this* man drowning in this river; you have not responded to *this* moment, you have followed an ideology.

To follow an ideology is good: Help everybody, become a servant to people, have compassion! — you have an ideology, and through the ideology you react. It is out of the past that the action comes, it is already dead. When the *situation* creates the action and you respond with full awareness, only then does something of beauty happen to you.

If you react because of the ideology, old habit patterns, you will not gain anything out of it. At the most you can gain a little ego, which is not a gain at all. You may start bragging about the fact that you have saved a man who was drowning in the river. You may go to the market-place and shout loudly, 'Look, I have saved another human life!' You may gain a little more ego, you have done something good, but it is not a gain. You have lost a great opportunity to be spontaneous, to be spontaneous in compassion. If you had responded to the situation, then something would have flowered in you, a blossoming; you would have felt a certain silence, a stillness, a blessing.

Whenever there is a response you feel a blossoming inside.

Whenever there is a reaction you remain dead;

corpse-like you behave, robot-like you act.

Reaction is ugly, response is beautiful.

Reaction is always of the part,

reaction is never of the whole.
Response is always of the whole,
your whole totality jumps into the river.
You don't think about it,
the situation simply lets it happen.

If your life becomes a life of response and spontaneity, you will become some day a Buddha. If your life becomes a life of reaction, dead habits, you may look like a Buddha but you will not become a Buddha. You will be a painted Buddha, inside you will be just a corpse. Habit kills life. Habit is against life.

Every day in the morning you have made it a habit to get up early; at five you get up. In India I have seen many people do it because in India, for centuries, it has been taught that the *Brahmamuhurt*, before the sun has arisen, is the most auspicious moment, the holiest. It is — but you cannot make a habit out of it, because the holy exists only in a living response. They get up at five, but you will never see on their faces the glory that comes if you get up early as a response.

The whole life is awakening all around you; the whole earth is waiting for the sun, the stars are disappearing. Everything is becoming more conscious! The earth has slept, the trees have slept, the birds are ready to take to the wing. Everything is getting ready. A new day starts, a new celebration.

If it is a response, then you get up like a bird — humming, singing; you have a dance to your step. It is not a habit, it is not that you *have* to get up, it is not that because it is written in the scriptures, and you are a devoted Hindu so you have to get up in the early morning. If you make a habit out of it you will not hear the birds because birds are not written in the scriptures; you will not see the sun rising because that is not the point — you are following a dead discipline.

You may even be angry; you may even be against it because last night you were late going to bed and you are not feeling well to get up. It would have been better if you could have slept a little more. You were not ready, you were tired. Or last night was not good, and you dreamt too much and your whole body feels lethargic — you would like to have a little more sleep. But no — the scriptures are against it and you have been taught from your very childhood. . . .

In my childhood my grandfather was very much for the morning. He would drag me out of my sleep near about three in the morning — and since then I have not been able to get up early. He would

156

drag me and I would curse him inside, but I couldn't do anything and he would take me for a walk — I was sleepy and I had to walk with him. He destroyed the whole beauty.

Whenever later I had to go for a morning walk, I could not forgive him. I would always remember him. He destroyed the whole thing, for years continuously he was dragging me — and he was doing something good, and he was thinking that he was helping me to create a life-style. This is not the way. Sleepy, and he was dragging me; and the path was beautiful and the morning was beautiful, but he destroyed the whole beauty, he put me off. Only after many years could I regain and move into the morning without remembering him; otherwise his memory was with me. Even when he was dead he would follow me like a shadow in the morning.

If you make it a habit, if you make it a forced thing, then the morning becomes ugly. Then it is better to go to sleep. But be spontaneous! Some days you may not be able to get up — nothing is wrong in it, you are not committing a sin. If you are feeling sleepy, sleep is beautiful — as beautiful as any morning and as beautiful as any sunrise, because sleep belongs to the Divine as much as the sun does. If you are feeling like resting the whole day, it is good!

This is what Tantra says: the Royal Way — behave like a king, not like a soldier; there is nobody on top of you to force you and order you; there should not really be a style of life. That is the Royal Way. You should live moment to moment, enjoying moment to moment — spontaneity should be the way. And why bother about tomorrow? — this moment is enough. Live it! Live it in totality. Respond, but don't react. 'No habits' should be the formula.

I am not saying live in a chaos, but don't live through the habits. Maybe, just living spontaneously, a way of life will evolve around you — but that is not forced. If you enjoy the morning every day, and through enjoyment you get up early in the morning, not as a habit, then you get up every day and you may get up for your whole life, but that is not a habit. You are not forcing yourself to get up — it happens. It is beautiful, you enjoy it, you love it.

If it happens out of love it is not a style, it is not a habit, not a conditioning, not a cultivated dead thing. Less habits — you will be more alive. No habits — you will be perfectly alive. Habits surround you with a dead crust and you become enclosed in it, you become encapsulated; like a seed a cell surrounds you, hard. Be flexible.

Yoga teaches you to cultivate the opposite of all that is bad. Fight with the evil and attend to the good. There is violence — kill the violence within you and become non-violent, cultivate non-violence. Always do the opposite and force the opposite to become your pattern. This is the soldier's way — a small teaching.

Tantra is the Great Teaching — the Supreme. What does Tantra say? Tantra says: Don't create any conflict within yourself. Accept both and through the acceptance of both, a transcendence happens, not victory but transcendence. In Yoga there are victories, in Tantra there are none. In Tantra there is simply transcendence. It is not that you become non-violent against violence, you simply go beyond both, you simply become a *third* phenomenon — a witness.

I was sitting once in a butcher's shop. He was a very good man and I used to go to visit him. It was evening and he was just going to close the shop when a man came and asked for a hen. And I knew the situation because just a few minutes before he had told me that everything had been sold that day — only one hen was left. So he was very happy; he went in, brought the hen, threw it on the scale and said, 'That will be five *rupees.'*

The man said, 'It is good, but I am going to give a party and many friends are coming and this hen seems to be too small. I would like to have a little bigger one.'

Now I knew that he had no more hens left, this was the only one. The butcher brooded a little, took the hen back inside the room, stood here and there a little, came back again, threw the hen on the scale — the same one — and said, 'This will be seven *rupees.'*

The man said, 'Tell you what, I will take both of them.'

Then the butcher was really in a fix.

And Tantra gives the same fix to the Whole, to the Existence itself. Tantra says, 'I will take both of them.'

There are not two. Hate is nothing but another aspect of love. And anger is nothing but another aspect of compassion. And violence is nothing but another face of non-violence. Tantra says, 'Tell you what, I will take both of them. I accept both.' And suddenly through this acceptance there is a transcendence, because there are not two. Violence and non-violence are not two. Anger and compassion are not two. Love and hate are not two.

That's why you know, you observe it, but you are so unconscious that you don't recognize the fact. Your love changes into hate within a second. How is it possible if they are two? Not even a second is needed: this moment you love and the next moment you hate the same

person. In the morning you love the same person, by the afternoon
you hate, in the evening you love again. This game of love and hate
goes on. In fact, love and hate are not the right words: love-hate,
anger-compassion — they are one phenomenon, they are not two.
That's why love can become hate, hate can become love, anger can
become compassion, compassion can become anger.

Tantra says the division is brought about by your mind and then
you start fighting. You create the division first; you condemn one
aspect and you appreciate another. You create the division first, then
you create the conflict and then you are in trouble. And you will be
in trouble. A yogi is constantly in trouble because whatsoever he does
the victory cannot be final, at the most it can be temporary.

You can push down anger and act compassionate, but you know
well that you have pushed it down into the unconscious and it is there
— any moment, a little unawareness, and it will bubble up, it will
surface. So one has to constantly push it down. This is such an ugly
phenomenon if one has to constantly push down negative things —
then the whole life is wasted. When will you enjoy the Divine? You
have no space, no time. You are fighting with the anger and greed
and sex and jealousy and a thousand things — and those one thousand
enemies are there, you have to be constantly on watch, you can never
relax. How can you be loose and natural? You will be always tense,
strained, always ready to fight, always afraid.

Yogis become afraid even of sleep, because in sleep they cannot
be on watch. In sleep all that they have forced down surfaces. They
may have attained to celibacy while they are awake, but in dreams it
becomes impossible — beautiful women come on floating inside. And
the yogi cannot do anything. Those beautiful women are not coming
from some heaven as it is written in Hindu stories: God sent them.
Why should God be interested in him? A poor yogi, not doing anybody any harm, simply sitting in the Himalayas with closed eyes,
fighting with his own problems — why should God be interested in
him? And why should He send *apsaras,* beautiful women, to distract
him from his path? Why? Nobody is there. There is no need for anybody to send anybody. The yogi is creating his own dreams.

Whatsoever you suppress surfaces in the dreams. Those dreams
are the part the yogi has denied. And your waking hours are *as* much
yours as your dreams are yours. So whether you love a woman in your
waking hours, or you love a woman in a dream, there is no difference
— there cannot be, because it is not a question of a woman being there

or not, it is a question of you. Whether you love a picture, a dream picture, or you love a real woman, there is in fact no difference — there cannot be, because a real woman is also a picture inside. You never know the real woman, you only know the picture.

I'm here. How do you know that really I am here? Maybe it is just a dream and you are dreaming me here. What will be the difference whether you dream me here or you see me actually here? — and how will you make the distinction? What is the criterion? Because whether I am here or not makes no difference — you see me inside your mind. In both cases — dream or real — your eyes take the rays in and your mind interprets that somebody is there. You have never seen any actual person, you cannot see.

That's why Hindus say this is a *maya*, this is an illusory world. Tilopa says, 'Transient, ghostlike, phantomlike, dreamlike is this world.' Why? Because between the dream and the actuality there is no difference. In both cases you are confined in your mind. You only see pictures, you have never seen any reality — you cannot, because the reality can only be seen when *you* become real. You are a ghost-like phenomenon, a shadow — how can you see the real? The shadow can see only the shadow. You can see reality only when the mind is dropped. Through the mind everything becomes unreal. The mind projects, creates, colours, interprets — everything becomes false. Hence the emphasis, continuous emphasis on how to be no-minds.

Tantra says: Don't fight. If you fight you may continue your fight for many lives and nothing will happen out of it, because in the first place you have missed — where you have seen two, there was only one. And if the first step has been missed, you cannot reach the goal. Your whole journey is going to be a continuous missing. The first step has to be taken absolutely rightly, otherwise you will never reach the goal.

And what is the absolutely right thing? Tantra says it is to see the one in two, to see the one in many. Once you can see one in duality, already the transcendence has started. This is the Royal Path.

Now we will try to understand the *sutra*.

To transcend duality is the kingly view.

To transcend, not to win — to transcend. This word is very beautiful. What does it mean to 'transcend'?

It is just like a small child playing with his toys. You tell him to put them away and he becomes angry. Even when he goes to sleep he goes with his toys, and the mother has to remove them when he has fallen asleep. In the morning the first thing that he demands is where his toys are and who has taken them away. Even in the dream he dreams about the toys. Then suddenly one day he forgets about the toys. For a few days they remain in the corner of his room, and then they are removed or thrown away; never again does he ask for them. What has happened? He has transcended, he has become mature. It is not a fight and a victory; it is not that he was fighting against the desire to have toys. No, suddenly one day he sees this is childish and he is no more a child; suddenly one day he realizes that toys are toys, they are not real life and he is ready for real life. His back is turned to toys. Never again in dreams will they come; never again will he think about them. And if he sees some other child playing with toys, he will laugh; he will laugh a knowing laugh, a wise laugh. He will say, 'He's a child, still childish, playing with toys.' He has transcended.

Transcendence is a very spontaneous phenomenon. It is not to be cultivated. You simply become more mature. You simply see the whole absurdity of a certain thing . . . and you transcend.

One young man came to me and he was very worried. He has a beautiful wife but her nose is a little too long. So he was worried and he said, 'What to do?' Even plastic surgery had been done — the nose became a little more ugly; because there was nothing wrong, and when you try to improve something where nothing is wrong, it becomes more ugly, it makes a bigger mess. Now he was more troubled and he asked me what to do.

I talked to him about the toys and I told him, 'One day you will have to transcend. This is just childish — why are you so obsessed with the nose? The nose is just a tiny part and your wife is so beautiful and such a beautiful person — and why are you making her so sad because of the nose?' Because she had also become touchy about the nose. And the nose had become as if it was the whole problem of life. And all problems are like this! Don't think that your problem is something greater — all problems are like this. All problems are created out of childishness, juvenility, they are born out of immaturity.

He was so concerned with the nose that he would not even look at his wife's face, because whenever he saw the nose he would be troubled — but you cannot escape things so easily. If you are *not* looking at the face because of the nose, still you are reminded of the nose. Even if you are trying to evade the issue, the issue is there. You are obsessed. So I told him to meditate on his wife's nose.

He said, 'What? I cannot even look at it.'

But I told him, 'This is going to help — you simply meditate on the nose. In the ancient days people used to meditate on the tip of their own noses, so what is wrong in meditating on the tip of your wife's nose? Beautiful! You try it.'

He said, 'But what will happen out of it?'

'You just try,' I told him, 'and after a few months you tell me what happens. Every day, let her sit before you and you meditate on her nose.'

One day he came running to me and he said, 'What nonsense I have been doing! Suddenly, I have transcended. The whole foolishness of it has become apparent — now it is no more a problem.'

He has not become victorious because, in fact, there is no enemy there so that you can win, there is no enemy to you — this is what Tantra says. The whole life is in deep love with you. There is nobody who is to be destroyed, nobody who is to be conquered, nobody who is an enemy, a foe to you. The whole life loves you. From everywhere the love is flowing.

And within you also, there are no enemies — they have been created by priests, they have made a battleground, they have made you a battleground. They say, 'Fight this, this is bad! Fight that, that is bad!' And they have created so many enemies that you are surrounded by enemies and you have lost contact with the whole beauty of life.

I say to you: anger is not your enemy, greed is not your enemy; neither is compassion your friend, nor is non-violence your friend — because friend or foe, you remain with the duality.

Just look at the whole of your being and you will find they are one. When the foe becomes the friend and the friend becomes the foe, all duality is lost. Suddenly there is a transcendence, suddenly an awakening. And I tell you, it is sudden, because when you fight you have to fight inch by inch. This is not a fight at all. This is the way of the kings — the Royal Path.

Says Tilopa, 'To transcend duality is the kingly view.'

Transcend duality!

Just watch and you will see there is no duality.

Bodhidharma went to China, one of the rarest jewels ever born. The King came to see him, and the King said, 'Sometimes I am very much disturbed. Sometimes there is much tension and anguish within me.'

Bodhidharma looked at him and said, 'You come tomorrow morning early at four o'clock, and bring all your anguish, anxieties, disturbances with you. Remember, don't come alone — bring all of them!'

The King looked at this Bodhidharma — he was a very weird looking fellow; he could have scared anybody to death — and the King said, 'What are you saying? What do you mean?'

Bodhidharma said, 'If you don't bring those things, then how can I set you right? Bring all of them and I will set everything right.'

The King thought, 'It is better not to go. Four o'clock in the morning — it will be dark, and this man looks a little mad. With a big staff in his hand, he may even hit me. And what does he mean that he will put everything right?'

He couldn't sleep the whole night because Bodhidharma haunted him. By the morning he felt that it would be good to go, 'because who knows? — maybe he can do something.'

So he went, grudgingly, hesitatingly, but he reached. And the first thing Bodhidharma asked — he was sitting there before the temple with his staff, was looking even more dangerous in the dark, and he said, 'So you have come! Where are the other fellows that you were talking about?'

The King said, 'You talk in puzzles, because they are not things that I can bring — they are inside.'

Bodhidharma said, 'Okay. Inside, outside, things are things. You sit down, close your eyes and try to find them inside. Catch hold of them and immediately tell me and look at my staff. I am going to set them right!'

The King closed his eyes — there was nothing else to do — he closed his eyes, afraid a little, looked inside here and there, watched, and suddenly he became aware the more he looked in that there was nothing — no anxiety, no anguish, no disturbance. He fell into a deep meditation. Hours passed, the sun started rising, and on his face there was tremendous silence.

Then Bodhidharma told him, 'Now open your eyes. Enough is enough! Where are those fellows? Could you get hold of them?'

The King laughed, bowed down, touched the feet of Bodhidharma, and he said, 'Really you have set them right, because I couldn't find them — and now I know what is the matter. They were not there in the first place. They were there because I never entered within myself and looked for them. They were there because I was not present inside. Now I know — you have done the miracle.'

And this is what happened. This is transcendence: not solving a problem, but seeing whether there is really a problem in the first place. First you create the problem and then you start asking for the solution. First you create the question and then you roam around the world asking for the answer. This has been my experience also, that if you watch the question, the question will disappear; there is no need for any answer. If you watch the question, the question disappears — and this is transcendence. It is not a solution because there is no question at all to solve. You don't have a disease. Just watch inside and you will not find the disease, then what is the need of a solution?

Every man is as he should be.

Every man is a born king.

Nothing is lacking,

you need not be improved upon.

And people who try to improve you, they destroy you, they are the real mischief-makers. And there are many who are just watching like cats for mice: you come near them and they pounce upon you and they start improving you immediately. There are many improvers — that's why the world is in such chaos — there are too many people trying to improve on you.

Don't allow anybody to improve upon you.

You are already the last word.

You are not only the alpha, you are the omega also.

You are complete, perfect.

Even if you feel imperfection, Tantra says that imperfection is perfect. You need not worry about it. It will look very strange to say that your imperfection is also perfect, that nothing is lacking in it. In fact, you appear imperfect not because you are imperfect but because you are a growing perfection. This looks absurd, illogical, because we think perfection cannot grow, because we mean by perfection that which has come to its last growth — but that perfection will be dead. If it cannot grow then that perfection will be dead.

God goes on growing. God is not perfect in that way, that he has no growth. He is perfect because he lacks nothing, but he goes from one perfection to another, the growth continues — God is evolution; not from imperfection to perfection but from perfection to more perfection, to still more perfection.

When perfection is without any future, it is dead. When perfection has a future to it, still an opening, a growth, still a movement, then it looks like imperfection. And I would like to tell you: be imperfect and growing, because that is what life is. And don't try to be perfect, otherwise you will stop growing. Then you will be like a Buddha statue, stone, but dead.

Because of this phenomenon — that perfection goes on growing — you feel it is imperfect. Let it be as it is. Allow it to be as it is. This is the Royal Way.

To transcend duality is the kingly view;
to conquer distractions is the royal practice.

Distractions are there, you will lose your consciousness again and again. You meditate, you sit for meditation, a thought comes — and immediately you have forgotten yourself; you follow the thought, you have got involved in it. Tantra says only one thing has to be conquered, that is distractions.

What will you do? Only one thing: when a thought comes, remain a witness. Look at it, observe it, allow it to pass your being, but don't get attached to it in any way, for or against. It may be a bad thought, a thought to kill somebody — don't push it, don't say, 'This is a bad thought.' The moment you say something about the thought, you have become attached, you are distracted. Now this thought will lead you to many things, from one thought to another. A good thought comes, a compassionate thought, don't say, 'Aha, so beautiful! I am a great saint. Such beautiful thoughts are coming to me that I would like to give salvation to the whole world. I would like to liberate everybody.' Don't say that. Good or bad, you remain a witness.

Still, in the beginning, many times you will be distracted. Then what to do? If you are distracted, be distracted. Don't be too worried about it, otherwise that worry will become an obsession. Be distracted! For a few minutes you will be distracted, then suddenly you will remember, 'I am distracted,' then it is okay, come back. Don't feel depressed. Don't say, 'It was bad that I was distracted,' then again you are creating a dualism: bad and good. Distracted, okay — accept it, come back. Even with distraction, don't create a *conflict.*

That's what Krishnamurti goes on saying. He uses a very paradoxical concept for it. He says if you are inattentive, be attentively inattentive. That's okay! Suddenly you find you have been inattentive, give attention to it and come back home. Krishnamurti has not been understood and the reason is that he follows the Royal Path. If he had been a yogi he would have been understood very easily. That's why he goes on saying there is no method — on the Royal Path there is no method. He goes on saying that there is no technique — on the Royal Path there is none. He goes on saying no scripture will help you — on the Royal Path there is no scripture.

Distracted? — the moment you remember, the moment this attention comes to you that you have been distracted, come back! That's all! Don't create any conflict. Don't say this was bad, don't feel depressed, frustrated that you have been again distracted. Nothing is wrong in distraction — enjoy it also.

If you can enjoy the distraction, it will happen to you less and less. And a day comes when there is no distraction — but this is not a victory. You have not pushed the distracting trends of your mind deep into the unconscious. No. You allowed them also. They too are good.

This is the mind of Tantra, that everything is good and holy. Even if there is distraction, somehow it is needed. You may not be aware why it is needed; somehow it is needed. If you can feel good for everything that happens, then only are you following the Royal Path. If you start fighting with *anything* whatsoever, you have fallen from the Royal Path and you have become an ordinary soldier, a warrior.

To understand duality is the kingly view;
to conquer distractions is the royal practice;
the path of no-practice is the way of all Buddhas.

Nothing is to be practised because practice creates habits. One has to become more aware, not more practised. The beautiful happens through the spontaneous, not through the practised. You can practise love, you can go through some training. In America they are thinking of creating a few training courses for love, because people have even forgotten that, how to love. It is really strange! Even birds, animals, trees, they don't ask anybody, they don't go to any college — and they love. And many people come to me. . . .

Just a few days ago, one young man wrote a letter to me. And he said, 'I understand — but how to love? How to proceed? How to approach a woman?' It seems ridiculous but we have lost the natural, loose way completely. Not even love is possible without training. And if you are trained you will become absolutely ugly, because then everything you do will be part of the training. It will not be real, it will be acting. It will not be real life, it will be just like actors.

Actors create love, they act in a loving way, but have you noticed that actors are the greatest failures as far as love is concerned? Their love-lives are almost always failures. This should not be so, because twenty-four hours a day they are practising love; with so many women, with so many stories, in different ways they are practising love; they are professional lovers, they should be perfect when they fall in love — but when they fall in love they are always failures.

The love-lives of actors and actresses are always failures. What is the matter? Practice is the matter, they have practised it too much — now the heart cannot function. They simply go on making impotent gestures: they kiss, but the kiss is not there, only lips meet. Only lips meet and the transfer of inner energy is not there; their lips are closed, cold. And if lips are cold, closed and energy is not being released through them, the kiss is an ugly thing, unhygienic. It is just a transfer of millions of cells, germs, diseases — that's all.

A kiss is ugly if the inner energy is not present. You can embrace a woman or a man — only bones meet, bodies clash, but there is no jump of the inner energy. The energy is not there. You are just moving through an impotent gesture. You can even make love; you can move through all the gestures of love, but that will be more like gymnastics and less like love.

Remember: practice kills life. Life is more alive when unpractised. When it flows in all directions without any pattern, without any forced discipline, then it has its own order and discipline.

The path of no-practice is the way of all Buddhas;
he who treads that path reaches Buddhahood.

Then what to do? If no-practice is the path, then what to do? Then just live spontaneously. What is the fear? Why are you so afraid of living spontaneously? Of course there may be dangers, hazards are there — but that is good! Life is not like a railway-track, the trains moving on the same track again and again, shunting. Life is like a river: it creates its own path; it is not a channel. A channel is not good — a channel means a life of habits. Danger is there, but danger is life, it is involved in life. Only dead persons are beyond danger. That's why people become dead.

Your houses are more like graves. You are too much concerned with security. And too much concern for security kills, because life is insecure. It is so! Nothing can be done about it, nobody can make it secure. All securities are false, all securities are imagined. A woman loves you today, tomorrow — who knows? How can you be secure about tomorrow? You may go to the court and register, and make a legal bond that she will remain your wife tomorrow also. She *may* remain your wife because of the legal bond, but love can disappear. Love knows no legality. And when love disappears and the wife remains the wife and the husband remains the husband, then there is a deadness between them.

Because of security we create marriage. Because of security we create society. Because of security we always move on the channelized path.

Life is wild.

Love is wild.

And God is absolutely wild.

He will never come into your gardens, they are too human. He will not come to your houses, they are too small. He will never be met on your channelized paths. He is wild.

Remember, Tantra says life is wild. One has to live through all the dangers, hazards — and it is beautiful because then there is adventure. Don't try to make a fixed pattern of your life. Allow it to take its own course. Accept everything; transcend duality through acceptance and allow life to take its own course — and you will reach, you will certainly reach. This 'certainly' I say, not to make you secure — this is a fact, that's why I say it. This is not your certainty of security. Those who are wild always reach.

> *Transient is this world:*
> *like phantoms and dreams, substance it has none.*
> *Renounce it and forsake your kin,*
> *cut the strings of lust and hatred,*
> *and meditate in woods and mountains.*

> *If without effort*
> *you remain loosely in the natural state,*
> *soon Mahamudra you will win*
> *and attain the Non-attainment, the Non-attainable.*

This *sutra* has to be understood very deeply because misunderstanding is possible. There has been much misunderstanding about *this* sutra of Tilopa's. And all those who have commented before me, they have missed the point. There is a reason. This sutra says: *Transient is this world* — this world is made of the same stuff as dreams are made of. Between dreams and this world there is no difference. Walking or asleep you live in a dream-world of your own. Remember there is not one world — there are as many worlds as there are persons;

everybody lives in his own world. Sometimes our worlds meet and clash, sometimes they merge, but we remain enclosed in our own worlds.

> *Transient is this world,* mind-created.
> *Like phantoms and dreams, substance it has none.*

This is what physicists say also: Substance it has none. Matter has disappeared completely from the vocabulary of the physicist within just thirty or forty years. Seventy years ago, seventy-five years ago, Nietzsche declared, 'God is dead.' And he said it to emphasize that only matter exists — and the century was not even complete. Just twenty-five years after Nietzsche died — Nietzsche died in 1900 — and in 1925 physicists came to understand that we don't know anything about God, but one thing is certain: matter is dead. There is nothing material around you, everything is just vibrations; criss-crossing vibrations create the illusion of matter.

It is the same as you see in a movie: there is nothing on the screen — only criss-crossing electric lights, and they create the whole illusion. And now there are three-dimensional films; they create the complete illusion of three dimensionality. Exactly like the movie film on the screen is the whole world, because it is all an electric phenomenon — *only you are real*, only the witness is real and everything else is a dream. And Buddhahood means when you transcend all these dreams and there is nothing left to be seen — only the seer sits silently; there is nothing, no object to be seen, only the seer is left — then you have attained to Buddhahood, to reality.

> *Transient is this world;*
> *like phantoms and dreams, substance it has none.*
> *Renounce it and forsake your kin. . .*

These words, 'Renounce it and forsake your kin,' have been misunderstood. There is reason why, because they are all renouncers, and they thought that Tilopa was saying what they believe. Tilopa cannot say it because it is against Tilopa's whole trend. If they are like dreams, what is the meaning of renouncing them? You can renounce reality, you cannot renounce dreams — it will be too foolish. You can renounce a substantial world, you cannot renounce a phantom world. In the morning do you go to the housetop and call everybody around and declare, 'I have renounced dreams! Last night there were many dreams and I have renounced them? They will laugh, they will think you

169

have gone crazy — nobody renounces dreams. One simply awakes; nobody renounces dreams.

One Zen Master woke up one morning and he asked one of his disciples, 'I had a dream last night. Would you interpret it for me, what it means?'

The disciple said, 'Wait! Let me bring a cup of tea for you.'

The Master took the cup of tea and then asked, 'Now what about the dream?'

The disciple said, 'Forget about it, because a dream is a dream and needs no interpretation. A cup of tea is enough interpretation — awake!'

The Master said, 'Right, absolutely right! If you had interpreted my dream I would have thrown you out of my monastery, because only fools interpret dreams. You did well, otherwise you would have been thrown out completely and I would not have looked at your face again.'

When there is a dream you need a cup of tea and then be finished with it. Freud and Jung and Adler would have been much worried had they known this story, because they wasted their whole lives interpreting others' dreams. A dream has to be transcended. Simply by knowing it is a dream you transcend — *this* is the renunciation.

Tilopa has been misunderstood because there are in the world so many renouncers, condemners. They thought he was saying renounce the world. He was not saying that. He was saying, 'Know that it is transient and this is renunciation.' 'Renounce it', he says, means, know that it is a dream.

'Forsake your kin' — it has been thought that he is saying, 'Leave your family, your relations, your mother, your father, your children.' No, he is not saying that; he cannot say that, it is impossible for Tilopa to say that. He is saying renounce the inner relationship with people. You should not think that somebody is your wife; that 'yourness' is a phantom, it is a dream. You should not say, 'This child is my son;' that 'myness', that 'mine' is a dream. Nobody is yours, nobody can be yours. Renounce these attitudes that somebody is yours — husband, wife, friend, enemy; renounce all these attitudes. Don't bridge: 'mine', 'thine' — these words, drop them.

Suddenly, if you drop these words, you have renounced your kin — nobody is yours. That doesn't mean that you escape, that you run away from your wife, because the running away will show that you think she is substantial. Running away will show that you still think she is yours, otherwise why are you running?

It happened: One Hindu *sannyasin*, Swami Ramteerth, came back from America. He was staying in the Himalayas; his wife came to see him — he became a little disturbed. His disciple, a very penetrating mind, Sardar Poorn Singh, was sitting beside him. He watched, he felt that he was disturbed. When the wife went, suddenly Ramteerth threw his orange robes. Poorn Singh asked, 'What is the matter? I was watching, you were a little disturbed. I felt you were not yourself.'

He said, 'That's why I'm throwing these robes. I have met so many women, and I was never disturbed. Nothing is special about this woman — except that she was my wife. That "my" is still there. I am not worthy to wear these robes. I have not renounced the "mine", I have renounced only the wife. The wife is not the problem; *no* other woman has ever disturbed me. I have walked all over the earth, but comes my wife — she is as ordinary a woman as any — and suddenly I am disturbed. The bridge is still there.' He died in ordinary clothes, he never again used the orange. He said, 'I am not worthy.'

Tilopa cannot say renounce your wife and children and your kin. No. He is saying renounce the bridges, drop them — that is your affair; it is not concerned with the wife. If she continues to think about you as her husband, that is her problem, not yours. If the son continues to think of you as his father, that is his problem; he is a child, he needs maturity.

I say to you: Tilopa means renouncing the inner dreams and bridges, the inner worlds.

. . . and meditate in woods and mountains.

And with that too he is not saying run away to the mountains and the woods. It has been interpreted like that, and many have escaped from their wives and children and gone to the mountains — that is absolutely wrong. What Tilopa is saying is deeper; it is not so superficial, because you can go to the mountains and remain in the market. Your mind is the question. You may sit in the Himalayas and think of the market and your wife and your children and what is happening to them.

It happened: A man renounced his wife, children, family, and came to Tilopa to be initiated as his disciple. Tilopa was staying in a temple outside the town. Came the man. When he reached inside he was alone and Tilopa was alone. Tilopa looked around him and said, 'You have come, that's okay — but why this crowd?' The man also looked back because there was none. Tilopa said, 'Don't look back! Look in! — the crowd is there.' And the man closed his eyes and the crowd was there: the wife was still crying there, the children were weeping and sad; they were standing there, they had come to leave him at the boundary of the town — friends, family, others, they were all there. And Tilopa said, 'Go out, leave the crowd! I initiate persons not crowds.'

No, Tilopa cannot mean that you renounce the world and go into the mountains. He is not so foolish. He cannot mean that — he is an Awakened man. What he means is this: he says if you renounce the dreams, the bridges, the relationships — not the relations — if you renounce your mind, suddenly you are in the woods and in the mountains. You may be sitting in the market — the market has disappeared. You may be sitting in your house — the house has disappeared. Suddenly you are in the woods and in the mountains. Suddenly you are alone. Only you are there, nobody else.

You can be in the crowd and alone, and you can be alone and in the crowd. You can be in the world and not of the world. You can be in the world, but you can belong to the mountains and the woods.

This is an inner phenomenon. There are inner mountains and inner woods, and Tilopa cannot say anything about the outer mountains and woods, because they are also dreams. A Himalaya is as much a dream as the market-place in Poona, because a Himalaya is as outer a phenomenon as the market-place is. The woods are also a dream. You have to come to the inner — the reality is there. You have to move more and more deeply, in the depth of your being, then you will come to the real Himalayas, then you will come to the real woods of your being, peaks and valleys of your being, heights and depths of your being. Tilopa means that.

> *If without effort*
> *you remain loosely in the natural state...*

And he has to mean that because he is for the loose and natural state. To escape from the wife and the children is not natural, and it is not loose at all. A man who leaves his wife and children and friends and the world becomes tense, he cannot be loose. In the very effort of renouncing a tension comes in.

To be natural means — to be there where you are. To be natural means: wherever you find yourself, be there. If you are a husband, good; if you are a wife, beautiful; if you are a mother, right — it has to be so. Accept wherever you are and whatsoever you are and whatsoever is happening to you, only then can you be loose and natural, otherwise you cannot be loose and natural. Your so-called monks, *sadhus,* people who have escaped from the world, in fact, cowards sitting in their monasteries, can*not* be loose and natural — they have to be uptight, they have done something unnatural, they have gone against the natural flow.

Yes, to a few people it can be natural. So I am not saying *force* yourself to be in the market-place, because then you will go to the other extreme, and you will again do the same foolishness. To a few people it may be absolutely natural to be in a monastery; then they have to be in the monastery. To a few people it may be absolutely natural to move in the mountains; they have to be in the mountains. The thing to be remembered as a criterion is being loose and natural. If you are natural in the market, beautiful — the market is also Divine. If you feel loose and natural in the Himalayas, beautiful — nothing is wrong in it. Remember only one thing: Be loose and natural. Don't strain! — and don't try to create a tension within your being. Be relaxed.

> . . .*soon Mahamudra you will win.* . . .

Remaining loose and natural, soon you will come to the orgasmic peak with the Existence.

> . . .*and attain the Non-attainment.*

And you will attain that which cannot be attained. Why? Why say it cannot be attained? Because it cannot be made a goal. It cannot be attained by a goal-oriented mind. It cannot be attained by an achieving mind.

Many people are here of the same trend of the achieving mind. They are uptight because they have made that a goal which cannot be made a goal. It happens to you! — you cannot attain it. You cannot reach for it — it comes to you. You can only be passive, loose and natural, and wait for the right time, because everything has its own season. It will happen in its own season. What is the hurry? If you are in a hurry then you will become uptight, then you will be constantly expecting.

That's why Tilopa says. '. . . and attain the Non-attainment.' It is not a goal. You cannot make a target out of it that you are going to attain, you cannot reach towards it like an arrow, no. The mind which is arrowed towards a goal is a tense mind.

Suddenly it comes, when you are ready —
not even the footsteps are heard.
Suddenly it comes.
You do not even become aware that it is coming.
It has bloomed.
Suddenly you see the blooming —
you are filled with the fragrance.

The Song continues:

Cut the root of a tree and the leaves will wither;
cut the root of your mind and samsara falls.
The light of any lamp dispels in a moment
the darkness of long kalpas;
the strong light of the Mind in but a flash
will burn the veil of ignorance.

Whoever clings to mind
sees not the truth of what's beyond the mind.
Whoever strives to practise Dharma
finds not the truth of beyond-practice.
To know what is beyond both mind and practice
one should cut cleanly through the root of mind
and stare naked.
One should thus break away from all distinctions
and remain at ease.

VIII   CUT THE ROOT
18th February 1975

C HOICE IS BONDAGE, choicelessness freedom.
The moment you choose something,
you have fallen into the trap of the world.
If you can resist the temptation to choose,
if you can remain choicelessly aware,
the trap disappears of its own accord,
because when you don't choose
you don't help the trap to be there —
the trap is also created by your choice.

So this word 'choice' has to be understood very deeply, because only through that understanding can choicelessness flower in you.

Why can't you remain without choosing? Why does it happen that the moment you see a person or a thing, immediately a subtle wave of choice has entered into you, even if you are not aware that you have chosen. A woman passes by and you say she is beautiful. You are not saying anything about your choice but the choice has entered, because to say about a person that she is beautiful means: I would like to choose her. In fact, deep down you have chosen; you are already in the trap. The seed has fallen to the soil; soon there will be sprouts, there will be a plant and a tree.

The moment you say this car is beautiful, choice has entered. You may not be aware at all that you have chosen, that you would like to possess this car, but in the mind a fantasy has entered, a desire has arisen. When you say something is beautiful, you mean that you would like to have it. When you say something is ugly, you mean that you would not like to have it.

Choice is subtle and one has to be very minutely aware about it. Whenever you say something remember this: that saying is not only

179

saying, not a mere saying — something has happened in the unconscious. Don't make the distinction: this is beautiful and that is ugly,
this is good and that is bad. Don't make distinctions. Remain aloof!
Things are neither bad nor good. The quality of goodness and badness
is introduced by you. Things are neither beautiful nor ugly; they are
simply there as they are — the quality of being beautiful or ugly is introduced by you, it is your interpretation.

What do you mean when you say something is beautiful? Is there
any criterion for beauty? Can you prove that it is beautiful? Just standing by your side, somebody may think, 'This is ugly!' — so it is nothing
objective; nobody can prove anything beautiful. Thousands and
thousands of books have been written on aesthetics, and it has been a
long arduous journey for intellectuals, thinkers and philosophers to
define what beauty is — they have not yet been able to. They have
written great books, great treatises, they go round about and round
about, but nobody has ever been able to pin-point what beauty is. No,
it seems impossible — because there exists nothing like beauty or ugliness, it is your interpretation.

First you make a thing beautiful. This is why I say that first you
create the trap and then you fall into it. First you think this face is
beautiful — this is *your* creation, this is just your imagination, this is
just your mind interpreting; this is not existential, this is just psycholog-
ical — and then you yourself fall into the trap. You dig the hole and then
you fall into it and then you cry for help, and then you cry for people
to come for your salvation.

Nothing is needed says Tantra. Simply see the whole trick — it is
your own creation.

What do you mean that something is ugly? If man is not on the
earth will there be ugliness and beauty? Trees will be there, of course,
and they will bloom; of course, rains will come, and summer and seasons
will follow one another — but there will be nothing like beautiful or
ugly, it will disappear with man and his mind. The sun will rise and in
the night the sky will be filled with stars — but nothing will be beautiful
and nothing will be ugly. It was just man creating noise. Now he is no
more there the interpretations have disappeared; what will be good
and what will be bad?

In nature nothing is good and nothing is bad. And remember,
Tantra is the loose and the natural way. It wants to bring you to the
deepest natural phenomena of life. It wants to help you drop from the

mind — and mind creates distinctions, and mind says this is to be chosen and that has to be avoided. To this you cling and that you avoid and escape from. Look at the whole phenomenon. Just a look is needed, nothing else; no practice is needed — just a view of the whole situation.

The moon is beautiful; why? Because for centuries you have been indoctrinated that the moon is beautiful; for centuries poets have been singing about the moon, for centuries people have believed it — now it has become engrained. Of course there are a few things that happen with the moon: it is very soothing, you feel calmed down, and the light of the moon gives a mysterious aroma to the whole of nature; it gives a sort of hypnosis, you feel a little sleepy yet awake and things look more beautiful; it gives a dreamlike quality to the world — that's why we call madmen lunatics. The word 'lunatic' comes from the word 'luna', the moon. They have gone mad, moonstruck.

The moon creates a sort of lunacy, a sort of madness, a neurosis. It may be concerned with the water in your body, just like the sea is affected by the moon and tides come. Your body is ninety percent sea-water. If you ask the physiologists they will say that something must be happening in the body because of the moon, because your body remains a part of the sea. Man has come from the sea to the earth; basically life was born in the sea. When the whole sea is affected, of course all sea animals are affected by the moon, they are part of the sea, and man has also come from the sea. Very, very long he has travelled but it makes no difference, the body still reacts in the same way; and ninety percent of your body is water, and not only water, sea-water, with the same chemicals, the same saltiness.

In the womb the child swims for nine months, floats in sea-water; the mother's womb is filled with sea-water. That's why when women are pregnant they start using, eating more salt. More salt is needed for their womb, to keep the same balance of saltiness. And the child passes through all the phases humanity has passed through. In the beginning he is just like a fish, he moves in the ocean of the mother's womb, floats. By and by, in nine months he passes millions of years. Physiologists have come to realize that he passes through all the stages of life in nine months.

That may be so, that the moon affects you, but there is nothing like beauty — it is a chemical phenomenon.

Certain eyes you feel are very beautiful. What is happening? Those eyes must have a quality, a chemical quality, an electric quality in them, they must be releasing some energy — you become affected by them. You say some eyes are hypnotic, like Adolf Hitler's eyes. Just the moment he sees you something happens in you, you say his eyes are very beautiful. What do you mean by beauty? You are affected.

In fact, when you say something is beautiful you are not saying that something is beautiful, you are saying that you are affected in a nice way, that's all. When you say something is ugly you are saying that you are affected in an antagonistic way. You are repelled or you are attracted. When you are attracted it is beautiful, when you are repelled it is ugly. *But it is you*, not the object, because the same object can attract somebody else.

It happens every day; people are always amazed about other people. They say, 'That man has fallen in love with that woman, amazing!' Nobody can believe that this can happen, that woman is ugly. But to that man, that woman is the very incarnation of beauty. What to do? There can be no objective criterion, there is none.

Tantra says remember that whenever you choose something, whenever you decide for this or against this, it is your mind playing tricks. Don't say the thing is beautiful! Just simply say, 'I am affected in a nice way,' so the base remains 'I'. If once you transfer the whole phenomenon onto the object, then it can never be solved because from the first step you missed, you missed the root. The root is you, so if you are affected it means your mind is affected in a certain way. And then that affection, that affectedness, creates the trap and you start moving.

First you create a beautiful man and then you start chasing, then you run after him. And after a few days of living with a beautiful man or woman, all fantasies fall to the ground. Suddenly you become aware, as if you have been deceived, that this woman looks ordinary. And you were thinking she was a Laila or a Juliet, or you were thinking he was a Majnu or a Romeo, and suddenly, after a few days, the dreams have evaporated and the woman has become ordinary, or the man has become ordinary; then you feel disgusted, as if the other has deceived you.

Nobody has deceived and nothing has fallen from the man or the woman, it is your own fantasy that has fallen — because fantasies cannot be maintained. You can dream about them but you cannot maintain them for a long time. Fantasies are fantasies! So if you really want to continue in your fantasy, then when you see a woman beautiful, immediately escape from her as far as you can. Then you will always remember her as the most beautiful woman in the world. Then the fantasy will never come in contact with reality. Then there will be no shattering. You can always sigh and sing and weep and cry for the beautiful woman — but never go near her!

The nearer you come, the more reality, the more objective reality reveals itself. And when there is a clash between objective reality and your fantasy, of course you know which is going to be defeated — your fantasy. Objective reality cannot be defeated.

This is the situation. And Tantra says become aware: nobody is deceiving you except yourself. The woman was not trying to be very beautiful, she was not creating the fantasy around herself, *you* created it around her; you believed it, and now you are at a loss as to what to do, because the fantasy cannot be continued against the reality. A dream has to break — and that is the criterion.

Hindus in the East have made a criterion for truth: they say truth is that which lasts forever, forever, forever; and untruth is that which lasts only for a moment. There is *no* other distinction. The momentary is the untrue and the everlasting is the truth. And life is everlasting; existence is everlasting. Mind is momentary — so whatsoever mind gives to life it remains momentary, it is a colour that the mind gives to the life, it is an interpretation. By the time the interpretation is complete, the mind has changed. You cannot maintain the interpretation because mind cannot be maintained for two consecutive moments in the same situation in the same state. Mind goes on changing, mind is a flux. It has already changed — by the time you realize that this man is beautiful, the mind has already changed. Now you will be falling in love with something which is there no more, even in your mind.

Tantra says: Understand the mechanism of the mind and cut the root. Don't choose, because when you choose you get identified. Whatsoever you choose you become, in a certain way, one with it.

If you love a car, you become one with that car in a certain way. You come closer and closer; and if the car is stolen, something of your being is stolen. If something goes wrong with the car, something goes wrong with you. If you fall in love with a house you become one with the house. Love means identification; coming so close, like when you put two wax candles closer, closer, closer, and put them very close — they become one. Because of the heat, the burning of the flame, by and by they become one. This is identification. Two flames coming closer and closer and closer, they become one.

And when you are identified with something you have lost your soul. This is the meaning of losing your soul in the world: you have become identified with millions of things, and with everything a part of you has become a thing.

Choice brings identification.

Identification brings a hypnotic state of sleep.

Gurdjieff has only one thing to teach to his disciples and that is not to be identified. His whole school, all his techniques, methods, situations, are based on one single base, and that base is: not to be identified.

You are crying; when you are crying, you have become one with the crying; there is nobody to watch it, there is nobody to see it, be alert and aware of it; you are lost in crying. You have become the tears and the red swollen eyes and your heart is in a crisis. Teachers like Gurdjieff, when they say not to be identified, they say, 'Cry, nothing is wrong in it, but stand by the side and look at it — don't be identified.' And it is a wonderful experience if you can stand by the side. Cry, let the body cry, let the tears flow, don't suppress it because suppression helps nobody, but stand by the side and watch.

This can be done — because your inner being is a witness, it is never a doer. Whenever you think it is a doer there is an identification. It is never a doer. You can walk the whole earth — your inner being never walks a single step. You can dream millions of dreams — your inner being never dreams a single dream. All movements are on the surface. Deep in the depth of your being there is no movement. All movements are on the periphery, just like a wheel moves, but at the center nothing moves. At the center everything remains as it is, and on the center the wheel moves.

Remember the center! Watch your behaviour, your actions, your identifications, and a distance is created; by and by a distance comes into existence — the watcher and the doer become two. You can see yourself laughing, you can see yourself crying, you can see yourself walking, eating, making love; you can act many things, whatsoever is going on around — and you remain the seer. You don't jump and become one with whatsoever you are seeing.

This is the trouble. Whatsoever happens you start saying it: you are hungry, you say, 'I am hungry' — you have become identified with the hunger. But just look inside; are you hunger, or is hunger happening to you? Are you hunger or are you simply aware of the hunger happening in the body? You cannot be hunger, otherwise, when the

184

hunger has disappeared, where will you be? When you have eaten well and the belly is full and you are satiated, where will you be if you are hunger? Evaporated? No, then immediately you become the satiety. Before the hunger disappears a new identification has to be created, you become the satiety.

You were a child and you thought you were a child; now where are you because you are a child no more? You have become young or you have become old — who are you now? Again you are identified with youth or old age.

The innermost being is just like a mirror. Whatsoever comes before it, it mirrors, it simply becomes a witness. Disease comes or health, hunger or satiety, summer or winter, childhood or old age, birth or death — whatsoever happens happens before the mirror, it never happens *to* the mirror.

This is non-identification, this is cutting the root, the very root — become a mirror. And to me this is *sannyas*: to become like a mirror. Don't become like a very sensitive photo-plate, that is identification. Whatsoever comes before the lens of the camera, the photo-plate immediately takes it in, becomes one with it. Become like a mirror. Things come and pass and the mirror remains vacant, empty, void.

This is the no-self of Tilopa. The mirror has no self to be identified with. It simply reflects. It does not react, it simply responds. It doesn't say, 'This is beautiful, that is ugly.' An ugly woman stands before it, the mirror is as happy as when a beautiful woman stands before it. It makes no distinction. It reflects whatsoever is the case but it doesn't interpret. It doesn't say, 'Go away, you disturb me very much,' or 'come a little closer, you are so beautiful.' The mirror says nothing. The mirror simply watches without making any distinction, friend or foe. The mirror has no distinctions to make.

And when somebody passes, goes away from the mirror, the mirror doesn't cling to it. The mirror has no past. It is not that you have passed and the mirror will cling a little to your phantom. It is not that the mirror will cling to your shadow for a little while. It is not that the mirror will try to retain the reflection that has happened in it. No. You have passed, the reflection has gone; not even for a single second does the mirror retain it. This is the mind of a Buddha. You come before it, he is filled with you; you go away, you have gone. Not even a memory flashes. A mirror has no past, neither has a Buddha. A mirror has no future, neither has a Buddha. The mirror doesn't wait: 'Now who is coming before me; now who am I going to reflect? I would like this person to come and not that person.' The mirror has no choice, it remains choiceless.

Try to understand this metaphor of the mirror because this is the real situation of the inner consciousness. Don't get identified with things that are happening around you. Remain centered and rooted in your being. Things are happening and they will continue to happen, but if *you* can be centered in your mirror-like consciousness, nothing will be the same — the whole has changed. You remain virgin, innocent, pure. Nothing can become an impurity to you, absolutely nothing because nothing is retained. You reflect, for a moment somebody is there and then everything is gone. Your emptiness is untouched.

Even while a mirror is reflecting somebody,
there is nothing happening to the mirror.
The mirror is not changing in any way;
the mirror remains the same.
This is cutting the very root.

There are two types of people. One, which goes on fighting with the symptoms, which goes on fighting, not with the root-cause, but just the symptoms of the disease. For example, you have a fever, a one hundred and five degrees fever. You can do one thing: you can go and take a good shower, a cold shower; that will cool down the body, that will bring the fever low — but you are fighting with the symptom because the temperature is not the disease. The temperature is simply an indication that something has gone wrong in the body. The body is in a turmoil, that's why the temperature has gone high; the body is in a crisis, something like a war is going on inside the body, some germs are fighting with other germs, that's why the temperature has gone high. You are feeling hot — this heat is not the problem, this heat is just a symptom. This heat is very very friendly to you, this heat simply shows you that you should do something, inside there is a crisis — and if you treat the symptom you will kill the patient. Putting ice on his head won't do. Giving him a cold shower won't help. It is destructive, because it will give a false coolness on the surface. But how, just by giving a cold shower, do you hope that the inner turmoil and the inner fight between the germs will stop? — they will continue and they will kill you.

The fool is always treating the symptoms. The wise man looks to the cause, to the very root. He doesn't try to cool down the body, he tries to change the root-cause of why the body is becoming hot. And when that root is changed, the cause is changed, the cause is treated, the temperature comes down by itself. The temperature is not the problem. But in life there are more fools than wise men. In medicine we have become wiser but in life still not.

In life we go on doing foolish things. If you are angry you start fighting with the anger. Anger is nothing but a temperature; precisely that, it is a temperature, it is a fever. If you are really angry your body becomes hot, but that shows only that in your blood-stream some chemicals are being released. But that is not the root either. Those chemicals are released for a certain reason — because you have created a situation in which either fight or flight becomes necessary.

When an animal is in a situation of danger he has two choices: one choice is to fight, the other choice is to escape. For both these choices certain poisons are needed in the blood, because when you fight you will need more energy than ordinarily. When you fight you will need more blood circulating than ordinarily. When you fight you will need emergency sources of energy to work, to function — the body has emergency sources. It collects poisons, hormones, many things in the glands, and when the time comes and the need is there it releases them into the blood-stream.

That's why when you are angry you become almost thrice as powerful as you are ordinarily. If your anger can be created, you can do many things you can never do ordinarily: you can throw a big rock — ordinarily you cannot even move it. In fight it will be needed — nature provides. Or if you have to escape and run away, then too energy will be needed because the enemy will chase you, follow you.

Everything has changed, man has created a civilization, a society, a culture, where animal situations no longer exist — but deep inside the mechanism remains the same. Whenever you are in a situation when you feel somebody is going to be aggressive to you, somebody is going to hit you, insult you, do some harm, immediately the body comes into the situation: it releases poisons into the blood-stream, your temperature rises high, your eyes become red, your face is filled with more blood — you are ready for fight or flight.

This too is not the deepest thing because this too is just a help from the body. Anger on the face, anger in the body, are not real things; they follow your mind, they follow your interpretation. It can be that there was nothing. You pass through a lonely street on a dark night, you see a lamp-post, you think it is a ghost — immediately the body has released things into the blood-stream, the body is preparing to fight the ghost or escape. Your mind interpreted the lamp-post as a ghost — immediately the body follows. You think somebody is your enemy, the body follows. You think somebody is a friend, the body follows.

So the root-cause is in the mind, it is in your interpretation. Buddha says, 'Think that the whole earth is your friend.' Why? Jesus says, 'Even forgive your enemies;' not only that, 'even love your enemies.' Why? Buddha and Jesus are trying to change your interpretations. But Tilopa goes still higher. He says that even if you think that all are your friends, you continue to think in terms of friendship and enmity. Even if you love the enemy you think that he is the enemy. You love because Jesus has said to. Of course, you will be in a better situation than an ordinary man who hates the enemy, less anger will happen to you. But Tilopa says that to *think* that someone is an enemy, to think that someone is a friend, is to divide — you have already fallen into the trap. Nobody is a friend and nobody is an enemy. This is the highest teaching.

Sometimes Tilopa surpasses even Buddha and Jesus. Maybe the reason is that Buddha was talking to the masses and Tilopa is talking to Naropa. When you talk to a very developed disciple, you can bring the highest down. When you talk to the masses you have to make a compromise. I was talking to the masses for fifteen years continuously, then by and by I felt I had to drop it. I was talking to thousands of people. But when you talk to twenty thousand people you have to compromise, you have to come down, otherwise it will be impossible for them to understand. Seeing this I dropped it. Now I like to talk only to Naropas. And you may not be aware of it, but even if a single new person comes here, and I am not aware that a new person is there, he changes the whole atmosphere. He brings you down and suddenly I feel that I have to make a compromise.

The higher you go, the higher your energy, the higher the teaching that can be delivered to you. And a moment comes when Naropa becomes perfect — Tilopa becomes silent. Then there is no need to say anything, because even talking is a compromise. Then silence suffices, then silence is enough; then just sitting together is enough. Then the Master sits with the disciple, they don't do anything, they just remain together — and only then does the highest glimpse happen.

So it depends on the disciples. It will depend on you how much you can allow me to bring to you. It is not only for your own understanding, of course, that is there, but it will depend on you how much I can bring to the earth because it is going to come through you.

Jesus has very ordinary disciples in that way, very ordinary, because he is starting a thing and he has to make compromises — with foolish things. Jesus is going to be caught the same night and the disciples are asking, 'Master, tell us: in the Kingdom of God you will, of course, be sitting to the right of God, on the right side of the throne — but we twelve, what will be our hierarchical situation? How will we be sitting? Who will be sitting by the side of you? And who next?' Jesus is going to die and these foolish disciples are asking something absurd. They are worried what the hierarchy will be in the Kingdom of God, who will be next to Jesus. Of course, Jesus will be next to God, they can see that much, but then who will be next to Jesus?

Foolish egos. And Jesus has to compromise with these people. That's why Jesus' teachings could not go to that height where Buddha can go easily, because he is not talking to such foolish people, never in his life has a single person asked such a foolish thing. But — nothing to compare with Tilopa.

Tilopa never talked to the masses. He sought a single man, a single developed soul, Naropa, and said, 'Because of you Naropa, I will tell you things which cannot be told; because of you and your trust, I have to.' That's why the teaching has gone, taken flight to the very farthest corner of the sky.

Now try to understand the *sutra:*

Cut the root of a tree and the leaves will wither;
cut the root of your mind and samsara, the world, falls.
The light of any lamp dispels in a moment
the darkness of long kalpas, long ages, millennia;
the strong light of the Mind in but a flash
will burn the veil of ignorance.

'Cut the roots of a tree and the leaves will wither.' But people ordinarily try to cut the leaves. That is not the way; the root cannot wither that way. On the contrary, if you cut the leaves, more leaves will come to the tree; if you cut one leaf, three will come, because by cutting leaves the roots become more active to protect the tree. So every gardener knows how to make a tree dense and thick — you just go on pruning. It will become thicker and thicker and thicker, because you give a challenge to the roots: you cut one leaf, the roots will send three to protect the body of the tree, because leaves are the body surface of the tree.

Leaves are not just there for your enjoyment, to look at and sit under the shade; no, leaves are the tree's body surface. Through leaves the tree absorbs sun-rays, through leaves the tree releases vapour, through leaves the tree is in contact with the cosmos. The leaves are the skin of the tree. You cut one leaf and the roots take the challenge: they send three instead; they become more alert, they cannot remain sleepy. Somebody is trying to destroy the tree and they have to protect it — and the same happens in life also, because life is also a tree.

Roots and leaves are there. If you cut anger, three leaves will come instead; you will be thrice angry. If you cut sex, you will become abnormally obsessed with sex. Cut anything and watch and you will see that thrice as much of it is happening to you. And then the mind will say, 'Cut more, this is not enough!' Then you cut more and then more comes of it — then you are in a vicious circle. The mind will go on, 'Cut more, it is still not enough.' That's why so many leaves are coming. You can cut all the branches, but it will make no difference because the tree exists in the root not in the leaves.

Tantra says don't try to cut leaves — anger, greed, sex, don't bother about them; it is simply foolish. You just find the root and cut the root, and the tree will wither away by itself, of its own accord. The leaves will disappear, the branches will disappear — you simply cut the root.

Identification is the root and everything else is nothing but leaves. Being identified with greed, being identified with anger, being identified with sex, is the root. And remember, it is the same whether you are identified with greed, or sex, or even meditation. Love, *moksha,* God, it makes no difference, it is the same identification. Being identified is the root, and all else is just like leaves. Don't cut the leaves, leave them, nothing is wrong in them.

That's why Tantra does not believe in improving your character. It may give you a good shape — if you prune a tree you can make any shape out of it — but the tree remains the same. Character is just an outer shape — but you remain the same, no transmutation happens. Tantra goes deeper and says, 'Cut the root!' That's why Tantra was misunderstood too much — because Tantra says, 'If you are greedy be greedy; don't bother about greed. If you are sexual be sexual, don't bother about it at all.' The society cannot tolerate such a teaching: 'What are these people saying? They will create chaos. They will destroy the whole order, but they have not understood that only Tantra can change the society, the man, the mind, nothing else; and only Tantra brings a real order, a natural order, a natural flowering of the inner discipline, nothing else. But it is a very deep process — you have to cut the root.

Watch the greed, watch sex, watch anger, possessiveness, jealousy. One thing has to be remembered: don't get identified, simply watch; simply look, become a spectator. By and by, the quality of witnessing grows; you become able to see all the nuances of greed. It is very subtle. You become capable of seeing how subtly the ego functions, how subtle are its ways. It is not a gross thing; it is very subtle and delicate and deep-hidden.

The more you watch, the more your eyes become capable of seeing, the more perceptive they become, the more you see and the deeper you can move, and the more distance is created between you and whatsoever you do. Distance helps because without distance there can be no perception. How can you see a thing which is too close? If you are standing too close near a mirror, you cannot see your reflection. If your eyes are touching the mirror, how can you see? A distance is needed. And nothing can give you a distance except witnessing. You try it and see.

Move into sex; nothing is wrong in it, but remain a watcher. Watch all the movements of the body; watch the energy flowing in and out, watch how the energy is falling downwards; watch the orgasm, what is happening — how two bodies move in a rhythm; watch the heartbeat — faster and faster it goes, a moment comes when it is almost mad. Watch the warmth of the body, the blood circulates more. Watch the breathing, it is going mad and chaotic. Watch the moment when a limit comes to your voluntariness and everything becomes involuntary. Watch the moment from where you could have come back, but beyond which there is no return. The body becomes so automatic that all control is lost. Just a moment before the ejaculation you lose all control, the body takes over.

Watch it: the voluntary processes, the non-voluntary process. The moment when you were in control and you could have come back, the return was possible, and the moment when you cannot come back, the return has become impossible — now the body has taken over completely, you are no more in control. Watch everything — and millions of things are there. Everything is so complex and nothing is as complex as sex, because the whole body-mind is involved — only the witness is not involved, only one thing remains always outside.

The witness is an outsider. By its very nature the witness can never become an insider. Find this witness and then you are standing on the top of the hill, and everything goes on in the valley and you are not concerned. You simply see; what is your concern? It is as if it is happening to somebody else. And the same with greed and the same with anger; everything is very complex. And you will enjoy it if you can watch — the negative, the positive, all the emotions. You simply remember one thing: that you have to be a watcher, then the identification is broken, then the root is cut. And once the root is cut, once you think you are not the doer, everything suddenly changes. And the change is sudden, there is no gradualness to it.

> Cut the root of the tree and the leaves will wither,
> cut the root of your mind and samsara falls.

The moment you cut the root of the mind, the identification with it, the *samsara* falls, the whole world falls like a house of cards. Just a small wind of awareness and the whole house falls. Suddenly you are here, but no longer in the world — you have transcended. You can live just the old way, doing the old things — but nothing is old, because you are no longer the old. You are a perfectly new being — this is rebirth. Hindus call it *dwij*, twice-born. A man who has attained to this is twice-born, this is a second birth — and this is the birth of the soul. This is what Jesus means by resurrection. Resurrection is not the rebirth of the body; it is a new birth of consciousness.

> Cut the root of your mind and samsara falls.
> The light of any lamp dispels in a moment
> the darkness of long long kalpas, long long ages.

So don't be worried about how a sudden light will dispel the darkness of many many, millions of lives. It dispels it because darkness has no density to it, darkness has no substance to it. Whether one moment old or many thousands of years old, it is the same. Absence cannot grow more or less, absence remains the same; light is substantial, it is something — darkness is just an absence. The light is there and darkness is there no more.

It is not that the darkness is dispelled really, because there was nothing to be dispelled. It is not that when you burn the light the darkness goes out — there was nothing to go out. In fact there was nothing, just the absence of light. Light comes and darkness is not.

> The strong light of the Mind in but a flash
> will burn the veil of ignorance.

Buddhists use 'mind' in two senses: mind with a small 'm' and Mind with a capital 'M'. When they use Mind with a capital 'M', they mean the witness, consciousness. When they use mind with a small 'm' they mean the witnessed. And both are mind — that's why they use the same word for both — with just a small difference, with a capital 'M'. With a capital 'M' you are the witness and with a small 'm' you are the witnessed — thoughts, emotions, anger, greed, everything.

Why use the same word? Why create confusion? There is a reason for it — because when the Mind with a capital 'M' arises, the mind with the small 'm' simply is absorbed in it. As rivers fall into the ocean, the millions of minds around the great Mind all fall into it, the energy is re-absorbed.

Greed, anger, jealousy, they were energies moving outwards, centrifugal. Suddenly when the Mind with a capital 'M' arises, the witness sits there silently watching and all the rivers change their course. They were moving centrifugally towards the periphery; suddenly they turn back, they become centripetal; they start falling into the great Mind — everything is absorbed. That's why the same word is used.

The strong light of the Mind in but a flash
will burn the veil of ignorance.

Just in a single moment all ignorance is burned — this is sudden Enlightenment.

Whoever clings to the mind
sees not the truth of what's beyond the mind.

If you cling to the mind, thoughts, emotions, then you will not be able to see that which is beyond the mind — the great Mind — because if you cling how can you see? If you cling, your eyes are closed by your clinging. And if you cling to the object, how can you see the subject? This 'clinging-ness' has to be dropped.

Whoever clings to the mind is identified,
and sees not the truth of what's beyond the mind.
Whoever strives to practise Dharma
finds not the truth of beyond-practice.

All practice is of the mind. Whatsoever you do is of the mind. Only witnessing is not of the mind, remember this.

So, even while you are doing meditation, remain a witness, continuously see what is happening. You are whirling in a Dervish meditation? — whirl, whirl as fast as you can, but remain a witness inside and go on seeing that the body is whirling. The body goes on, faster and faster and faster, and the faster the body goes, the deeper you feel that your center is not moving. You are standing still, the body moves like a wheel, you stand still just in the middle of it. The faster the body goes, the deeper you realize the fact that you are not moving, and the distance is created.

Whatsoever you are doing, even meditation, I make no exception, don't cling to meditation either, because a day has to come when even that clinging has to be dropped. Meditation becomes perfect when it too is dropped. When there is perfect meditation, you need not meditate.

So keep it constantly in your awareness that meditation is just a bridge, it has to be passed over. A bridge is not a place to make your house on. You have to pass it and go beyond it. Meditation is a bridge; you have to be watchful about it also, otherwise you may stop being identified with anger, greed, and you may start being identified with meditation, compassion. Then you are in the same trap again; through another door you have entered the same house.

It happened once: Mulla Nasrudin came to the town bar and he was already too drunk, so the bar-keeper told him, 'You go away! You are already drunk and I cannot give you any more. You just go back to your house.' But he was insisting, so the bar-keeper had to throw him out.

He walked a long distance in search of another bar. Then he came into the same bar through another door. He entered, looked at the barman with a little suspicion because he looked familiar, asked again — the man said, 'I have told you once and forever that this night I am not going to give you anything. You get away from here!' Insisting again, he was thrown out again.

He walked a long distance in search of another bar, but in that town there was only one bar. Again, through the third gate, he entered, looked at the man, looked too familiar, he said, 'What is the matter? Do you own all the bars in the town?'

This happens. You are thrown out through one door; you enter through another door. You were identified with your anger, your lust; now you become identified with your meditation. You were identified with your sexual pleasure; now you become identified with the ecstasy that meditation gives. Nothing is different — the town has

194

only one bar. Don't try to enter the same bar again and again. And from *wherever* you enter you will find the same owner — that is the witness. Be mindful of it, otherwise much energy is unnecessarily wasted. Long distances you travel to enter into the same thing again.

Whoever clings to the mind
sees not the truth of what's beyond the mind.

What is beyond the mind? You. What is beyond the mind? Consciousness. What is beyond the mind? *Satchitananda*, the Truth, the Consciousness, the bliss.

Whoever strives to practise Dharma
finds not the truth of beyond-practice.

And whatsoever you practise, remember, practice cannot lead you to the natural, the loose and the natural, because practice means practising something which is not there. Practising means always practising something artificial. Nature does not have to be practised; there is no need, it is already there. You learn something which is not there. How can you learn something which is already there? How can you learn nature, Tao? It is already there! You are born in it. There is no need to find any teacher so that you can be taught — and that is the difference between a teacher and a Master.

A teacher is one who teaches you something; a Master is one who helps you to unlearn all that you have already learned. A Master is to help you unlearn. A Master is to give you the taste of the non-practised. It is already there, but through your learning you have lost it. Through your unlearning you will regain it.

Truth is not a discovery, it is a rediscovery.
It was already there in the first place.
When you came into this world it was with you,
when you were born into this life it was with you,
because *you are it.*
It cannot be otherwise. It is not something external, it is intrinsic to you, it is your very being. So if you practise, says Tilopa, you will not know that which is beyond practice.

Remind yourself again and again, that whatsoever you practise will be a part of the mind, the small mind, the outer periphery, and you have to go beyond it. How to go beyond it? Practise, nothing is wrong in it, but be alert; meditate, but be alert — because in the final meaning of the term, meditation is witnessing.

195

All techniques can be helpful but they are not exactly meditation, they are just a groping in the dark. Suddenly one day, doing something, you will become a witness. Doing a meditation like the dynamic, or *kundalini* or whirling, suddenly one day the meditation will go on but you will not be identified with it. You will sit silently behind, you will watch it—that day meditation has happened; that day technique is no longer a hindrance, no longer a help. You can enjoy it if you like, like an exercise, it gives a certain vitality, but there is no need now—now the real meditation has happened.

Meditation is witnessing. To meditate means to become a witness. Meditation is not a technique at all! This will be very confusing to you because I go on giving you techniques. In the ultimate sense meditation is not a technique; meditation is an understanding, awareness. But you need techniques because that final understanding is very far away from you; hidden deep in you, but still very far away from you. Right this moment you can attain it, but you will not attain it, because your moment goes on, your mind goes on. *This* very moment it is possible and yet impossible. Techniques will bridge the gap, they are just to bridge the gap.

So in the beginning techniques are meditations; in the end you will laugh, techniques are not meditation. Meditation is a totally different quality of being, it has nothing to do with anything. But it will happen only in the end, don't think it has happened in the beginning, otherwise the gap will not be bridged.

This is the problem with Krishnamurti, and this is the problem with Maharishi Mahesh Yogi—they are the two opposite poles. Mahesh Yogi thinks that technique is meditation, so once you are attuned to a technique—transcendental meditation or any other—the meditation has happened. This is right and wrong. Right, because in the beginning a beginner has to attune himself to some technique, because his understanding is not ripe enough to understand the Ultimate. So, approximately, a technique is a meditation.

It is just like a small child learning the alphabet—so we tell the child that 'm' is the same as when you use 'monkey'; the monkey represents 'm'. With the 'm' the monkey is there, the child starts learning. There is no relationship between a monkey and 'm'. 'M' can be represented by millions of things, and still it is different from every one of them. But a child has to be shown something and a monkey is nearer the child; he can understand the monkey, not the 'm'. Through the monkey he will be able to understand 'm' — but this is just a beginning not the end.

Mahesh Yogi is right in the beginning, to push you on the path, but if you are stuck with him you are lost. He has to be left, he is a primary school; good as far as it goes, but one need not remain always in the primary school. The primary school is not the university, and the primary school is not the universe; one has to pass from there. It is a primary understanding that meditation is a technique.

Then there is Krishnamurti on the other pole. He says there are no techniques, no meditations; don't fool around with techniques, meditation is simple awareness, choiceless awareness. Perfectly right! — but he is trying to help you enter into the university without the primary school. He can be dangerous because he is talking about the Ultimate. You cannot understand it, right now in your understanding it is not possible — you will go mad. Once you listen to Krishnamurti you will be lost, because you will always understand intellectually that he is right, but in your being you will know that nothing is happening.

Many Krishnamurti followers have come to me. They say intellectually they understand: 'Of course it is right, there is no technique and meditation is awareness — but what to do?' And I tell them the moment you ask what to do, it means you need a technique. 'What to do?' You ask *how* to do it, you are asking for a technique. Krishnamurti will not help you. Go rather to Maharishi Mahesh Yogi, that will be better. But people are stuck with Krishnamurti and there are people who are stuck with Mahesh Yogi.

I am neither — or I am both; and then I am very confusing. They are both clear, their standpoints are simple, there is no complexity in understanding Mahesh Yogi or Krishnamurti. If you understand language, you can understand them, there is no problem. The problem will arise with me, because I will always talk about the beginning and never allow you to forget the end. And I will always talk about the end and always help you to start from the beginning. You will be confused because you will say, 'What do you mean? If meditation is simply awareness then why go through so many exercises?'

You have to go through them; only then will that meditation happen to you which is simple understanding.

Or you say, 'If techniques are all, then why do you go on saying again and again that techniques have to be left, dropped?' Because then you feel: 'Something learned so deeply, with so much effort and arduous labour has to be left again?' You would like to cling to the beginning. I will not allow you. Once you are on the path I will go on pushing to the very end.

This is a problem; with me this problem has to be faced, encountered and understood. I will look contradictory. I am; I am a paradox — because I am trying to give you both the beginning and the end, the first step and the last.

Tilopa is talking of the Ultimate. He is saying:

Whoever strives to practise Dharma
finds not the truth of beyond-practice.
To know what is beyond both mind and practice,
one should not cling,
one should cut cleanly through the root of the mind
and stare naked.

That's what I call witnessing: staring naked. Just staring naked will do, the root is cut. This staring naked becomes like a sharp sword.

One should thus break away from all distinctions
and remain at ease.

Loose, natural, staring naked within yourself — that is the final word.

But go slowly, because mind is a very delicate mechanism. If you are in too much of a hurry and you take too great a dose of a Tilopa, you may not be able to absorb and digest it. Go slowly; take only proportions which you can digest and absorb.

Even I am here; I will be saying many things because you are many, and I will be taking many dimensions because you are many. But absorb only that which is a nourishment to you, digest it.

Just the other day a *sannyasin* came, a sincere seeker, but puzzled because I talked about Yoga and Tantra, and told that Tantra is the higher teaching and Yoga is a lower teaching, and he has been practising Hatha Yoga for two years and feeling good. He became puzzled as to what to do. Don't become so easily puzzled. If you are feeling good with Yoga, follow your own natural inclination. Don't allow me to confuse you. I can be confusing to you, but simply follow your natural inclination — loose, natural. If it is good, it is good for you. Why bother whether it is higher or lower? Let it be lower. The ego comes in; the ego says, 'If it is a lower thing, then why follow?' That will not help. Follow it; it is right for you. Even if it is lower what is wrong in it? A moment will come when through the lower you will reach the higher.

The staircase has two ends: on one end it is the lowest, on the other end it is the highest. So Tantra and Yoga are not opposities, they are complementary. Yoga is the primary, the basic, from where you have to start. But then one should not cling. A moment comes when one has to transcend Yoga and move into Tantra; and finally you have to leave the whole staircase — Yoga and Tantra both. Alone in yourself, deep in rest, one forgets everything.

Look at me: I am neither a yogi nor a tantrica.
I do nothing — no practice, no non-practice.
Neither do I cling to method nor to no-method.
I am simply here resting, not doing anything.
The staircase doesn't exist to me now,
the path has disappeared,
there is no movement, it is absolute rest.
When one comes home there is nothing to do;
one simply forgets everything and rests —
God is ultimate rest.

Remember this, because sometimes I will be talking of Tantra for there are many who will be helped through it; sometimes I will be talking about Yoga, and there are many who will be helped by it. You just think of your own inclination, follow your own feeling. I am here to help you to be yourself, not to distract you. But I have to say many things because I have to help many. So what will you do? You just go on listening to me. Whatsoever you find nourishing, you digest it; chew it well, digest it; let it become your blood and bones, the very marrow of your bones — but follow your own inclination.

And when I talk about Tantra I am so absorbed in it, because that's how I am; I cannot be partial, I am total whatsoever I do. If I am talking about Tantra, I am totally in it, then nothing matters, only Tantra matters; that may give you a false impression. I am not talking comparatively, nothing matters to me. Tantra is the highest, ultimate flower. This is because if I look totally at it, it is. When I talk about Yoga the same will happen again, because I am total. This has nothing to do with Tantra or Yoga — it is my totality that I bring to anything. When I bring it to Yoga and Patanjali, I will be again saying that this is the last.

So don't be distracted; always remember this is *my* totality and my quality that I bring to it. If you can remember that, you will be helped; even through my parodoxical being you will not be confused.

The song continues:

One should not give or take,
but remain natural—for Mahamudra
is beyond all acceptance and rejection.
Since alaya is not born,
no one can obstruct or soil it;
staying in the unborn realm
all appearance will dissolve into the Dharmata,
and self-will and pride will vanish into nought.

IX   BEYOND AND BEYOND
19th February 1975

THE ORDINARY MIND wants to take more and more from the world; from everywhere, from every direction and dimension. The ordinary mind is a great taker, it is a beggar, and the begging is such that it cannot be satisfied — it is infinite. The more you get, the more the longing arises; the more you have, the more you desire. It becomes an obsessive hunger. There exists no need for it in your being, but you are obsessed, and you become more and more miserable because nothing satisfies it. Nothing can satisfy the mind which is constantly asking for more. The 'more' is feverish, it is not healthy, and there is no end to it.

The ordinary mind goes on eating, in a metaphorical sense, not only things but persons also. The husband would like to possess the wife so deeply and so absolutely that it is a sort of eating her; he would like to eat and digest her so she becomes part of him. The ordinary mind is cannibalistic. The wife wants the same: to absorb the husband so totally that nothing is left behind. They kill each other. Friends do the same; parents do the same to children, children to parents; all relationships of the ordinary mind are of absorbing the other completely. It is a sort of eating.

And then there is the extraordinary mind, just the opposite of the ordinary mind. And because of the ordinary mind, the extraordinary mind has come into existence. Religions teach about it. They say, 'Give, share, donate!' All the religions teach basically that you should not take, rather on the contrary, you should give. Charity is preached. This is preached to create an extraordinary mind.

The ordinary mind will always be in misery, because the longing for the 'more' cannot be fulfilled; you will find him always depressed, sad. The extraordinary mind the religions have been cultivating, you will find him always happy, a certain cheerfulness is there because he is not asking for more; on the contrary, he goes on giving — but deep down he is still the ordinary mind.

The cheerfulness cannot be of the deepest being, it can only be of the surface. He has totally turned around and become just the reverse of the ordinary. He is standing on his head, he is in a *shirshasan,* but he remains the same. Now a new desire arises to give more and more and more; again there is no end to it. He will be cheerful, but deep down in his cheerfulness you can detect a certain quality of sadness.

You will always find that quality of sadness in religious people. Cheerful, of course, because they give, but sad because they cannot give more; cheerful because they share, but sad because it is not enough. Nothing will be enough.

So there are two types of misery: the ordinary misery; you can find those miserable people all around, everywhere, the whole earth is filled with them because they ask for more and it cannot be fulfilled. Then there is another misery which has a face of cheerfulness; you will find in the priests, monks, in the monasteries, *ashrams,* people who seem to be always smiling, but their smile carries a certain sadness behind it. If you observe deeply you will find they are also miserable — because you cannot give infinitely, you don't have it!

These are the two types of people easily met. The religious man is cultivated by Christianity, Judaism, Islam, Hinduism. It is better than the ordinary mind but cannot be the final word about consciousness. It is good to be miserable in a religious way, better to be miserable like an emperor, not like a beggar.

A very rich man was dying and he had called me to be near him when he died, so I was there. At the last moment he opened his eyes and he spoke to his son — and that had always been on his mind, he had told it to me many times: he was worried about his son because he was a spendthrift and he loved material things, and this old man was a religious man. The last word he said to his son was, 'Listen: money is not everything and you cannot buy everything with money. There are things which are beyond money, and money alone cannot make anybody happy.'

The son listened and said, 'You may be right, but with money a person can choose the sadness of his own liking' — it may not purchase happiness but you can choose the sadness of your own liking, you can be miserable in your own way.

A poor man has to be miserable with no choice; a rich man can be miserable with his own choice — that's the only difference. He chooses his own misery, there is a certain freedom. The poor man's misery simply happens to him like a fate, a destiny; he has no choice. The religious man has chosen his misery, that is why he is a little cheerful; and the non-religious man is suffering his misery because he has not chosen it. Both live in the same world of the 'more', but the religious man lives like an emperor, sharing, giving, charitable.

Buddhism, Jainism and Tao, they have created a third type of mind which is neither ordinary nor extraordinary; in fact, which is not a mind at all. To give it a name it will be good to call it a 'no-mind'. So try to understand the classification. Ordinary mind, extraordinary mind — just the opposite of it, but still in the same dimension of more — then no-mind which Buddhism, Jainism, Tao have created. What is this no-mind? — the third approach towards reality.

Buddhism and Jainism don't preach charity, they preach indifference. They don't say, 'Give!' because giving is part of taking, the same circle. In taking you take from somebody, in giving you give to somebody, but the same circle. Dimensions don't change, only the direction changes. Buddhism preaches indifference, non-possessiveness. The emphasis is on non-possession, not on giving. You should not possess, that's all. You should not try to possess things or persons; you simply drop out of the world of possessions. There is no question of taking or giving, because both belong to the world of possessions. You can give only that which you possess; how can you give that which you don't possess? You can give only that which you have acquired before; you can give only that which you have taken before — otherwise, how can you give it? You come into the world without anything, with no possessions; you go out of the world without any possessions.

In the world you can be on these two sides: either on the side of those who long for more and more, to take more and more and absorb more and more, and go on fattening themselves; and then there is the other side of those who go on giving and giving more and more, and become thinner and thinner and thinner. Buddha says you should not possess; you should not choose either side. Simply be in the state of non-possession.

This man, this third type of man, whom I call the man of no-mind, will not be as happy, cheerful as the extraordinary man. He will be more silent, he will be more quiet, still; he will have a deep contentment — but not cheerfulness. You will not even find a smile on his face; you will not find a single statue of Buddha smiling or of Mahavir smiling, no. They are not cheerful, they are not happy. They are not miserable, of course, but they are not happy — they have dropped out of the world of misery and happiness. They are simply at rest, indifferent to things and the world of things; non-possessing, they are aloof, detached. This is what *anashakti* is, detachment, indifference. This man will have a certain quality of silence around him, you can feel that silence.

But Tilopa goes beyond all three; Tilopa goes beyond *all* three and now it is difficult to classify him. Ordinary mind, asking for more; extraordinary mind, trying to give more; no-mind, indifferent, unattached, neither giving nor taking — then what to call Tilopa's mind? Tilopa is of the fourth type, and the fourth is the last and the highest, there is no beyond to it. It is *not* even a no-mind, it is not a mind at all — because in the no-mind also, negatively the mind is present. The emphasis is still on being indifferent to things and the world of things, but your focus is on things: Remain indifferent, unattached! You are not possessing things, but you have to be alert not to possess; you have to remain detached, you have to move being very alert so you don't possess anything. Make a clear point of it: the emphasis is still on things — Be indifferent to the world!

Tilopa says the emphasis should be on your own self, not on things. Rest in yourself; don't even be indifferent to the world, because that indifference still is a very subtle bridge to the world. The focus should not be on the other. Turn your lives completely inwards. Don't bother about the world, things, not even to be indifferent towards them. You neither ask for more, nor do you try to give more, nor are you indifferent to the world. It is as if the world has simply disappeared. You are self-centered, sitting inside doing nothing. Your whole focus has turned, taken a total about-turn.

It is as if the world has completely disappeared;
there is nothing to give, nothing to take,
nothing to be indifferent about.
Only you are.
You live in your consciousness
and that is your only world.
Nothing else exists.

This is the state of beyond mind *and* beyond no-mind. This is the supreme-most state of understanding. Nothing is beyond it. And I would like to tell you: never be satisfied unless you attain this. Why? Because the man is miserable, the ordinary man. He asks for more and it can never be satisfied, so continuously the misery is there, and the misery goes on becoming more and more and more.

The man of extraordinary mind, that the religions teach, is cheerful, but deep down sad. Even his very cheerfulness has an undercurrent of sadness. It seems as if he is trying to smile, the smile is not coming to him; it seems he is posing, as if some photographers are there and he is posing a certain gesture which doesn't exist in fact. Better than the first, at least you can smile; the smile is not very deep .but at least it is there. But this will not last for long. Soon whatsoever you can give will be exhausted, then, then the smiling cheerfulness will disappear. You would like to give more, then you will be in the same plight as the first, the ordinary man.

It may take a little longer for the second man to understand and realize the misery, but the misery will come. The cheerfulness that you practise in the mosques, temples, monasteries, cannot go very deep and it cannot become a permanent state of affairs. It cannot be eternal. You will lose it. The very nature of it is such that it can be only momentary. Why can it be only momentary? Because a point will come, is bound to come, when you cannot give because you don't have. That's why people of these two minds settle on a compromise. The ordinary mind and the extraordinary mind are the same in their quality; they settle for a compromise. And the compromise you will find everywhere.

First a man goes on taking things and then he starts donating. Or he will earn a hundred *rupees* and donate ten percent of it, because that is the only possible way. If you donate one hundred *rupees* completely, then you don't have any more to donate. Go on taking things and then a part of it distribute. The Mohammedans say one fifth of your income you should donate; be charitable with one fifth of your income. Why? Because this is a compromise; otherwise, you won't have anything to donate. So first accumulate and then distribute. Accumulate to distribute, be rich so that you can be charitable, exploit so that you can help. This is absurd! But this is the only possible way: the bridge between the ordinary and the extraordinary.

And even the ordinary mind goes on thinking and believing that when he has much he will donate, he will help people. And of course he also does it, when he has enough he gives a donation to a hospital, a donation to a cancer research center, a donation to a library or a college. First he exploits and then he donates; first he robs you and then he helps you. Helpers and robbers are not different; in fact they are the same persons: by the right hand they rob and by the left hand they help; they belong to the same dimension of affairs.

The third man, the man of no-mind, is in a better situation than these first two. His silence can be longer, but he is not blissful. He doesn't feel blissful—he is not unhappy, he is not miserable, but his state is of the nature of negativity. He is like a man who is not ill because doctors cannot find anything wrong with him, and he is not healthy because he doesn't feel any well-being. He is not ill and he is not healthy—he is just in the middle. He is not miserable, he is not happy—he is simply indifferent. And indifference may give you silence, but silence is not enough. It is good, it is beautiful, but you cannot be content with it; sooner or later you will be bored with it.

That is what happens if you go to the hills. You were too bored with the city-life—the Bombay, the London, the New York—you were bored with the noise, the traffic, and the whole madness going on and on, so you escaped to the Himalayas. But after a few days—three, four, five, at the most seven—you start feeling bored with the silence. The hills are silent, the trees are silent, the valley is silent—no excitement. You start longing for the city-life: the club, the movie-house, the friends.

Silence is not enough, because silence has the nature of death, not the nature of life. It is good as a holiday, it is good as a picnic, it is good to get out of your over-concern with life for a few days, a few moments, and be silent; you will enjoy it, but you cannot enjoy it forever. Soon you will get fed up with it; soon you will feel this is not enough. This is not *nourishing*. A silence will protect you from misery and happiness, from excitements, but there is no nourishment in it. It is a negative state.

The fourth state that Tilopa is indicating—that which cannot be said and he is trying to say for Naropa and his trust and his love and his faith—is a blissful state, silent and blissful, it has a positivity in it. It is not simply silence. It has not come through indifference to life, rather on the contrary, it has come through the deepest experience of one's own being. It has not been driven by renouncing; it has bloomed by being loose and natural. Subtle are the differences. But if you try to understand and meditate on these distinctions, your whole life-path will be clear, and then you can travel very easily.

Never be satisfied before the fourth state, because even if you become satisfied, sooner or later the discontentment will arise. Unless you attain *Satchitananda* — absolute truth, absolute consciousness, and absolute blissfulness — the home has not been reached yet, you are still travelling on the path. Okay, sometimes you rest by the side of the path, but don't make it a home. The journey has to continue; you have to get up again and you have to move.

From the first state of mind move to the second, from the second move to the third, from the third move to the beyond.

If you are in the first state of mind, as ninety-nine percent people are, then Jewish thinking, Islam, Christianity, will be helpful. They will bring you out of the ordinary trap of misery — good, but you are still on the path and don't deceive yourself that you have reached. Now you have to get beyond this, beyond this cheerfulness which has a sadness in it, beyond both this taking and giving, beyond charity. Who are you to give? What have you got to give? Who are you to help? You have not helped even yourself; how can you help others? Your own light is not burning and you are trying to burn others' lights? You may put them off — your own inner being is dark. You cannot help, you cannot give, you have nothing to give.

Buddhism, Jainism, Taoism, Lao Tzu, Mahavir and Siddhartha Gautam can help you out of it, but Tilopa says don't be satisfied even with that indifference, silence, detached standing, aloofness, because it is still not a happening, still you are concerned with the world. Tilopa can help you beyond that. He can bring you to your innermost center of being. He can help you center, rooted in yourself, unconcerned with the world — not even is the unconcern there.

Everything has dissolved;
only you remain in your crystal purity,
only you remain in your absolute innocence —
as if the world has not arisen,
was not there ever.

You come to the point in this fourth state of consciousness, to the point where you were not born, to the absolute source of being; not even has the first step been taken in the world, or, you have come to the last, the last step has been taken.

This is what Zen people call attaining the original face. Zen Masters say to the disciples, 'Go, and find your face you had before you were born;' or, 'Go, and find the face you will have when you are dead' — either when the world was not, or when the world has disappeared — you attain to your original purity. That is what nature is.

Now try to understand Tilopa:

One should not give or take
but remain natural — for Mahamudra
is beyond all acceptance and rejection.

'One should not give or take,' because when you give you have moved out of yourself, when you take you have moved out of yourself. Both are distractions, both lead you to the other; you get mixed, your energy has flowed outwards. Whether you give or take is irrelevant — the other has come into being, your eyes are focused on the other, and when the eyes are focused on the other you forget yourself. This is what has happened to you all. You don't remember yourself because your eyes have become focused, paralysed in fact on the other. Whatsoever you do, you do it for the other; whatsoever you are, you are for the other.

Even if you escape from the world, your mind goes on, continues: 'What are people thinking about me?' Even if you escape to the Himalayas, sitting there you will think, 'Now people must be thinking that I have become a great sage, renounced the world; in the newspapers there must be talk about me.' And you will wait for some lonely traveller, wanderer, to reach and give you news of what is happening in the world *about you.*

You don't have your own face, you have only the opinions of others about you. Somebody says you are beautiful and you start thinking you are beautiful. Somebody says you are ugly and you feel hurt and you carry a wound that somebody has said 'ugly' — you have become ugly. You are just an accumulation of the opinions of others, you don't know who you are. You know only what others think you are. And this is strange, because those others who think what you are, don't know themselves — they know themselves through you. This is a beautiful game: I know myself through you, you know yourself through me, and we both don't know who we are.

The other has become too important, and your whole energy has become obsessed with the other. Always thinking of others, always either taking something from them or giving something to them.

Tilopa says one should not give or take. What is he saying? Is he saying one should not share? No. If you take it in that way you will misunderstand him. He is saying one should not be concerned with taking or giving; if you can give naturally, beautiful, but then there

210

is nothing in the mind, no accumulation that you have given something. That is the difference between giving and sharing.

A giver knows that he has given and he would like you to recognize it, give him a receipt that, 'Yes you have given me.' You should thank him, you should feel grateful that he has given to you. This is not a gift; this is again a bargain. In fact he would like you to give him something in return. Even if it is your gratefulness, that's okay, but something he would like; it is a bargain, he gives to get. Tilopa is not saying don't share. He is saying don't be concerned with taking or giving. If you have and naturally it happens that you feel like giving, give. But it should be a sharing, a gift. This is the difference between a gift and giving.

A gift is not a bargain; nothing is expected, absolutely nothing; not even a recognition, not even a nod of the head of appreciation — no, nothing is expected. If you don't mention it, there will be no scar in the person who has given you a gift. In fact, if you mention it he will feel a little embarrassed because that was never expected. On the contrary, he feels grateful towards you because you accepted his gift. You could have rejected it; the possibility was there. You could have said no, but how nice of you that you didn't say no. You accepted it — that's enough. He feels grateful towards you. A man who gives you a gift always feels grateful that you accepted. You could have rejected it. That's enough.

Tilopa is not saying don't give, and he is not saying don't take, because life cannot exist without giving and taking. Even Tilopa has to breathe, even Tilopa has to beg for his food, even Tilopa has to go to the river to drink water. Tilopa is thirsty, he needs water; Tilopa is hungry, he needs food; Tilopa feels suffocated in a closed room, he comes out and breathes deeply. He is taking life every moment — you cannot exist without taking. People have tried, but those are not natural people, they are the supreme-most egoists.

Egoists always try to be independent of everything. Egoists always try to exist as if they don't need anything from anybody. This is foolish, absurd! Tilopa cannot do such a thing. He is a very very natural man, you cannot find a more natural man than Tilopa. And if you understand nature you will be surprised to find, to discover a very deep basic fact, and that fact is this: no one is dependent, no one is independent — everyone is interdependent. Nobody can claim: 'I am independent.' This is foolish! You cannot exist for a single moment in your independence. And nobody is absolutely dependent.

These two polarities don't exist. One who looks dependent is also independent, and one who looks independent is also dependent. Life is an interdependence, it is a mutual sharing. Even the emperor depends on his slaves; and even the slaves are not dependent on the emperor — at least they can commit suicide; that much independence they have.

Absolutes don't exist here. Life exists in relativity. Of course, Tilopa knows that. He prescribes the natural way — how can he not know it? He knows that life is a give and take. You share, but you should not be concerned about it, you should not think about it — you should allow it to happen. Allowing it to happen is totally different, then you neither ask for more than you can get, nor do you ask to give more than you can give; you simply give that which naturally can be given, you simply take that which naturally can be taken. You don't feel obliged to anybody and you don't make anybody feel obliged to you. You simply know that life is interdependent.

We exist mutually, we are members of each other.

The consciousness is a vast ocean and nobody is an island.

We meet and merge with each other.

There are no boundaries.

All boundaries are false.

That Tilopa knows — then what does he say?

One should not give or take, but remain natural. . .

The moment you think you have taken you become unnatural. Taking is okay, but thinking that you have taken you become un-natural. Giving is beautiful, but the moment you think that you have given it becomes ugly, you become unnatural. You simply give be-cause you cannot help it; you have, so you have to give. You simply take because you cannot help it; you are part of the Whole. But no unnatural ego is created through taking or through giving — that is the point to be understood. You neither accumulate, nor do you renounce — you simply remain natural.

If things come your way, you enjoy them. If you have more, and the more always becomes a burden, you share. It is just a deep balanc-ing, you simply remain natural. No holding and no renouncing; no possessiveness, no non-possessiveness. Look at the animals or the birds: no taking, no giving. Everybody enjoys out of the Whole, out of the Whole everybody shares, in the Whole everybody shares. Birds and trees and animals, they exist naturally. Man is the only unnatural animal—that's why religion is needed.

Animals don't need any religion, birds don't need any religion — because they are not unnatural. Only man needs religion. And the more man becomes unnatural, the more religion is needed. So remember this: whenever a society becomes more and more unnatural, technological, more religion will be needed.

People come and ask me why in America there is so much searching for religion, so much turmoil, seeking. Because America is the most unnatural country today, the most technological, technical. A technocracy has come into existence which has made everything unnatural. Your inner being thirsts for freedom from technology. Your inner being thirsts to be natural, and your whole society has become unnatural; more cultured, more civilized — more unnatural. When a society becomes too cultured then religion comes to balance it. It is a subtle balancing. A natural society doesn't need it.

Says Lao Tzu, 'I have heard from the ancients that there was a time when people were natural, there was no religion. When people were natural, they never thought about heaven and hell. When people were natural they never thought about moral precepts. When people were natural there was no code, no law.' Lao Tzu says that because of the law people have become criminals, and because of morality people have become immoral, and because of too much culture . . . and China has known too much culture, no other country has known that much culture.

Confucius made an absolute discipline of how to culture a man — three thousand three hundred rules of discipline. Suddenly Lao Tzu came into being to balance it, because this Confucius would have killed the whole society — three thousand three hundred rules? — this is too much. You will make the man so cultured that the man will disappear completely, he will not be a man at all! Lao Tzu erupts and Lao Tzu throws all the rules to the dust, and he says the only, the golden rule is to have no rules. This is a balancing. Lao Tzu is religion, Confucius is culture.

Religion is needed like a medicine, it is medicinal. If you are ill, you need medicine; more ill, of course, more medicine. A society becomes ill when the natural is lost. A man becomes ill when the natural is forgotten. And Tilopa is all for the natural and the loose.

And remember always the loose *with* the natural — because you can try to be natural so hard that the very effort can become unnatural. That's how fads are created. I have come across many people, faddists, who have made something absolutely unnatural out of a natural teaching. For example, it is good to have organic food, nothing is wrong in it, but if you become too concerned, and you become so minutely concerned that every moment you are thinking of organic food, and nothing inorganic should be allowed in the body, then you have overdone it.

I know people who believe in natural therapies, naturopathy, and they have become so unnatural through their naturopathy that you cannot believe how it can happen. It happens. If it becomes a straining on the mind, then it has already become unnatural. The word 'loose' has to be continuously remembered, otherwise you can become faddists, you can become maniacs; and then you can take one part of it and you can strain so much that even the natural turns into the unnatural.

Loose and natural is Tilopa and that is his whole teaching. He cannot say you should not give and you should not take, but he does say it, so he must mean something else.

One should not give or take but remain natural. . .

Therein is hidden the meaning: remaining natural. And if, remaining natural, it happens that you give — beautiful! If, remaining natural, somebody gives something to you and you take, natural. But don't make a profession out of it. Don't make an anxiety out of it.

. . . for Mahamudra is beyond all acceptance and rejection.

Lao Tzu teaches acceptance. And Tilopa teaches something beyond rejection and acceptance both. Tilopa is really one of the greatest Masters.

You reject something and you become unnatural — that we can understand. You have anger inside and you reject it because of the moral teachings, and because of the difficulties that anger brings you into — conflicts, violence. And to live with anger is not easy, because if you want to live with anger you cannot live with anybody else. It creates trouble and then the moral teachers are there who are always ready to help you and they say, 'Suppress it, throw it, don't be angry, reject it!' You start rejecting.

The moment you reject you start becoming unnatural, because whatsoever you have, nature has given it to you — who are you to

214

reject it? A part of the mind playing the role of the master with another part of the mind? — and both are parts of the same. It is not possible. You can go on playing the game. And the part which is the anger does not bother about your other part which is trying to suppress it, because when the moment comes it erupts. So there is no trouble for the part which is anger, the part which is sex, the part which is greed. You go on fighting, wasting, putting yourself together in millions of ways and always remaining divided, in conflict, fragmentary.

Once you reject, you become unnatural. Don't reject. Of course, immediately the acceptance comes in: if you don't reject then accept. This is subtle, delicate. Tilopa says even in acceptance there is a rejection, because when you say, 'Yes I accept,' deep down you have rejected already. Otherwise why do you say, 'I accept'? What need is there to say that you accept? Acceptance is meaningful only if there is rejection, otherwise it is meaningless.

People come to me and they say, 'Yes, we accept you.' I see their faces, what they are saying; not knowing what they are doing, they have already rejected me. They are forcing their minds to accept me and a certain part of the mind is rejecting. Even when they say 'yes', there is a 'no'; that very 'yes' carries the 'no' in it. The 'yes' is just a superficial garb, a decoration. Inside I can see their 'no' kicking and alive, and they say, 'We accept' — they have already rejected.

If there is no rejection how can you accept, how can you say, 'I accept'? If there is no fight how can you say, 'I surrender'? If you can see this point then an acceptance happens which is beyond both rejection and acceptance, then a surrender happens which is beyond both fight and surrender — then it is total . . . *for Mahamudra is beyond all acceptance and rejection.*

And when you remain simply natural, neither rejecting nor accepting, neither fighting nor surrendering, neither saying no nor saying yes, but allowing things, then whatsoever happens, happens, you have no choice of your own. Whatsoever happens you simply note down that it has happened; you don't try to change anything, you don't try to modify anything. You are not concerned with improving yourself, you simply remain whatsoever you are. Very, very arduous for the mind, because the mind is a great improver.

The mind always says, 'You can reach higher. You can become great. You can polish here and there and you can become pure gold. Improve, transform, transmute, transfigure yourself!' The mind goes on again and again and again saying, 'More is possible, more is still

215

possible, do it!' Then rejection comes. And when you reject part of yourself you are in deep trouble. Because that part is organically yours, you cannot throw it. You can cut the body but you cannot cut the being, because being remains the whole. How can you cut the being? There is no sword that can cut the being.

If your eyes go against you, you can throw them away; if your hand commits a crime you can cut it off; if your legs lead you to sin, you can cut them off — because the body is not you, it is already separate, you can cut it — but how will you cut your consciousness? How will you cut your innermost being? It is not substantial, you cannot cut it. It is like emptiness — how can you cut emptiness? Your sword will go through it, it will remain undivided. If you try too much, your sword may break, but the emptiness will remain undivided; you cannot cut it.

Your innermost being is of the nature of emptiness.

It is a no-self, it is non-substantial.

It is, but it is not matter.

You cannot cut it, there is no possibility.

Don't reject — but immediately the mind says, 'Then okay, we accept.' The mind never leaves you alone. The mind follows you like a shadow; wherever you go the mind says, 'Okay, I am with you just as a help, as a helper. Whenever you are in need I will give you help. Don't reject — of course, right! Tilopa is right: accept!' And if you listen to this mind, again you are in the same trap. Rejection and acceptance are both aspects of the same coin.

Says Tilopa:

. . . *for Mahamudra is beyond all acceptance and rejection.*

Don't accept, don't reject. There is nothing to do in fact. You are not asked to do anything. You are simply asked to be loose and natural; be yourself and let things happen. The whole world is going on without you: the rivers go to the sea, the stars move, the sun rises in the morning, the seasons follow each other, the trees grow and bloom and disappear, and the Whole is moving without you — can't you leave yourself loose and natural and move with the Whole? This is *sannyas* for me.

People come to me and they ask, 'Give us a definite discipline. You simply give us *sannyas* and you never talk about discipline. What do you expect us to do?' I don't expect anything. I want you to be loose and natural. You just be yourself and let things happen — whatsoever happens, *whatsoever* unconditionally: good and bad, misery and happiness, life and death — whatsoever happens let it happen. Just don't you come in the way. You relax. The whole existence goes on and goes on so perfectly well, why are you worried about yourself?

There is no need to improve,
there is *no* need to change.
You simply remain loose and natural
and improvement happens of its own accord,
and changes follow, and you will be transfigured completely —
but not by you.

If you are trying, you are doing the same thing as when somebody is pulling himself up by his own shoe-strings. Foolish! Don't try it. It is just like a dog catching his own tail. On a winter morning when the sun has arisen you can find many dogs doing that. They are sitting silently, enjoying, and then suddenly they see their tails by their sides — looks tempting. And how can they know, poor dogs, that the tails belong to them? And the same is your plight; on the same boat you are also travelling: the temptation becomes too much and the tail looks delicious, it can be eaten! The dog tries, at first very slowly and silently so the tail is not disturbed, but whatsoever he does the tail simply moves itself farther and farther away. Then a hectic activity starts, then the dog becomes alert: 'What does this tail think about herself?' It becomes a challenge. Now he jumps but the more he jumps, the more the tail jumps. A dog can go crazy.

And this is all that spiritual seekers are doing to themselves. Catching their own tails on a winter morning when everything is beautiful, unnecessarily bothering with their tails. Let them rest! Be natural and loose — and who can catch his own tail? You jump; the tail jumps with you and then you feel frustrated. And then you come to me and say, 'The *kundalini* is not rising.' What can I do? You are chasing your own tail and missing the beautiful morning meanwhile. You could have rested with your tail silently; many flies were coming of their own accord and there would have been a good breakfast — but catching the tail the flies also become scared and the very possibility of a good breakfast . . . you simply wait! — just knowing that things cannot be improved; they are already the best that they can be.

You have just to enjoy.
Everything is ready for the celebration, nothing is lacking.
Don't get caught up in absurd activities — and spiritual improvement is one of the most absurd activities.

. . . remain natural — for Mahamudra
is beyond all acceptance and rejection.
Since alaya is not born. . .

Alaya is a Buddhist term, it means the abode, the inner abode, the inner emptiness, the inner sky.

Since alaya is not born
no one can obstruct or soil it.

Don't you be worried! Since your innermost being is never born, it cannot die; since it is never born nobody can soil it or obstruct it. It is deathless! And since the Whole has given you life, since the life comes from the Whole, how can the part improve it? From the source comes everything, let the source supply it — and the source is eternal. You unnecessarily get in the way and you start pushing the river which was already flowing towards the sea . . . *no one can obstruct or soil it.* Your inner purity is absolute! You cannot soil it. This is the essence of Tantra.

All the religions say that you have to attain it — Tantra says it is already attained.

All the religions say you have to work hard for it — Tantra says because of your hard activity you are missing it.

Please, relax a little; just by relaxation you attain the Nonattainable.

. . . no one can obstruct or soil it.

You may have done millions of things — don't be worried about *karmas,* because no act of yours can soil or make your inner being impure.

This is the base of the myth of Jesus' virgin birth. It is not that Jesus' mother Mary was a virgin; it is a Tantric attitude. On his travels in India Jesus came across many tantricas — and he understood the fact that 'virginness' cannot be destroyed, and every child is born out of a virgin. Christian theologians have been very worried about how to prove that Jesus was born out of a virgin. There is no need! — every child is always born out of a virgin, because the virginity cannot be soiled.

How can you soil the virginity? Just two beings, man and wife, or two lovers, moving into a deep sexual orgasm — how can you soil the virginity by it? The innermost being remains a witness, it is not a part of it. The bodies meet, the energies meet, the mind meets, and there is a blissful moment through it; but the innermost being remains a witness — out of it. That virginity cannot be soiled. So they are worried in the West how to prove that Jesus was born out of a virgin.

And I tell you that not even a single child has ever been born without a virgin mother. All children are born out of virginity.

Every moment, whatsoever you do, *you* remain out of it. No action is a scar on you, cannot be. And once you relax and see this, then you are not worried about what to do and what not to do. Then you let things take their own course. Then you simply float like a white cloud, not moving anywhere, simply enjoying the movement. The very wandering is beautiful.

> *. . . no one can obstruct or soil it.*
> *Staying in the unborn realm*
> *all appearance will dissolve into the Dharmata.*

Dharmata means that everything has its own elementary nature. If you remain in your inner abode everything, by and by, will dissolve into its own natural element. You are the disturber. If you remain inside your being, in the *alaya*, in the inner sky, in that absolute purity, then just like the sky, clouds come and go, no trace is left. Actions come and go, thoughts come and go, many things happen, but inside, deep down, nothing happens.

There you simply *are*.

Only existence is there.

No actions reach, no thoughts reach.

If you remain loose and natural in that inner abode, by and by, you will see that all elements move into their own nature. The body is made of five elements. The earth, by and by, will move into the earth; the air into the air, the fire into the fire. That is what happens when you die: every element moves to its own rest — *Dharmata* means the elementary nature of everything — everything moves to its own abode. You move to your own abode and then everything moves to its own; then there is no disturbance.

There are two ways to live and two ways to die. One way is to live like everybody is living: getting mixed up with everything, forgetting completely the inner sky. Then there is another way of living: resting within and allowing the elementary forces to have their own way. When the body feels hunger it will move and seek food.

A man who is Enlightened remains inside his abode. The body feels the hunger, he watches. The body starts moving to feed hunger, he watches. The body finds the food, he watches. The body starts eating, he watches. The body absorbs, feels satiated, he watches. He goes on watching. He is an actor no more. He is not doing anything; he is not a doer. The body feels thirst, he watches. The body stands and moves; these are elementary forces working on their own; you unnecessarily say, 'I am thirsty' — you are not! You get mixed up. The *body* is thirsty and the body will find its own course. It will move wherever the water is.

If you remain inside, you will see everything happens by itself. Even trees find their water sources with no ego and no mind; the roots will go and seek the sources, even sometimes hundreds of feet they will travel to find a source of water. And this has been one of the most amazing things for botanists because they cannot understand how it happens. A tree is there: towards the north one hundred feet away, there is a water source, a little spring hidden inside the earth. How does the tree know that the roots have to move towards north, not to the south? And it is one hundred feet away, so even a guess is not possible; and the tree has no mind of its own, no ego. But through the elemental forces, by itself the tree starts growing roots towards the north, and one day it reaches the water source.

The tree reaches towards the sky. . . In African jungles trees grow very high, they have to because the forest is so dense that if the trees don't grow very high they will not be able to reach the sun and the light and the air. So they grow higher and higher and higher, they seek their way. Even trees can find their water sources — why are you worried?

That's why Jesus says, 'Look, consider the lilies in the field: they toil not, they don't do anything, but everything happens.'

When you sit inside your abode, your elemental forces will start functioning in their crystal purity. Don't you come in. The body feels hunger, the body itself moves — and it is so beautiful to see the body moving itself. It is really one of the most wonderful experiences to see one's own body moving itself and finding the source of water or food. There is a thirst for love and the body moves itself. You go on sitting inside your abode, then suddenly you see actions don't belong to you: you are not a doer, you are simply a watcher.

Realized this, you have attained the Non-attainable. Realizing this, you have realized all that can be realized.

Staying in the unborn realm
all appearance will dissolve into the Dharmata,
all self-will and pride will vanish into nought.

And when you see that things are happening by themselves, then
how can you gather an ego, pride about it?
How can you say 'I' when hunger has its own way,
fulfills itself, becomes satiety;
when life has its own way,
fulfills itself, reaches death and rest?
Who are you to say, 'I am'?
The pride, the self, the self-will, all dissolve.
Then you don't do anything,
then you don't will anything—
you simply sit in your inner-most being
and the grass grows by itself. . .
Everything happens by itself.
Difficult to understand this because you have been brought up,
conditioned, that you have to do, that you have to be a doer, constantly alert and moving and fighting. You have been brought up in a
milieu which says that you have to fight for your survival otherwise
you will be lost, otherwise you will achieve nothing. You have been
brought up with the poison of ambition in you. And in the West particularly, a very nonsense word 'will-power' exists. This is simply
absurd. There is nothing like will-power — a fantasy, a dream. There
is no need for any will. Things are happening by themselves, it is
their nature.
It happened: The Master of Lin Chi died. The Master was a well-
known man, but Lin Chi was even more well-known than the Master,
because the Master was a silent man, but through Lin Chi, in fact, he
had become very famous. Then the Master died — through Lin Chi
it was also known that he was Enlightened — and a crowd of thousands
gathered to pay their respects and bid him the last farewell, and they
saw Lin Chi crying and weeping and tears flowing down like a small
child whose mother has died. People could not believe it because
they thought that he had attained — and he was crying like a small
child. This is okay when a person is ignorant, but when a person is
Awakened, and he himself has been teaching that the innermost
nature is immortal, eternal, it never dies, why then?
A few who were very very intimate with Lin Chi, they came and

221

told him, 'It is not good, and what will people think about you? — already there is a rumour: people are thinking that they were wrong in thinking that you have attained. Your whole prestige is at stake. You stop crying! And a man like you need not cry.'

Lin Chi said, 'But what can I do? Tears are coming! It is their *Dharmata.* And who am I to stop them? I neither reject nor accept; I remain inside myself. Now tears are flowing, nothing can be done. If the prestige is at stake, let it be. If the people think I am not Enlightened, that is their own business. But what can I do? I left the doer long before. There is no longer any doer. It is simply happening. These eyes are crying and weeping of their own accord, because they will not be able to see the Master again — and he was a nourishment to them, they lived on that food. I know very well that the soul is eternal, nobody ever dies, but how to teach these eyes? What to tell them? They don't listen, they don't have any ears. How to teach these eyes not to weep, not to cry, that life is eternal? And who am I? It is their business. If they feel like crying, they are crying.'

Remaining natural and loose means this: things happen, you are not the doer. Neither accepting nor rejecting, self-will dissolves. The very concept of will-power becomes empty and impotent, it simply withers away; and pride vanishes into nothingness.

Difficult to understand an Enlightened person. No concepts will be helpful. What will you think about Lin Chi? He says, 'I know — but the eyes are crying; let them cry, they will feel relaxed. And they will not be able to see this man again; that body is to be burned soon and they were nourished by him, and they knew no beauty other than this man, and they knew no grace. They have lived too long being nourished on this man's form and the body. Now, of course, they feel thirsty, hungry; now, of course, they feel that the very ground is disappearing underneath them — they are crying!'

A natural man simply sits inside and allows things to happen.
He does not 'do'.
And Tilopa says only then does Mahamudra appear,
the final, the utterly final orgasm with the Existence.
Then you are separate no more.
Then your inner sky has become one with the outer sky.
There are not two skies then, only one sky.

The Song ends:

The supreme understanding
transcends all this and that.
The supreme action
embraces great resourcefulness without attachment.
The supreme accomplishment
is to realize immanence without hope.

At first a yogi feels his mind
is tumbling like a waterfall;
in mid-course, like the Ganges,
it flows on slow and gentle;
in the end it is a great vast ocean
where the lights of son and mother merge in one.

X   THE SUPREME UNDERSTANDING
20th February 1975

EVERYBODY IS BORN IN FREEDOM, but dies in bondage. The beginning of life is totally loose and natural, but then enters the society, then enter rules and regulations, morality, discipline and many sorts of training; and the looseness and the naturalness and the spontaneous being are lost. One starts to gather around oneself a sort of armour. One starts becoming more and more rigid. The inner softness is apparent no more.

On the boundary of one's being one creates a fort-like phenomenon, to defend, to not be vulnerable, to react, for security, safety, and the freedom of being is lost. One starts looking at others' eyes; their approvals, their denials, their condemnations, their appreciations become more and more valuable. The 'others' become the criterion, and one starts to imitate and follow others because one has to live with others.

And a child is very soft, he can be moulded in any way; and the society starts moulding him — the parents, the teachers, the school — and by and by he becomes a character not a being. He learns all the rules. Either he becomes a conformist, that too is a bondage, or he becomes rebellious, that too is another sort of bondage.

If he becomes a conformist, orthodox, square, that is one sort of bondage; he can react, can become a hippy, can move to the other extreme, but that too is again a sort of bondage — because reaction depends on the same thing it reacts against. You may go to the farthest corner of the world, but deep down in the mind you are rebelling against the same rules. Others are following them, you are reacting, but the focus remains on the same rules. Reactionaries or revolutionaries, all travel in the same boat. They may be standing against each other, back to back, but the boat is the same.

A religious man is neither a reactionary nor a revolutionary. A religious man is simply loose and natural: he is neither for something nor against, he is simply himself; he has no rules to follow and no rules to deny, simply, he has no rules. A religious man is free in his own being, he has no mould of habits and conditionings. He is not a cultured being — not that he is uncivilized and primitive, he is the highest possibility of civilization and culture, but he is not a cultured being. He has grown in his awareness and he doesn't need any rules, he has transcended rules. He is truthful not because this is the rule to be truthful; being loose and natural he is simply truthful, it happens to be truthful. He has compassion, not because he follows the precept: Be compassionate! No. Being loose and natural he simply feels compassion flowing all around, there is nothing to be done about it on his part; it is just a by-product of his growth in awareness. He is not against society, nor for society — he is simply beyond it. He has again become a child, a child of an absolutely unknown world, a child in a new dimension — he is reborn.

Every child is born natural, loose; then the society comes in, has to come in for certain reasons — nothing wrong in it, because if the child is left to himself or herself the child will never grow, and the child will never be able to become religious, he will become just like an animal. The society has to come in; the society has to be passed through — it is needed. The only thing to remember is that society is just a passage to pass through; one should not make one's house in it. The only thing to remember is that society has to be followed and then transcended, the rules have to be learned and then unlearned. The rules will come in your life because there are others, you are not alone.

When the child is in the mother's womb he is absolutely alone, no rules are needed. Rules come only when the other comes into relationship with you; rules come with relationship — because you are not alone you have to think of others and consider others. In the mother's womb the child is alone; no rules, no morality, no discipline is needed, no order, but the moment he is born, even the first breath he takes is social. If the child is not crying, the doctors will force him to cry immediately, because if he doesn't cry for a few minutes then he will be dead. He has to cry because the cry opens the passage through which he will be able to breathe, it clears the throat. He has to be forced to cry — even the first breath is social; and others are there and the moulding has started.

228

Nothing wrong in it! It has to be done, but it has to be done in such a way that the child never loses his awareness, does not become identified with the cultured pattern, remains deep inside still free, knows that rules have to be followed but that rules are not life, and knows also that he has to be taught. And that's what a good society will do, teach that: 'These rules are good but there are others, and these rules are not absolute, and you are not expected to remain confined to them — one day you must transcend them.' A society is good if it teaches to its members civilization *and* transcendence; then the society is religious. If it never teaches transcendence then that society is simply secular and political, it has no religion in it.

You have to listen to others up to a certain extent, and then you have to start listening to yourself. You must come back to the original state in the end. Before you die you must become an innocent child again — loose, natural; because in death again you are entering the dimension of being alone. Just like you were in the womb, in death again you will enter in the realm of being alone. No society exists there. And throughout your life you have to find a few spaces in your life, a few moments like oases in deserts, where you simply close your eyes and go beyond society, move into yourself, into your own womb — this is what meditation is. The society is there; you simply close your eyes and forget the society and become alone. No rules exist there, no character is needed, no morality, no words, no language. You can be loose and natural inside.

Grow into that loose-and-naturalness. Even if there is a need for outer discipline, inside you remain wild. If one can remain wild inside and still practise things which are needed in the society, then soon one can come to a point where one simply transcends.

I will tell you one story and then I will enter into the *sutras*.

This is a Sufi story: An old man and a young man were travelling with a donkey. They reached near a town; they both were walking with their donkey. School children passed them and they giggled and they laughed and they said, 'Look at these fools: they have a healthy donkey with them and they are walking. At least the old man can sit on the donkey.'

Listening to those children the old man and the young man said, 'What to do? Because people are laughing and soon we will be entering the town, so it is better to follow what they are saying.' So the old man sat on the donkey and the young man followed.

Then they came near another group of people and they looked at them and said, 'Look! — the old man is sitting on the donkey and the poor boy is walking. This is absurd! The old man can walk, but the boy should be allowed to sit on the donkey.' So they changed: the old man started walking and the boy was allowed to sit.

Then another group came and said, 'Look at these fools. And this boy seems to be too arrogant. Maybe the old man is his father or his teacher and he is walking, and the boy is sitting on the donkey — this is against all rules!' So what to do? They both decided that now there was only one possibility: that they should both sit on the donkey; so they both sat on the donkey.

Then other groups came and they said, 'Look at these people, so violent! The poor donkey is almost dying — two persons on one donkey. It would be better if they carried the donkey on their shoulders.'

So they again discussed, and then they came to the river and the bridge. They had now almost reached the boundary of the town, so they thought: 'It is better to behave as people think in this town, otherwise they will think we are fools.' So they found a bamboo; on their shoulders they put the bamboo and hung the donkey by his legs, tied him onto the bamboo and carried him. The donkey tried to rebel, as donkeys will, they cannot be forced very easily. He tried to escape because he was not a believer in society and what others are saying. But the two men were too much and they forced him, so the donkey had to yield.

Just in the middle of the bridge a crowd passed and they all gathered around them and they said, 'Look at these fools! We have never seen such idiots — a donkey is to ride upon, not to carry on your shoulders. Have you gone mad?'

They listened to them and a great crowd gathered. The donkey became restless, so restless that he jumped and fell from the bridge down into the river and died. Both the men went down — the donkey was dead. They sat by his side and the old man said, 'Now listen. . .' This is not an ordinary story — the old man was a Sufi Master, an Enlightened person, and the young man was a disciple and the old Master was trying to give him a lesson, because Sufis always create situations; they say that unless the situation is there you cannot learn deeply. So this was just a situation for the young man. Now the old man said, 'Look: just like this donkey you will be dead if you listen to people too much. Don't bother about what others say, because there are millions of others and they have their own minds and everybody will say something different; everybody has his opinion and if you listen to opinions this will be your end.'

Don't listen to anybody, you remain yourself. Just bypass them, be indifferent. If you go on listening to everybody, everybody will be prodding you to go this way or that. You will never be able to reach your innermost center.

Everybody has become eccentric. This English word is very beautiful: it means off the center, and we use it for the mad people. But everybody is eccentric, off the center, and the whole world is helping you to be eccentric because everybody is prodding you. Your mother is prodding you towards the north, your father towards the south, your uncle is doing something else, your brother something else, your wife, of course, something else, and everybody is trying to force you somewhere. By and by, a moment comes when you are nowhere. You remain just on the cross-roads being pushed from north to south, from south to east, from east to west, moving nowhere. By and by, this becomes your total situation — you become eccentric.

This is the situation. And if you go on listening to others and not listening to your inner center, this situation will continue. All meditation is to become centered, not to be eccentric, to come to your own center. Listen to your inner voice, feel it, and move with that feeling. By and by, you can laugh at others' opinions, or you can be simply indifferent. And once you become centered you become a powerful being; then nobody can prod you, then nobody can push you anywhere — simply, nobody dares. You are such a power, centered in yourself, that anyone who comes with an opinion simply forgets his opinion near you; anybody who comes to push you somewhere simply forgets that he had come to push you. Rather, just coming near you he starts feeling overpowered by you.

That's how even a single man can become so powerful that the whole society, the whole history, cannot push him a single inch. That's how a Buddha exists, a Jesus exists. You can kill a Jesus but you cannot push him. You can destroy his body, but you cannot push him a single inch. Not that he is adamant or stubborn, no, he is simply centered in his own being — and he knows what is good for him, and he knows what is blissful for him. It has already happened; now you cannot allure him towards new goals, no salesmanship can allure him to any other goal. He has found his home. He can listen to you patiently but you cannot move him. He is centered.

This centering is the first thing towards being natural and loose;

otherwise if you are natural and loose, anybody will take you any-where. That's why children are not allowed to be natural and loose, they are not mature enough to be that. If they are natural and loose and running all around, their life will be wasted. Hence, I say, society does a needful work: it makes them protected; a cell-like character becomes the citadel, they need it, they are very vulnerable, they may be destroyed by anybody; the multitude is there, they will not be able to find their way — they need a character armour.

But if that character armour becomes your total life, then you are lost. You should not become the citadel, you should remain the master and you should remain capable of going out of it. Otherwise it is not a protection; it becomes a prison. You should be capable of going out of your character. You should be capable of putting aside your principles. You should be capable, if the situation demands, of responding in an absolutely novel way. If this capacity is lost then you become rigid, then you cannot be loose. If this capacity is lost then you become unnatural, then you are not flexible.

Flexibility is youth, rigidness is old age; the more flexible, the more young; the more rigid, the more old.

Death is absolute rigidity.

Life is absolute looseness and flexibility.

This you have to remember and then try to understand Tilopa. His final words:

The supreme understanding
transcends all this and that.
The supreme action
embraces great resourcefulness without attachment.
The supreme accomplishment
is to realize immanence without hope.

Very very significant words.

The supreme understanding transcends all this and that.

Knowledge is always either of this or of that. Understanding is neither. Knowledge is always of duality: a man is good, he knows what good is; another man is bad, he knows what bad is — but both are fragmentary, half. The good man is not whole because he does not know what bad is; his goodness is poor, it lacks the insight that badness gives. The bad man is also half; his badness is poor, it is not rich because he does not know what goodness is. And life is both together.

A man of real understanding is neither good nor bad, he understands both. And in that very understanding he transcends both. A sage is neither a good man nor a bad man. You cannot confine him to any category, there exists no pigeon-hole for him, you cannot categorize him. He is elusive, you cannot catch hold of him. And whatsoever you say about him will be half, it can never be total. A sage may have friends and followers, and they will think he is God because they see only the good part. And the sage may have enemies and foes, and they will think that he is the Devil incarnate because they know only the bad part. But if you know a sage he is neither—or both together; and both mean the same.

If you are both together, good and bad, you are neither — because they annihilate each other, negate each other, and a void is left.

This concept is very difficult for the Western mind to understand, because the Western mind has divided God and Devil absolutely. Whatsoever is bad belongs to the Devil and whatsoever is good belongs to God; their territories are demarked, Hell and Heaven are set apart.

That's why Christian saints look a little poor before Tantric sages, very poor; just good, simple; they don't know the other side of life. And that's why they are always afraid of the other side, always trembling with fear. A Christian saint is always praying for God to protect him from the evil. The evil is always by the corner; he has avoided it and when you avoid something, continuously it is in the mind. He is afraid, trembling.

A Tilopa knows no trembling, no fear, and he never goes to pray to God to protect him; he is protected. What is *his* protection? Understanding is his protection. He has lived all, he has moved to the farthest corner into evil, and he has lived the Divine, and now he knows both are two aspects of the same. And now he is neither worried about good nor worried about bad; now he lives a loose and natural, simple life, he has no predetermined concepts. And he is unpredictable.

You cannot predict a Tilopa; you can predict St. Augustine, you can predict other saints, but you cannot predict a Tantric sage; you cannot — simply unpredictable. Because in each moment he will respond and nobody knows in what way, nobody knows; even he himself does not know. That's the beauty of it, because if you know your future then you are not a free man, then you are moving according to certain rules, then you have a prefabricated character, then somehow you have to react, not respond.

Nobody can say what a Tilopa will do in a certain situation; it will depend; the whole situation will bring the response. And he has no likings, no dislikings—neither this nor that. He will act, he will not react; he will not react out of his past, he will not react according to his future concepts, from his own ideals. No. He will act here and now, the response will be total; nobody can say what will happen.

Understanding transcends duality.

It is said that once Tilopa was staying in a cave and a passer-by, a seeker of a certain type, came to visit him. He was taking his food and he was using a human skull as a bowl. The traveller became afraid. It was weird!—and he had come to see a sage and this man seemed to be something of the world of black magicians. He was eating from a human skull and he was enjoying; and a dog was sitting by the side of Tilopa and the dog was also eating from the same bowl, and when this man came Tilopa invited him to participate. 'Come here,' he said, 'so beautiful you reached in time because this is all that I have got. Once it is finished then for twenty-four hours there is nothing. Only tomorrow somebody may bring something. So you come and join in and participate.'

The man felt very much disgusted—a human skull, food in it, and a dog also a participant! The man said, 'I feel disgusted.'

Tilopa said, 'Then you escape as soon as possible from here and run fast and never look back, because then Tilopa is not for you. Why are you disgusted with this human skull? You have been carrying it for so long and what is wrong if I am taking my food in it? It is one of the cleanest things. And you are not disgusted with your own skull inside yourself? Your whole mind, your beautiful thoughts and your morality and your goodness and your saintliness—all are in the skull. I am taking only my food in it; and your Heaven and your Hell and your gods and your Brahma, all are in your skull. They must have become absolutely dirty by now—you should be disgusted about that. And you yourself are there in the skull. Why do you feel disgusted?'

The man tried to avoid and rationalize; he said, 'Not because of the skull but because of this dog.'

And Tilopa laughed and said, 'You have been a dog in your past life and everybody has to pass through all the stages. And what is wrong in being a dog? And what is the difference between you and a dog? The same greed, the same sex, the same anger, the same violence, aggressiveness, the same fear — why do you pretend that you are superior?'

Tilopa is difficult to understand because ugly and beautiful make no sense to him; purity, impurity make no sense to him; good and bad make no sense to him. He has an understanding of the total.

Knowledge is partial, understanding is total.

And when you look at the total, all distinctions drop.

What is ugly and what is beautiful?

What is good and what is bad?

All distinctions simply drop if you have a bird's-eye view of the total, then all boundaries disappear. It is just like looking down from an aeroplane. Then where is Pakistan and where is India? And where is England and where is Germany? All boundaries become lost, the whole earth becomes one.

And if you go still higher in a spaceship and look from the moon, the whole earth becomes so small — where is Russia and where is America? And who is a communist and who is a capitalist? And who is a Hindu and who is a Mohammedan? The higher you go, the less are the distinctions — and understanding is the highest thing, there is nothing more beyond it.

From that highest peak everything becomes everything else.

Things meet and merge and become one,

boundaries are lost . . .

an unbounded ocean with no source to it

. . . infinity.

The supreme understanding
transcends all this and that.
The supreme action
embraces great resourcefulness without attachment.

Tilopa says be loose and natural — but he doesn't mean by that be lazy and go to sleep. On the contrary, when you are loose and natural much resourcefulness happens to you. You become tremendously creative. Activity may not be there — action is there. Obsession with occupation may not be there, will not be there, but you become tremendously resourceful, creative. You do millions of things, not because of any obsession but just because you are so filled with energy that you have to create.

Creativity comes easy to a man who is loose and natural. Whatsoever he does becomes a creative phenomenon. Wherever he touches, it becomes a piece of art; whatsoever he says becomes poetry. His very movement is aesthetic. If you can see a Buddha walking, even his walking is creativity; even through his walking he is creating a rhythm, even through his walking he is creating a milieu, an atmosphere around him. If a Buddha raises his hand he changes the climate around him immediately. Not that he is doing these things, they are simply happening. He is not the doer.

Calm, settled inside; tranquil, collected, together inside,
filled with infinite energy pouring over,
overflowing in all directions,
his every moment is a moment of creativity,
of cosmic creativity.

Remember that. It has to be remembered because many people can misunderstand. They can think, 'No activity is needed,' so they can think, 'no action is needed.' Action has a different quality altogether! Activity is pathological.

If you go into a madhouse you will see people in activity, every madman doing something, because that is the only way they can forget themselves. You may find somebody washing his hands three thousand times a day because he believes in cleanliness. In fact, if you stop him washing his hands three thousand times a day he will be unable to stand himself, it will be too much. This is an escape.

Politicians, people who are after wealth, power, they are all mad people. You cannot stop them because if you stop them they don't know what to do then; and then they are thrown to themselves and that is too much.

One of my friends was telling me once that he and his wife had to go to a certain party; and they have a very small child, a beautiful child, and of course very active as children are. So they locked the room and told him, 'If you behave well and don't create any disturbance in the house, whatsoever you ask we will give you, and within an hour we will be back.' The child was allured: whatsoever he can ask will be given. So he acted really well. In fact, he didn't do anything; he simply stood in the corner because: 'Whatsoever I do may turn out . . . nobody knows, nobody knows about these adult minds — what is wrong and what is good; and they go on changing their opinions also.' So he stood with closed eyes just like a meditator.

Then they opened the door when they came back and he was

standing in the corner, stiff: He opened his eyes and looked at them, and they asked, 'Did you behave well?'

He said, 'Yes, in fact I behaved so well that I couldn't stand myself.' It was too much.

People who are too occupied in activities are afraid of themselves. Activity is a sort of escape; they can forget themselves in it. It is alcoholic, it is an intoxicant. Activity has to be dropped because it is pathological, you are ill. Action has not to be dropped, action is beautiful.

What is action? Action is a response: when it is needed you act; when it is not needed you relax. Right now you go on doing things which are not needed; and right now when you want to relax, you cannot relax. A man of action, total action, acts; and when the situation is over he relaxes.

I am talking to you. Talking can be either activity or action. There are people who cannot stop talking: they go on, they go on. Even if you stop their mouths it will not make any difference *inside;* they will go on chattering, they cannot stop it. This is activity: a feverish obsession. You are here and I talk to you. Even I don't know what I'm going to say to you. Until the sentence is uttered, even I was not aware of what it was going to be. Not only are you the listeners, I am also a listener here. When I have said something then I know that I have said it. Neither can you predict, nor can I predict what I am going to say; not even is the next sentence there, it is *your* situation that brings it.

So whatsoever I say, I alone am not responsible, remember, you are also half responsible for it. It is half-half: you create the situation, I act. So if my listeners change, my talk changes. It depends, because I have nothing preformulated. I don't know what is going to happen, and that's why it is beautiful for me also. It is a response, an act. When you are gone I sit inside my abode, not even a single word floats in the inner sky. It is you.

So sometimes it happens that people come to me and say, 'We were going to ask a certain question and you answered it.' And every day it happens. It is happening: if you have a certain question, you create a climate around you of that question, you come filled with that question. Then what am I to do? I have to respond. Your question simply creates the situation and I have to respond. That's why many of your questions are simply solved. If some question is not solved the reason must be somewhere in you; you may have forgotten it. In the morning it was in mind but when you entered this room you forgot about it. Or there were many questions and you were not certain exactly which question to ask; you were in confusion, vague, cloudy. If *you* are certain about your question the answer will be there.

It is nothing on my part, it simply happens. You create the question, I simply float into it. I have to, because I have nothing to say to you. If I have something to say to you, you are irrelevant; whatsoever question you may have, it doesn't make any difference—I have my prepared thing in me and I have to tell it to you. Even if you are not there, it will not make any difference.

The All-India Radio used to invite me to speak, but I felt it very difficult because it was so impersonal: talking to nobody! I simply said, 'This is not for me. And it is such a strain and I don't know what to do—there is nobody.' So they arranged something. They said, 'This can be done: from our staff a few people can come and they can sit.' But then I told them, 'Then don't you give me the subject because those people will give me the subject. This will be totally irrelevant — people sitting there and you have given me a subject to talk on, and nobody is involved in that subject; they will be just a dead audience.'

When you are there you create the question, you create the situation and the answer flows towards you. It is a personal phenomenon. Then I simply stopped going there. I said, 'This is not for me, it is not possible. I cannot talk to machines, because they don't create any situation for me to float in. I can talk only to persons.'

That's why I have never written a book. I cannot!—because for whom? Who will read it? Unless I know that man who will read it, and unless he creates a situation, I cannot write—for whom? I have written only letters, because then I know that I am writing to somebody. He may be somewhere in the United States, it makes no difference—the moment I write a letter to him it is a personal phenomenon: he is there. While I am writing he helps me to write. Without him it is not possible; it is a dialogue.

This is action. The moment you are gone, all language disappears from me; no words float, they are not needed. And this should be so! When you walk you use your legs and when you sit in your chair, what is the point of moving your legs? It is mad! When there is a dialogue, words are needed; when there is a situation, action is needed—but let the Whole decide it; you should not be the deciding factor, you should not decide. Then there are no *karmas*, then you move from

238

moment to moment fresh. The past dies by itself every moment, and the future is born and you move into it fresh like a child.

The supreme action
embraces great resourcefulness without attachment.

Actions happen but there is no attachment; you don't feel, 'I have done this.' I don't feel I have said this. I simply feel it has been spoken, it has happened. The Whole has done it, and the Whole is neither me nor you — the Whole is both and neither; and the Whole hovers around and the Whole decides. You are not the doer. Much happens through you, but you are not the doer. Much is created through you, but you are not the creator. The Whole remains the creator, you become simply vehicles, mediums for the Whole.

A hollow bamboo,
and the Whole puts his fingers and his lips on it
and it becomes a flute, and a song is born.

From where does this song come? From that hollow bamboo you call 'flute'? No. From the lips of the Whole? No. From where does it come? Everything is involved: the hollow bamboo is involved, the lips of the Whole are also involved, the singer is involved, the listener is involved, everything is involved. Even a small thing can create a difference.

Just a rose-flower by the side of the room and this room will not be the same, because the rose-flower has his own aura, his own being. He will influence: he will influence your understanding, he will influence whatsoever is spoken by me — and the total moves, not parts. Much happens but nobody is the doer.

. . . great resourcefulness without attachment.

And when you are not the doer how can the attachment happen? You do a small thing and you become attached. You say, 'I have done this.' You would like everybody to know that you have done this and you have done that. This ego is the barrier for the supreme understanding. Drop the doer and let things happen. That's what Tilopa means by being loose and natural.

The supreme accomplishment
is to realize immanence without hope.

This is a very deep thing, very subtle and delicate. Tilopa says, 'What is the supreme accomplishment? It is to realize immanence

239

without hope; that inside, the inner space is perfect, absolute —
without hope.' Why does he bring this word 'hope' in?

Because with the hope comes the future,
with the hope comes desire,
with the hope comes the effort to improve,
with the hope comes the greed for more,
with the hope comes discontentment —
and then, of course, frustration follows.

He is not saying be hopeless, because that too comes with hope.
He is simply saying 'no hope'; not hopeful, not hopeless — because
they both come with hope. And this has become such a great problem
for the West, because Buddha says the same, and then Western thinkers
think that these people are pessimists. They are not. They are not
pessimists, they are not optimists. And this is the meaning of 'no hope'.

If somebody hopes we call him an optimist, we say that he can see the
silver lining in the darkest cloud, we say that he can see the morning
following the darkest night: he is an optimist. And then there is the
pessimist, just the opposite of him. Even around the brightest silver
lining he will always see the darkest cloud. And if you talk about the
morning he will say, 'Every morning ends in the evening.' But
remember: they may be opposites but they are not really separate;
their focus is different but their mind is the same. Whether you see the
bright lining, the silver lining in the dark cloud, or you see the dark
cloud around the silver lining, you always see the part; your division
is there, you choose, you never see the total.

Buddha, Tilopa, myself, we are neither optimists nor pessimists —
we simply drop hope. With hope they both come in — optimist, pessimist. We simply drop the coin of hope and both the aspects are
dropped with it. This is a totally new dimension, difficult to understand.

Tilopa sees the suchness of things; he has no choice.
He sees *both* the morning and the evening together,
he sees both the thorns and the flower together,
he sees both the pain and the pleasure together,
he sees both birth and death together.
He has no choice of his own.
He is neither a pessimist nor an optimist —
he lives without hope.

And that is a really wonderful dimension to live in: to live without
hope. Just to use the very term 'without hope' and inside you it simply

feels that this is something so pessimistic, but that is because of the language — and what Tilopa is saying is beyond language. He says, 'The supreme accomplishment is to realize immanence without hope.' You simply realize yourself as you are in your total suchness, and simply you are that! There is no need for any improvement, change, development, growth, no need.

Nothing can be done about it.

It is simply the case.

Once you go deep into this, that it is simply the case, suddenly all flowers and all thorns disappear, days and nights disappear, life and death disappear, summer and winter disappear. Nothing is left — because the clinging disappears. And with the acceptance of whatsoever you are, whatsoever is the case, there is no problem then, no question, nothing to be solved — you simply are that. Then a celebration comes; and this celebration is not of the hope, this celebration is just an overflowing of the energy. You start blooming, you simply bloom, not for something in the future, but because you cannot do otherwise.

When one realizes the suchness of being, the blooming happens; one goes on blooming and blooming and celebrating for *no* visible cause at all. Why am I happy? What have I got that you have not got? Why am I serene and quiet? Have I achieved something that you have to achieve? Have I attained to something that you have to attain? No. I have simply relaxed into the suchness. Whatsoever I am — good, bad, moral, immoral — whatsoever I am, I have simply relaxed into the suchness of it. And I have dropped all efforts to improve, and I have dropped all future. I have dropped hope, and with the dropping of hope everything has disappeared. I am alone and simply happy for no reason at all; simply silent because now, without hope, I don't know how to create any disturbance. Without hope how can you create any disturbance in your being?

Remember this: that all effort will lead you to a point where you leave all effort and become effortless. And the whole search will lead you to a point where you simply shrug your shoulders and sit down under a tree and settle.

Every journey ends into the innermost suchness of being — and that you have every moment. So it is only a question of becoming a little more aware. What is wrong with you? I have seen millions of people and I have not seen even a single person who really has something wrong, but he creates. You are creators, great creators of illnesses, wrongs, problems, and then you chase them — how to solve them? First you create them and then you go chasing them. Why in the first place create them?

Just drop hope, desire, and simply look at the case that you are already; just simply close your eyes and see who you are, and finished! Even in the blinking of an eye this is possible, it needs no time. If you are thinking it needs time, gradual growth, then it is because of your mind — you will need time, otherwise time is not needed.

The supreme accomplishment is to realize immanence . . . that all that is to be achieved is inherently there. That is the meaning of immanence: all that is to be achieved is already there inside you. You are born perfect, otherwise is not possible because you are born of the perfect. That is the meaning when Jesus says, 'I and my Father are one.' What is he saying? He is saying that you cannot be anything other than the Whole because you come out of the Whole!

You take a handful of water from the ocean, you taste it, it tastes the same everywhere. In a single drop of sea-water you can find the whole chemistry of the sea. If you can understand a single drop of sea-water you have understood all seas, past, future, present — because a small drop is a miniature ocean. And you are the Whole in a miniature form.

When you go deeper inside you and realize this, suddenly a laughter happens, you start laughing. What were you seeking? The seeker himself was the sought; the traveller himself was the goal. This is the supreme-most accomplishment: to realize oneself, one's absolute perfection — without hope. Because if a hope is there it will stir; it will continually stir in your disturbance. You will start thinking again, 'Something more is possible.' Hope always creates dreams: 'Something more is possible. Of course it is good. . . .'

People come to me and they say, 'Meditation is going very well; of course, it's good, but give us some other technique so that we can grow more.' Sometimes people have even come to me saying, 'Everything is beautiful!' And then they say, 'Now what?' Now the hope stirs. Everything is beautiful, then why ask, 'Now what?' Everything was wrong, then you were asking, 'Now what?' And now everything is beautiful, again you ask, 'Now what?' Now leave it, this hope!

Just the other day somebody came, and said, 'Everything is going very beautifully now, but who knows about tomorrow?' Why bring tomorrow in when everything is going absolutely right? Can't you remain without problems? Now everything is good, but you worry whether it will be good tomorrow or not. If it is good today from where is the tomorrow going to come? It will be born out of today, so why be worried? If today is silent, tomorrow is going to be more silent; it will be born out of today. But because of this worry you can destroy today; then the tomorrow will be there and you will be fulfilled in your frustration and you will say, 'This is what I was thinking and worrying about — it has happened.' *And it has happened because of you.* It was not going to happen! Had you remained without the future, it would not have happened.

This is the self-destructive tendency of the mind, suicidal; and in a way it is very self-fulfilling, so always the mind can say, 'I was warning you before. I had warned you beforehand, you didn't listen to me.' Now you will think, 'Yes, that's right; the mind was warning me and I did not listen to it.' But it has come only because of the warning of the mind.

Many things happen . . . . If you go to the astrologers, *jyotishi,* palmists, and they tell you something, when it happens you will think they predicted your future. Just the opposite is the case: because they predicted, your mind got into it and it happened. If somebody says that next month on the 13th March you are going to die, the possibility is there — not because he knew your future, but because he predicted the future. Now the 13th March will move in your mind continuously: you will not be able to sleep without it, you will not be able to dream without it, you will not be able to love without it. Twenty-four hours a day: 'The 13th March and I am going to die.' It will become a self-hypnosis, a chanting. It will go round and round; the nearer the 13th March comes, the faster it will move. And it will self-fulfill: 13th March . . . .

It happened once that a German palmist predicted his own death. He had been predicting many people's deaths and they happened, so he became certain that his prediction was something; otherwise, how was it happening? And he was getting old so a few friends suggested, 'Why not predict your own?' So he studied his hands and charts and everything — all foolish — and then he decided for his own death: that it was going to happen on such and such a date, at six o'clock early in the morning. And then he waited for it. Six was approaching, from five o'clock he was ready, sitting by the clock; each moment and death was coming nearer and nearer and nearer. And then came just the last moment — one moment more and the clock will say it is six, and he is still alive, how is it possible? The seconds started passing, and exactly

243

when the clock knocked six — he jumped out of the window. Because how is it possible? And of course, he died exactly as predicted.

Mind has a self-fulfilling mechanism. Be alert about it. You are happy; the mind says, 'Of course, you are happy, it is okay — but what about tomorrow?' Now already the mind has destroyed this moment, it has brought tomorrow in. Now the tomorrow will come out of this mind, not out of that blissful moment that was there.

Don't hope this way or that, for or against, drop all hope. Remain here to the moment, in the moment, with the moment, for the moment. There is no other moment than this. And whatsoever is going to happen will happen out of this moment, so why worry? If this moment is beautiful how can the next moment be ugly? From where will it come? It grows, it will be more beautiful — has to be. There is no need to think about it.

And once you accomplish this, remaining with your innate perfection. . . . Remember, I have to use words and there is a danger that you may misunderstand. When I say remain with your inner perfection you may be worried because sometimes you may feel that you are not perfect — then remain with your imperfection. Imperfection is also perfect! Nothing is wrong in it, remain with it. Don't move away from *this* moment; here and now is the whole existence. Everything that has to be accomplished is to be accomplished here and now, so whatsoever is the case, even if you feel imperfect — beautiful, be imperfect! That's how you are, that is your suchness. You feel sexual — perfect, feel sexual; that's how you are, that's how God meant you to be. Sad — beautiful, be sad, but don't move from the moment.

Remain with the moment and, by and by, you will feel the imperfection has dissolved into perfection, the sex has dissolved into inner ecstasy, the anger has dissolved into compassion.

This moment, if you can be with your total being, then there is no problem. This is the supreme accomplishment. It has no hope, it need not have. It is so perfect there is no need for hope. Hope is not a good situation; hoping always means something is wrong with you — that's why you hope for the against, for the opposite. You are sad and you hope for happiness; your hope says that you are sad. You feel ugly and you hope for a beautiful personality; your hope says you are ugly. Show me your hope and I can tell you who you are, because your hope immediately shows who you are — just the opposite. Drop hope and just be. If you try this, just being, this will happen:

At first a yogi feels his mind
is tumbling like a waterfall;
in mid-course, like the Ganges,
it flows on slow and gentle;
in the end
it is a great, vast ocean
where the lights of son and mother merge in one.

If you are being here and now, the first *satori* will happen, the first glimpse of Enlightenment. And this will be the situation inside: *At first a yogi feels his mind is tumbling like a waterfall* . . . because your mind starts melting. Right now it is like a frozen glacier. If you remain loose, natural, true to the moment, authentically here and now, the mind starts melting. You have brought sun energy to it. This very being in the here and now conserves such a vast energy; not moving in the future, not moving in the past, you have so much, tremendous energy in you that the very energy starts melting the mind.

Energy is fire, energy is of the sun. When you are not moving anywhere, completely still, here and now, no going, converging upon yourself, all leakage stops, because leakage is through desire and hope. You leak because of the future; leakage is because of a motivation: 'Do something, be something, have something; why are you wasting your time sitting? Go! Move! Do!' — then there is leakage. If you are simply here, how can you leak? Energy converges, falls back upon you, it becomes a circle of fire — and then the glacier of the mind starts melting.

At first a yogi feels his mind is tumbling like a waterfall.

Everything falls. The whole mind is falling, falling, falling — you may be scared. Near the first *satori* the Master is needed very very deeply and intimately, because who will tell you, 'Don't be afraid; it is beautiful — fall.'

Just the word 'fall' and fear comes in, because falling means falling into an abyss, losing your ground, moving into the unknown. And falling carries a sense of death; one becomes afraid.

Have you ever gone to some mountains — a high peak, and from there looked down into the abyss, the valley — nausea, trembling; fear comes in as if the abyss is death and you can fall into it. When the mind melts everything starts falling, *everything* I say. Your love, your ego,

245

your greed, your anger, your hate — all that you have been up to now suddenly starts becoming loose and falling — as if the house is falling apart, you become a chaos, no more order, all discipline falling. You have been maintaining yourself somehow; somehow you were together forcing a control upon yourself, a discipline. Now being loose and natural everything is falling. Many things that you have suppressed will bubble up, they will surface. You will find a chaos all around; you will be just like a madman.

The first step is really difficult to pass through, because whatsoever society has forced on you will fall, whatsoever you have learned will fall, whatsoever you have conditioned yourself to be will fall. All your habits, all your directions — all your paths will simply disappear. Your identity will evaporate; you will not be able to know who you are. Up to now you knew well who you were: your name, your family, your status in the world, your prestige, your honour, this and that: you were aware. Now suddenly everything is melting, the identity is lost. You knew many things, now you will not know anything. You were wise in the ways of the world; they will fall and you will feel completely ignorant.

This is what happened to Socrates. That was his first *satori* moment when he said, 'Now I know only one thing: that I don't know anything. Only one knowledge do I have, that I am ignorant.' This is the first *satori*.

Sufis have a particular term for this man, this type of man, who comes to this state, they call him *mast*, they call him the madman. He looks at you without looking at you. He roams around not knowing where he is going. He talks nonsense. He cannot keep a relevant coherence in his talk — one word and then a gap; then another word absolutely unrelated; one sentence, then another sentence not connected at all; no coherence, all consistency is lost. He becomes a contradiction, you cannot rely on him.

For *these* moments a school is needed, where people can take care of you. *Ashrams* came into existence because of this — because this man cannot be allowed in the society, otherwise they will think he is mad and they will force him into a prison or a madhouse, and they will try to treat him. They will try to bring him down, back to his normal state — and he is growing! He has broken all the chains of the society; he has become a chaos.

Hence my insistence on chaotic meditations. They will help you to come to this first *satori*. You cannot sit silently from the very beginning; you can befool yourself, but you cannot sit silently, that is not possible; that can happen only in the second *satori*. In the first *satori* you have to be chaotic, dynamic; you have to allow your energies to move so that all strait-jackets around you are broken and all chains are thrown away. You become for the first time an outsider, no more part of the society. A school is needed where care can be taken of you. A Master is needed who can say to you, 'Don't be afraid,' who can tell you, 'Fall easily, allow it to happen; don't cling to something because that will only delay the moment — fall!' The sooner you fall, the sooner madness will disappear, if you delay then the madness can be continued for a long time.

There are millions of mad people in the madhouse throughout the world who are not in fact mad, who needed a Master, who don't need a psychotherapist. They have attained their first *satori*, and all psychotherapies are forcing them back, to be normal. They are in a better situation than you; they have attained a growth but the growth is so outlandish — it has to be so in the beginning, they are passing the first *satori* — that you have made them guilty. You say, 'You are mad!' — and they try to hide it and they try to cling, and the longer they cling the longer the madness will follow.

Only just recently a few psychoanalysts, particularly R. D. Laing and others, have become aware of the phenomenon that a few mad people have not fallen down below the normal, really they have gone beyond the normal. Just a few people in the West, very perceptive people have become aware of it — but the East has always been aware, and the East has *never* suppressed mad people. The first thing the East will do is to bring the mad people to a school where many people are working and a living Master is present. The first thing is to help them to attain a *satori*.

Mad people have been respected highly in the East; in the West they are simply condemned; forced to have electric shocks, insulin shocks; forced somehow even if their brains are destroyed — because now there are surgical things going on. Their brains are operated on and some parts of the brain are removed. Of course, then they become normal, but dull, idiotic, their intelligence is lost. They are no longer mad, they will not harm anybody; they will become a silent part of the society — but you have killed them not knowing that they were reaching a point from where a man becomes superhuman. But of course, the chaos has to be passed through.

With a loving Master and a loving group of people in a school, in an *ashram*, it passes easily, everybody takes it easily, helps it; one moves to the second stage easily. This has to happen because all order is imposed on you, it is not real order. All discipline is forced on you, it is not your inner discipline. Before you attain to the inner, the outer has to be dropped; before a new order is born, the old has to cease — and there will be a gap. That gap is madness. One feels as though one is tumbling, falling like a waterfall into the abyss, and there seems to be no bottom to it.

In mid-course if this point is passed, if the first *satori* is lived well, then a new order arises that is from the within, that comes from your own being. Now it is no more of the society, it is not given to you by others, it is not an imprisonment. Now a new order arises which has a quality of freedom. A discipline comes to you naturally, it is your own; nobody asks about you, nobody says, 'Do this!' you simply do the right thing.

In mid-course, like the Ganges, it flows on slow and gentle.

The tumbling, the roaring waterfall has disappeared, the chaos is no more. This is the second *satori*. You become like the Ganges, flowing gently, slowly; not even a sound is created. You walk like a bridegroom, silently, gracefully; an absolutely new charm happens to your being — grace, elegance. This is the second stage in which we have caught all the Buddhas in the statues; because the third cannot be caught, only the second or the first.

All the Buddhas, Jain Teerthankaras, go and watch their statues: the elegance, the grace, the subtle roundness of their bodies, feminine. They don't look masculine, they look feminine; they have a roundness, their curvature is feminine; that shows their inner being has become very slow, very gentle; there is nothing of aggression in them.

Zen Masters like Bodhidharma, Rinzai, Bokoju, they have been pictured in the first state, that's why they are so ferocious: they look like roaring lions, they look like they will kill you. If you look at their eyes, their eyes are volcanoes, fire jumps at you; they are like shocks. They have been pictured in the first *satori* state for certain reasons, because Zen people know that the first is the problem; and if you know Bodhidharma in this state, when the same state happens to you you will understand that you need not be afraid; even to Bodhidharma . . . . But if you have always been watching Buddhas and Teerthankaras in their silent and slow-flowing rivers and their feminine grace, you will become very much afraid when ferociousness comes to you, when you become like a lion — exactly : one starts roaring; you become a tremendous waterfall.

That's why in Zen the ferocious state has been pictured more and more. Of course there were Buddhas in the shrine, but that is the next state. And that is not a problem at all; when you become silent there is no problem. In India the second stage has been over-emphasized and that became a barrier, because one should know from the very beginning how things are. A Buddha is already an accomplished being. It can happen to you, but in the gap from you to Buddha something else is going to happen — and that is complete madness.

What happens when you accept all madness, you allow it? — it subsides by itself. The old order that society forced goes, it simply evaporates; old knowledge is there no more; all that you knew about the scriptures is there no more. There is a picture of a Zen monk burning all scriptures — his picture is one of the most famous — that comes in the first state. One burns all the scriptures, one throws all knowledge; everything that has been given to you looks rubbish, rot. Now your own wisdom is arising; there is no need to borrow it from anybody. But it will take a little time, just like a seed takes time, to sprout.

If you can manage to pass through the chaotic state, then the second follows very very easily, automatically, of its own accord; you become silent, everything has calmed down, just like the Ganges when it comes to the plains. In the hills it is roaring like a lion, falling from great heights into depths, much turmoil; and then it comes to the plains, leaves the hills; now the terrain changes, now everything flows silently. You cannot even see whether it is flowing or not; everything moves as if it is not moving, at ease.

Attain to inner accomplishment,
innate, with no hope — not going to any goal,
not in any hurry, no haste;
just enjoying . . . each moment.

Like the Ganges it flows on slow and gentle.

This second stage has the quality of absolute silence, calm, quietude, tranquillity, collectedness, at-homeness, rest, relaxation.
And then:

It is a great vast ocean in the end,
where the lights of son and mother merge in one.

Then suddenly, flowing silently, it reaches the ocean and becomes one with the ocean — vast expanse, no boundaries. Now it is no longer a river, now it is no longer an individual unit, now there is no ego.

Even in the second stage there is a very very subtle ego. Hindus have two names: one is *ahamkar*, ego, that's what you have; the second they call *asmita*, 'am-ness', not ego. When you say, 'I am', not the 'I', but simply 'am', 'am-ness', that they call *asmita*. It is a very very silent ego, nobody will feel it, it is very passive, not aggressive. It will not leave any trace anywhere, but it is still there. One feels one is.

That's why it is called the second *satori*: the Ganges is flowing silently of course, at home, at peace, but still it is; it is *asmita*, it is am-ness. The 'I' has dropped and all the madness of the 'I' has gone; the aggressive, the ferocious 'I' is there no more, but a very silent am-ness follows, because the river has banks and the river has boundaries. It is still separate, it has its own individuality.

With the ego, personality drops but individuality remains. Personality is the outer individuality. Individuality is the inner personality. Personality is for others, it is a show-room thing, a display. That has dropped; that is the ego. But this inner feeling that 'I am', or rather 'am' is not on display, nobody will be able to see it. It will not interfere with anybody's life; it will not poke its nose into anybody's affairs. Simply it moves, but it is still there — because the Ganges exists as an individual.

Then the individuality is also lost. That is the third word: *atma*. *Ahamkar* is ego, the 'I-ness'; the 'am' is just a shadow to it, the 'I' is focused. Then the second state *asmita*: the 'I' has dropped; now the am-ness has become total, not a shadow. And then *atma*: now the am-ness has also dropped.

This is what Tilopa calls no-self. *You are*, but without any self; you are, but without any boundaries. The river has become the ocean; the river is in the ocean, it has become one with it. The individuality is there no more, no boundaries, but the being exists as a non-being. It has become a vast emptiness. It has become just like the sky.

The ego was like black clouds all over the sky. The am-ness, *asmita*, was like white clouds in the sky. And *atma* is like the sky without clouds, only the sky remains.

> *In the end it is a great vast ocean,*
> *where the lights of son and mother merge in one.*

Where you come back to the original source, the mother; the circle is complete. You have come back home, dissolved with the original source. The Ganges has come to the Gangotri, the river has come to its original source: the complete circle. Now you are, but in such a totally different sense that it is better to say that you are not.

This is the *most* parodoxical state because it is most difficult to bring it into language and expression. One has to taste it. This is what Tilopa calls Mahamudra, the great orgasm, the ultimate orgasm, the supreme orgasm. You have come back from where you had gone. The journey is over, and not only is the journey over, but also the journeyman is no more. Not only is the journey over as a path, but the goal is also over.

Now nothing exists and everything is.

Remember this distinction. A table exists, a house exists — but God *is*; because a table can go into non-existence, a house can go into non-existence, but God cannot. So it is not good to say that God exists; God simply is. It cannot go into non-existence. It is pure 'is-ness'. This is Mahamudra.

All that exists has disappeared, only is-ness remains.

The body has disappeared, it existed. The mind has disappeared, it existed. The path has disappeared, it existed. The goal has disappeared. All that existed has disappeared — only the purity of is-ness is there . . . an empty mirror, an empty sky, an empty being.

This is what Tilopa calls Mahamudra. This is the supreme, the last, there is no beyond to it. It is the very 'beyond-ness'.

Remember these three stages; you will have to pass through them. Chaos, everything gone topsy-turvy; you are no longer identified with anything, everything has become loose and fallen apart — you are completely mad. Watch it, allow it, pass through it, don't be scared; and when I am here you need not be scared. I know it will pass, I know it always passes, I can assure you. And unless it passes, the grace, the elegance, the silence of a Buddha will not happen to you.

Let it pass. It will be a nightmare, of course, but let it pass. With that nightmare all your past will be cleansed. It will be a tremendous catharsis. All your past will pass through a fire, but you will become pure gold.

Then comes the second state. The first has to be passed because you may get scared and run away from it. The second also has a different kind of danger, an absolutely different kind; not at all a danger. The first has to be passed; you have to be aware that it will pass; it will pass, just time is needed and trust. The second has a different kind of danger: you would like to cling to it, because it is so beautiful; one would like to

251

be in it forever and ever. When the inner river flows calm and quiet one wants to cling to the banks; one wants not to go anywhere else, this is so good. In a way it is a greater danger.

A Master has to assure you that the first will pass, and a Master has to force you so that you don't cling to the second. Because if you cling, the Mahamudra will never happen to you. There are many people clinging to the second, they are hanging. There are many people hanging with the second, because they have become so much attached to it. It *is* so beautiful — one would like to fall in love with it; one falls automatically. Aware, remain aware—that too has to be passed. Watch so that you don't start clinging.

If you can watch your fear with the first and your greed with the second. . . . Remember. fear and greed are two aspects of the same coin. In fear you want to escape from something, in greed you want to cling to it, but they are both the same. Watch fear, watch greed and allow the movement to continue; don't try to stop it. You can become stagnant, then the Ganges becomes, not a flowing thing, but a stagnant pool; howsoever beautiful, it will be dead soon. It will become dirty, it will dry up and soon all that was gained will be lost.

Go on moving. The movement has to be eternal—keep it in mind— it is an endless journey, more is always possible; allow it to happen. Don't hope for it, don't ask for it, don't go ahead of yourself, but allow it to happen. Because then the third danger comes when the Ganges falls into the ocean, and that is the last because you will be losing yourself.

That is the ultimate death. It appears like the ultimate death. Even the Ganges shudders, trembles before it falls; even the Ganges looks backwards, thinks of past days and memories, and the beautiful time on the plains and the tremendous energy phenomenon in the hills and the glaciers. At the last moment when the Ganges is going to fall into the ocean, it lingers a little while more. It wants to look back, think over memories, beautiful experiences. That also has to be watched. Don't linger.

When the ocean comes, allow: merge, melt, disappear.

Only at the last point can you say goodbye to the Master, never before it. Say goodbye to the Master and become the ocean. But up to that moment you need somebody's hand who knows.

There is a tendency in the mind to avoid intimate relationship with the Master; that's what becomes a barrier in taking *sannyas*. You would like to remain uncommitted; you would like to learn, but you would like to remain uncommitted. But you cannot learn, that is not the way; you cannot learn from the outside. You have to enter the inner shrine of a Master's being. You have to commit yourself. Without it you cannot grow.

Without it you can learn a little bit from here and there, and you can accumulate a certain knowledge—that will not be of any help, rather it may become an encumbrance. A deep commitment is needed, a total commitment in fact, because many things are going to happen. If you are just outside on the periphery, just learning as a casual visitor, then not much is possible, because what will happen to you when the first *satori* comes? What will happen to you when you go mad? And you are not losing anything when you commit yourself to a Master because you don't have anything to lose. By your commitment you are simply gaining; you are not losing anything because you don't have anything to lose. You have nothing to be afraid of. But still, still one wants to be very clever, and one wants to learn without commitment. That has never happened, because it is not possible.

So if you are really authentically, sincerely a seeker,
then find someone with whom you can move
in a deep commitment,
with whom you can take the plunge into the Unknown.
Without it you have wandered for many lives
and you will wander.
Without it the supreme accomplishment is not possible.
Take courage and take the jump.